CONSENSUS IN IRELAND

CONSENSUS IN
IRELAND

APPROACHES AND RECESSIONS

Edited by
CHARLES TOWNSHEND
Foreword by
BRIAN FARRELL

CLARENDON PRESS · OXFORD
1988

Oxford University Press, Walton Street, Oxford OX2 6DP

Oxford New York Toronto
Delhi Bombay Calcutta Madras Karachi
Petaling Jaya Singapore Hong Kong Tokyo
Nairobi Dar es Salaam Cape Town
Melbourne Auckland

and associated companies in
Berlin Ibadan

Oxford is a trade mark of Oxford University Press

Published in the United States
by Oxford University Press, New York

British Library Cataloguing in Publication Data

Consensus in Ireland: approaches and recessions.
1. Northern Ireland. Politics, 1969–1986
I. Townshend, Charles
320.9416
ISBN 0–19–827545–5

Library of Congress Cataloging in Publication Data

Consensus in Ireland: approaches and recessions /
edited by Charles Townshend; foreword by Brian Farrell.
p. cm.
Bibliography: p.
Includes index.
1. Northern Ireland—Politics and government—1969–
2. Great Britain Treaties, etc. Ireland, 1985 Nov. 15.
3. Great Britain—Foreign relations—Ireland.
4. Ireland—Foreign relations—Great Britain.
5. Irish question. I. Townshend, Charles.
DA990.U46C666 1988 327.410416—dc19 88–12493
ISBN 0–19–827545–5

Set by Hope Services, Abingdon
Printed in Great Britain
at the University Press, Oxford
by David Stanford
Printer to the University

FOREWORD

Brian Farrell

NEARLY fifty years ago Northern Ireland was aptly characterized as the factory of grievances (Buckland 1979, p. 1). Today it might be described as an academic industry. Since the current phase of the troubles began a prodigious flood of books, articles, reports, and investigative journalism has threatened to swamp us all with paper. It prompted John Whyte, the most assiduous and analytic chronicler of this continuously expanding literature, to pose the question: 'Is Research on the Northern Ireland Problem Worth While?' (1983*b*). It might prompt others to ask: do we need another book on Northern Ireland?

There is a positive answer to both questions. Northern Ireland was, in Charles Townshend's striking phrase, 'a polity born in a terminal condition'. It attracted little research curiosity in its early decades (see below, pp. 24–44). A bare handful of books comprised the total literature before 1968. The neglect of politicians in both Ireland and Britain was matched by the indifference of scholars to this narrow ground that could provide such a convenient testing-pad for issues ranging from immediate, sometimes deadly, local concerns to the loftiest, theoretical considerations of political theory. The troubled last years of the final Stormont administration forced both politicians and researchers to look again—more intensively and extensively—at Northern Ireland.

To date the results of all that activity—political and scholarly—have not been particularly encouraging. Northern Ireland continues in a chronic state of political crisis; a place apart in which the level of political passions appears an affront to the civilized norms of the western world. A variety of general theories have been tested and found wanting in this intense crucible; a variety of political 'solutions' have so far failed to take. John Whyte's sense of oppression about 'the disproportion between the enormous amount of work produced and the lack of practical difference it has made' (1983*b*, p. 16) has been voiced—sometimes less discreetly—by politicians and civil servants on both sides of the Irish Sea. Yet there has been some interaction between the researchers and the policy-makers; the analyses, and the language used to present them, have changed. The Anglo-Irish Agreement signed at Hillsborough on 15 November 1985 reflects some measure of this political education and marks a new departure. It was, then, entirely sensible that some effort should be made to focus academic attention on an intergovernmental initiative designed to foster 'lasting peace and stability' which had provoked further internal discord and upheaval. It was also appropriate that a conference should choose to concentrate its energies on the feasibility of consensus, and that the University of Keele, which had already identified Irish studies as an area of special interest, should be its location.

Richard Rose's monumental study *Governing without Consensus* (1971), perceptively fashioned before the civil rights crisis that inaugurated the present troubles, showed how scholarship could illuminate and order an intractable and chaotic political reality. It was, at first sight, an unlikely approach to analysis. Shils's influential article in the *International Encyclopaedia of the Social Sciences* (1968) had identified three necessary preconditions for consensus: a common acceptance of laws, rules, norms; attachment to the institutions which promulgate and apply the laws; a widespread sense of identity or unity. All were conspicuously lacking in Northern Ireland; they still are. So has that made a search for consensus—or, at least, the search for a better basis of government than sullen or reluctant acquiescence—irrelevant? On the contrary, as the preamble to the Hillsborough Agreement testifies, the pursuit of some agreed basis for managing differing, and even opposing, traditions within a framework accessible to all is a prime purpose of joint government action.

In one sense it could be argued that Hillsborough, with its recognition of two major traditions, identities, and aspirations, is an acknowledgement that consensus cannot be achieved. On the other hand, Article 4 offers the reward of devolved powers in return for an effort to secure 'widespread acceptance throughout the community'. Some will see in this inherent ambiguity a futile attempt to square the vicious circle of what passes for politics in Northern Ireland; no more than a political formula to enable the two governments to get a problem identified as 'too difficult' off their respective Cabinet agendas (Hennessy 1986, p. 168). That is, I believe, an interpretation which is not only based on a cynical misattribution of motive but, more fundamentally, is grounded in a failure to consider the genesis of the document itself.

For over a century politicians in both Britain and Ireland have struggled to produce a suitable framework of good government for the island of Ireland. The Westminster pendulum, swinging between high political analysis and low partisan calculation, has rarely achieved any sustained equilibrium. All too often, the attempt to apply the latest formula—whether Home Rule or power sharing—has been sacrificed on the altar of domestic elections. By comparison with this vacillation, Unionist politicians have remained committed to an intransigent 'not an inch' strategy that has seen their position decline from virtual local supremacy within the United Kingdom to an uneasy and ineffective opposition to the expressed will of the sovereign parliament that they should reach an accommodation with their neighbours. Nationalist political leaders, north and south of the border, have moved (however slowly and uncertainly) from an unthinking assertion of a majoritarian right-to-rule to a recognition that change—if it is to come at all—must be the result of a long and still obscure process. Meantime, a majority of militants, on both sides, have been busy asserting that the wasteland of their endeavours marks the boundaries of real politics. To date the efforts by politicians to frame 'solutions' have been the products of crisis management, brief spurts of concentrated activity seeking rapid and tangible results. Typically, the sweaty engine-rooms of the Cabinets (Hennessy 1986, pp. 27–30) have rapidly manufactured the broad outlines of some policy initiative and then left it to the civil servants—and, frequently enough, to the security forces—to adapt it to whatever circumstances were provoked by it.

The failure to consider in advance just what those circumstances might be has been a constant weakness in policy-making. The unanticipated depth and passion of loyalist antipathy to the Hillsborough Agreement—now readily admitted by politicians—might suggest that the same politically truncated time-perspective flaws this latest initiative. But that is to ignore a central difference between this and all other former agreements.

Much has been made of the fact that Hillsborough was the outcome of direct negotiations between two sovereign governments. Rather less emphasis has been placed on the even more significant fact that it is the end-product of a long series of close negotiations between senior officials on both sides of the Irish Sea. Preliminary discussions at official level typically precede meetings of ministers, and especially prime ministers; notoriously, drafts of joint communiqués are brought to Anglo-Irish summits and, indeed, often form the real agenda at heads of government meetings. But such material is normally prepared within time-constraints determined by the desires, exigencies, and convenience of elected politicians. Officials are forced to work to a political deadline; they must accept the narrow limits of manœuvre imposed by existing institutional realities. Above all, they are required to contain recommended proposals within the more or less precisely defined terms of their own government's position. A high degree of formality is a barrier to easy communication and a permanent brake on adventurous policy speculation; each side plays with cards held closely to the chest.

The background to Hillsborough was different. The Dublin Summit of 8 December 1980 commissioned joint studies, to be undertaken by senior officials of the two governments, designed to assist the Taoiseach and the Prime Minister 'in their special consideration of the totality of relationships within these islands'. The subsequent public, political gloss placed on this latter phrase by politicians in Dublin and extravagant hints that this implied a new set of constitutional arrangements soon became the focus of attention, comment, and political tension. Less attention was paid to the fact that the summit was followed by a series of meetings between officials, giving rise to the publication of the joint report published on 11 November 1981. That report contained the seed of an 'Anglo-Irish Intergovernmental Council' which was to flower in Hillsborough; the preparation of the joint studies provided a model of the close working relations between Irish and British officials which created the conditions for germination. It was a quiet, fruitful interaction which was able to survive more obvious strains at the level of public discourse. There were evident tensions among the political principals: the H-blocks crisis, the Falklands affair, and Mrs Thatcher's apparent rejection of all the New Ireland Forum options indicate that this was not simply a matter of personality disagreements. Yet, while carrying out the instructions of their governments, officials were able—even in periods of considerable discord—to continue a process of exploration, communication, and reconciliation. At official level the pursuit of consensus, not simply within Northern Ireland but between Ireland and Britain, became a central focus of policy.

Some of this was revealed in a damage-limitation exercise after Mrs Thatcher's post-summit press conference of 19 November 1985 had seemed to many to signal a dismissal of Ireland from any priority position on the British Cabinet agenda. The Prime Minister's vigorous 'out, out, out' to the Forum's preferred solutions was compared unfavourably to a lack-lustre performance by the Taoiseach. Yet, officials were at pains to point to the language of the agreed communiqué and insist that the two governments remained on course in their determination to provide a new context for Anglo-Irish reconciliation.

For those of us who were in London on the day it was not immediately convincing. It was known that earlier negotiations between the two heads of government had been unfruitful. It was not known that, at a side conference during the Milan EEC Summit, Dr FitzGerald had abandoned earlier quiet diplomacy and, in the face of Mrs Thatcher's apparent resistance to any initiative, had demanded that the problem be confronted. It appears that his passion on this occasion made an impression on the British prime minister. But observers after the London summit could only judge by appearances. The contrast in the demeanour of the two leaders appeared to suggest failure.

What was not evident—and could not be revealed—was that the links forged between officials were already close enough, and strong enough, to withstand even such a degree of public stress. In the next few crowded months those links were strengthened at the most senior levels of the public service; as far as the top officials were concerned Ireland remained high on the agenda. They were willing to devote an extraordinary amount of time and their very experienced and professional ingenuity to find a formula that could be accepted by their political principals. One official has spoken of a year in which there was never a weekend free; it was the only time available to men whose own schedules were already over-burdened. What is particularly striking is that the procedure adopted for this marathon series of conferences (something like seventy meetings at official level preceded the final Hillsborough meeting) was deliberately unstructured. The conventional strait-jackets of committee work were discarded. There was something like a continuous, and quite unbuttoned, conversation in which the differences between the two sides—and there continues to be real and substantial differences—were subsumed in a common, professional, endeavour to provide some resolution. At the same time, while the officials were as conscious as their principals of the urgency of the situation, they were able to consider the issues in a more generous time-frame than elected politicians. They were also committed to reaching an agreement which could lead to decisions rather than one which would satisfy rhetorical aspirations. On both sides, politicians and civil servants alike shared a conscious recognition that any agreement must be balanced between the fears, needs, and aspirations of the two communities in Northern Ireland, and that any sustainable line of balance (if it could be struck) would be narrow, probably inconstant, and affected by developments on the ground.

The seniority of the officials on both sides provided significant advantages. They worked at the top of their bureaucracies, at the sensitive interface between politics and public policy. They were skilled in anticipating—and drafting responses to—objections from interested departments; experienced at recognizing—and providing for—likely political responses. They recognized the advantage of small, working groups and managed, for the most part, to keep the numbers involved to a bare minimum. They also used their authority to draw on resources of information from many parts of the public service without being required to give any reciprocal right of participation. Sections of the public service likely to prove obstructive on the basis of past record were carefully managed. In one case, in Ireland, the head of the relevant department was included in the negotiations at the outset; in another, in Britain, the department was excluded until the negotiations had reached a point well beyond their predictable resistance-barrier.

All of this is not to deny the contribution of the politicians, and especially the heads of government, to the Hillsborough Agreement. It was a happy coincidence that in autumn 1983 there were political leaders on each side of the Irish Sea who had just won elections and could anticipate a period of three or four years in office before facing another election. Each was prepared to consider some shifts of position; each saw the possibility of developments at the level of relations between governments. As time went on, the supervision and co-ordination of the official negotiations by Ministerial Committee under the Taoiseach came to be increasingly close and active; on the British side, it seems Mrs Thatcher's chairmanship of the Cabinet Committee on Overseas and Defence ensured similar active involvement (Hennessy 1986, p. 27). It required commitment to give so much scarce executive time to the consideration of such a chronic and recalcitrant problem as Northern Ireland, and there were senior ministers in both countries who resented the priority given to the issues. It required courage to propose and support an agreement that was bound to be opposed and criticized, not least by some of those it was designed to satisfy. It required tenacity to persist as the depth and width of resistance within Northern Ireland manifested itself. Both Dr FitzGerald and Mrs Thatcher (and their foreign ministers) invested heavily in an imaginative initiative.

But it was the preliminary effort put in by senior civil servants and diplomats that provided the atmosphere of trust, commitment, and co-operation in which the final text was agreed. That text was designed with subtle resilience to continue the processes of inter-governmental consensus already in place. The skill and guile of the draftsmen is exemplified in Article 1, which reads:

STATUS OF NORTHERN IRELAND

ARTICLE 1

The two Governments

(a) affirm that any change in the status of Northern Ireland would only come about with the consent of a majority of the people of Northern Ireland;

(b) recognise that the present wish of a majority of the people of Northern Ireland is for no change in the status of Northern Ireland;

(c) declare that, if in the future a majority of the people of Northern Ireland clearly wish for and formally consent to the establishment of a united Ireland, they will introduce and support in the respective Parliaments legislation to give effect to that wish.

What is noticeable here is that, despite the heading of the Article and the affirmation, recognition, and declaration of the text, there is in fact no definition of the actual status of Northern Ireland. It is clearly a deliberate omission. This approach contrasts with the use of parallel paragraphs in paragraph 5 of the Sunningdale Communiqué which gave rise to a challenge in the Irish Supreme Court. The Hillsborough draftsmen hoped to provide against such a constitutional challenge. They also attempted to head-off potential criticism from Mr Haughey by deliberately incorporating the precise wording of his joint communiqué after the Downing Street summit of 21 May 1980 in the affirmation that 'any change in the status of Northern Ireland would only come about with the consent of a majority of the people of Northern Ireland'; indeed, as Dr FitzGerald subsequently pointed out in a television interview, even the misplaced use of 'only' was retained in an effort to ensure acceptance.

Two other features to the text are worth noting. On the one hand, by avoiding definition of status it provides a flexibility that allows incremental adaptations of status without requiring any legislative or constitutional clarification. On the other, the exclusion of Article 1 from the possibility of review envisaged in Article 11 secures this foundation stone of the Agreement against upset arising from governmental changes in either Ireland or Britain. The whole Agreement effectively binds the two sovereign governments to a joint pursuit of consensus.

Arguably what was not provided was a persuasive tool to gain the acquiescence of the loyalist majority within Northern Ireland. But, then, the Agreement was not simply intended as just another 'resolution' of the Northern Ireland crisis, another effort to provide for the good government of Ireland. It was intended to 'develop the unique relationship' between the peoples of these two islands and to diminish those internal divisions within Northern Ireland which disturb that relationship. It was a broad attempt to foster a wider consensus between Ireland and Britain; perhaps even the first recognition that two sovereign states, so closely linked and so often divided, required a firmer framework of institutionalized relationships, a more coherent understanding of the benefits and limits of consensus.

Certainly, the extraordinarily exhilarating and well-informed discussions at Keele following the conference papers presented in this volume revealed that pursuing the theme of the feasibility of consensus unlocked a much wider range of issues than just the Northern Ireland problem. Bernard Crick's insistence on the need for a conceptual shift in the sovereignty equation implicit in the conventional concept of the nation-state; David Trimble's assertion that Northern Ireland was not susceptible to rational discussion; Tom Garvin's observations that at heart the Republic remains Anglophile—these, and a dozen other insights and interventions, provoked an unusual degree of participation. It was a conference that fulfilled its central objective: it raised questions. It is hoped that the publication of its proceedings will provide a similar benefit to readers.

CONTENTS

NOTES ON THE CONTRIBUTORS

PAUL ARTHUR: Senior Lecturer in Politics, University of Ulster at Jordanstown.

BERNARD CRICK: Emeritus Professor of Politics, Birkbeck College, University of London.

JOHN DARBY: Professor of Social Administration and Director of the Centre for the Study of Conflict, University of Ulster at Coleraine.

MARTIN DENT: Senior Lecturer in Politics, University of Keele.

BRIAN FARRELL: Associate Professor of Politics, University College, Dublin; Presenter of the RTE current affairs programme *Today Tonight*.

TOM GARVIN: Lecturer in Politics, University College, Dublin.

JAMES O'CONNELL: Professor of Peace Studies, University of Bradford.

CHARLES TOWNSHEND: Professor of Modern History, University of Keele.

DAVID TRIMBLE: Senior Lecturer in Law, The Queen's University of Belfast. Unionist member of the Northern Ireland Constitutional Convention (1975); Chairman of the Lagan Valley Unionist Constituency Association.

JOHN WHYTE: Professor of Politics, University College, Dublin.

INTRODUCTION

Charles Townshend

THE essays assembled here were prepared for a conference held at Keele University in April 1986, aiming to explore the feasibility of consensus in Ireland, both North and South.* Politicians and civil servants, as well as academic specialists, took part under the vigorous chairmanship of Brian Farrell; and though nearly all the essays were contributed by the latter group (David Trimble being a rare hybrid), the range of their academic disciplines—comprising history, law, and sociology, as well as political science—created an unusually open-frontiered discussion. We have risked bringing this collection of approaches to public attention because we think the issue addressed is of fundamental public importance. Starting from the commonplace assumption that the legitimacy and operability of any modern political system rest on some sort of consensus, we set ourselves to ask just what sort, and how expressed? Where, as in the six counties of Northern Ireland, there are few if any conventional signs of consensus, can institutions be conceived that will work without, or maybe serve to foster, a working measure of public accord?

The negative side of the case is easy enough to make out. At its most negative, it would take consensus to mean wholehearted, thorough-going, unanimous, active, public support for—and where appropriate participation in—the ends and means of the polity. By this definition there can never have been consensus in Ireland, North or South, and never will be. Even modified somewhat, to become positive approval by the majority, with no irreconcilable opposition amongst the minority, this is still a demanding criterion to apply to any state. Like the first version of consensus, it probably belongs to the realm of political mythology and rhetoric rather than reality. The reality beneath the 'Whig interpretation', or still more the imagery of *Volksgemeinschaft*, is erratic in nature. Professor Bernard Crick suggested to the conference that in Northern Ireland active ('explicit') consent does not exist among a majority, while the level of tacit consent varies with political events (see below, p. 116; Crick 1986). This latter point at least is

---

* This approximate and contentious usage may appear from time to time in this volume; it is assumed to be comprehensible even where it is disputed.

probably true of most societies, and can be further refined by talking of the 'incidence' rather than the 'level' of consent (whether explicit or tacit). Individuals and groups will each give differing endorsement to different public policies at any time: their consent would be a jagged curve rather than a flat level.

Still, however carefully it is refined, the commonsense understanding of consensus must be exceptionally difficult to locate in Ireland. (We set aside here the specialized use of the term 'consensus democracy' by, for instance, Arend Lijphart to describe systems in which majority rule is replaced by some form of power-sharing.) The mild notion of 'accord' in its most general sense bespeaks an absence of fundamental discord over the existence of the state itself. Whether the strong term 'cultures' or the weaker term 'traditions' is used, it is beyond dispute that two sharply differentiated sets of political assumptions and outlooks exist in Ireland. That the differentiation is not diminishing, but is being constantly reinforced by separate socialization, and may well (as those who talk of polarization suggest) be further sharpening, is also evident (Rose 1971, ch. 11; McAllister 1980). Repeated efforts, both official and private, to find mechanisms of intercommunal integration have failed.

One result of this has been unusual pessimism amongst academic analysts as to the possibility of a 'solution' to the 'Irish problem'. Some political scientists have more or less given up on it for this reason. But at the same time there is emerging a new academic realism (a precursor, it may perhaps be hoped, of a new journalistic and political realism) which is endeavouring to reconstruct the nature of such problems so as not to invoke elegant, rapid, or complete solutions. From this perspective, which was well evidenced at the Keele conference, there is no need to minimize or disguise the intractability of the Northern Ireland situation. The six-county area is a sectarian political entity in a crucial historical sense: it would never have come into existence but for Protestant hostility to Catholic Irish nationalism. Its existence itself forms the most substantial evidence of the absence of consensus in Ireland. Within the six counties, the elementary preconditions for a political community are missing. There is no set of superordinate values, or 'political formula', as Tom Garvin puts it; a political culture which is personalistic, parochial, centrifugal; and few political conventions by which public trust can be assumed. There is disaffection (a notion which Bernard Crick urges us to prefer to the slippery, pseudo-psychological 'alienation'), producing obstruction, demonstrations, riots and strikes, and a diffuse tolerance of violence which can paralyse the enforcement of law. At the root of this is diametric opposition over the ultimate source of sovereignty and the *locus* of identity.

Over the fifty years of devolved government in Northern Ireland, Protestants denied full civil rights to Catholics, not so much on confessional grounds as because Catholics were manifestly, and self-confessedly, disloyal to the state (McCracken 1967, p. 154; McAllister 1982; Rose 1983; Bruce 1986).* The 'constitutional' issue continues to override all other political cleavages, not only for 'Ultra' Loyalists but in the last analysis for all those who see Protestantism as in some sense the bedrock of their 'way of life'. This uncompromising Ultra strain has destroyed sophisticated, elegant mechanisms like consociation or concurring-majority (power-sharing). Loyalist determination to uphold the British Crown 'being Protestant' (i.e. as a symbol of the Protestant way of life) has been proof against repeated appeals in the name of British national interest, or even of the Crowned Head. David Trimble unflinchingly contemplates the prospect that it will play its part, shoulder to shoulder with republican intransigence, in perpetuating the 'political impasse' indefinitely.

We must accept, with Bernard Crick, that 'if we believe that the national sovereign state is the best form that national sentiment can take and the almost unavoidable form of human government in the modern world, there is probably no lasting acceptable framework of government for Northern Ireland'. But as Professor Crick points out, and Martin Dent urges in his original proposal, the erosion of hermetic sovereignty since 1945 by a variety of international agencies, and the persistence of several local conflicts which are not merely unresolvable but are evidently exacerbated by the standard nation-state framework, must give some hope that less inflexible arrangements will be tolerated and eventually legitimized.

If this were merely a pious hope, there would be little excuse for

---

* This religio-political view has not substantially altered. Though McAllister's article was written to show that religious commitment does not correlate with political attitudes, it also wields data which demonstrate a strikingly high attribution of Catholic disloyalty on the part of Protestants. The vital bearing of religious identity on communal perceptions is confirmed in the reworking of the same material in McAllister and Rose (1983). The sophistication of such multiple regression analyses highlights the crudity of the variables employed; they offer no means of getting under the skin of Protestant political affiliations. Compare a sensitive work of social anthropology such as Bruce (1986).

wasting time on it. But there are more solid grounds for confidence. Some of these are, like what has gone before, negative. The evident failure, or apparent impossibility, of all the 'simple solutions' (Boyle and Hadden 1985), has had a cumulative mental impact on all sides. It may be that Boyle and Hadden, in common with other recent analysts such as the Liberal/SDP Alliance Commission on Northern Ireland (1985), exaggerate the impossibility of some of these allegedly 'simple' outcomes. Two outcomes or projects in particular have more to be said for them than these authorities are prepared to admit.

An independent 'Ulster' state is widely dismissed as being unviable, if not unthinkable. Dr Garret FitzGerald (1982), for instance, in his justly celebrated 1982 Dimbleby Lecture, declared that Ulster Protestants 'uneasily recognize that Ulster is not a nation and cannot credibly become a state'. Whether or not they do so recognize, this cannot be properly said to be a fact—at least not on the grounds usually cited, namely economic ones. Ulster would certainly not be more incredible than several already existing states. And determined leaders have manufactured national spirit out of less promising materials than are to hand in the six counties. Whilst it is no doubt true that Ulster is not yet a nation (notwithstanding the contentions of the Ulster Defence Association and others), it is pointless to imply that it is a mere province or region like any other. The 'Protestant Province of Ulster', in the mouths of Carson or Brookeborough, and in the minds of their hearers, is an entity with real self-hood. It may not have elected to express national identity, but its cultural identity has repeatedly found independent political expression. Still, one should beware of assuming that unionism is a sufficiently coherent idea to sustain an independent political community. For fundamentalist Protestants, as for their Muslim counterparts, religion may furnish an entire social-political edifice. But in this sense fundamentalists are (as yet) a small minority of Protestant unionists. The unionist grouping, as Paul Arthur has observed, is an uneasy 'alliance of people thrown together by what they were opposed to rather than by any positive or co-operative principles' (Arthur 1980, p. 65). The negative nature of unionism was revealed in the failure of Ulster Vanguard's attempt in the mid-1970s to construct a viable basis for renewed devolution. There remains a missing dimension in unionist political thought.

Ulster independence may be said to have been launched as a project as early as 1912 (whether or not it was a rhetorical flourish on Carson's part). The other possible outcome, repartition, is one with an almost equally venerable history, coeval with the border in its present form. As a project it derives its force from the assertion that, if partition was a regrettable necessity, avoidable injustice was a disastrous complication. The Alliance Commission observes that repartition is not supported by 'any significant political party in Northern Ireland or the Republic', but this does nothing to impair its theoretical validity. It is in fact the logical conclusion of traditional assumptions about national sovereignty and political community: in these terms there is a good argument that an Ulster unit with greater homogeneity (or to put it straightforwardly, acceptance of its existence as a unit) would be capable of functioning as a 'normal' democratic polity. A major reduction in the Nationalist/Catholic minority would render it less threatening to the majority, and permit the emergence of social-economic rather than constitutional political alignments (McKeown 1985; New Ulster Political Research Group 1979). At the very least, repartition would eliminate a transparent injustice, belatedly applying the 'Versailles principles' which were clearly invoked by the Irish delegation during the 1921 Treaty negotiations. The urban areas, above all Belfast, would remain outside the scope of practicable repartition, but the existence of insoluble problems is not a sound reason for failing to deal with soluble ones.

If the logic of repartition is a function of traditional nationalist assumptions, the powerful practical arguments adduced against repartition by Boyle and Hadden are in effect arguments against traditional nationalism. Or rather, perhaps one should say, arguments for the supersession of traditional nationalism, and above all of uniform national sovereignty. In this direction even the weakest argument against repartition—the *quieta non movere* sort—may contribute to reformulating the future. If it is and remains the case that no significant political group openly favours repartition, then the six counties under one label or another have started to show symptoms of that mental integration which Benedict Anderson holds to be a precursor of national identity (1983). His thesis that institutional continuities have the power to generate shared mental pictures and hence cohesive assumptions about political frameworks indicates a positive aspect of the border.

The Alliance Commission is on the right track when it suggests that 'the effect of seeing local politicians working together to administer day-to-day affairs of the province . . . would lead very gradually, to declining emphasis on those issues which divide communities. Thus political rhetoric would soften . . .'. One of the strongest lines taken in the Keele conference discussions was emphasis on the need to focus on low-level, day-to-day coexistence, rather than spectacular issues of overall sovereignty. Many participants stressed the power of governments to reshape public attitudes. Bernard Crick pointed out that governments do more than passively reflect pre-existing consent; they go out and work to create or enlarge it. 'Consent needs to be mobilized if governments would attempt rapid social change.'

Indeed, by merely existing, governments exert vast—albeit inert—influence. The administrative priorities reflected in the 1985 Agreement are rightly seen as constructive avoidance of unresolvable issues of principle. Whether or not we choose to speak of 'fractionating' conflict, it is evident that greater progress is routinely made by adjustment of small-scale matters than by attempts to shift major concepts. Public attitudes do change over the *longue durée*, and even if resistance to change in certain spheres of public life in Ireland is uncommonly strong, it cannot be absolute. Tom Garvin discerns a 'huge if shapeless cultural revolution' occurring in the Republic (see below, p. 103). The extent and pace of secularization remains astonishingly limited, no doubt, by the canons of modernization; this undermined Garret FitzGerald's 'crusade' to alter the unacceptable political face of Catholicism. More relevant, perhaps, is Garvin's analysis of public attitudes to partition. The first stage in the process of detaching rhetoric from reality was to see that 'reunification' (which, as Garvin points out, was always a misnomer, now more misleading than ever) is a 'low intensity aspiration' amongst voters in the twenty-six counties. This fact does not necessarily reduce its power over political leaders, or *ipso facto* increase their room for manœuvre on the question of ultimate unity. But it opens up the possibility that low-level adjustments could receive public endorsement.

In a characteristically meticulous formulation of his view of partition, Eamon de Valera said in 1927, 'we must, of course, recognize existing facts, but it does not follow that we must acquiesce in them' (Bowman 1982, p. 99). Here the subtlety of his distinction almost exhausted the resources of the English language, but the intended discrimination was clear enough. Since de Valera there has been, perhaps, a less doctrinaire attitude to facts. For people *can* reject and yet accept. Everyday life is full of unsatisfactory situations and outcomes; it is mostly marked by coexistence rather than community. Only when positions are sealed off by abstract political demands does coexistence become untenable. Acceptance of 'low practicability', likened by Garvin to a vote against the weather, may be the solvent of such abstract armour. The Anglo-Irish Agreement may not satisfy nationalist aspirations; it may indeed enshrine a permanent barrier to them. But in so far as it works, it is quite likely to be both recognized and acquiesced in.

Governments have power to make things work. Indeed, there is good anthropological evidence that administrative authority is a function of civil conflict as much as consensus (Colson 1974, pp. 62–9). Governmental power does have uncertain limits, however, and in Ulster these have been reached with disconcerting frequency. The disaffection of the minority has often been, in Professor Crick's view, 'more deadly than the fanaticism of the relatively few active terrorists'. The attitude of the majority has been more ambiguous. Loyalists have disobeyed, but as 'Queen's rebels' they have not been disaffected. The UDA puzzled many outside observers by taking as its motto *cedent arma togae*, which seems to display at least a predisposition towards normal politics—though just whose armed force was to give way was left uncertain (Aughey and McIlheney 1984). The Ulster Workers' Council strike of 1974 will always stand as a classic manifestation of civil resistance, but it did not give rise to a new form of politics. Power-sharing was seen at that moment by the majority as a danger comparable to that of Home Rule in 1912. Yet as John Darby says, power-sharing has remained the most consistently supported option across the unionist/nationalist divide. Not every form of consociation will necessarily trigger a repeat of 1974; mass civil resistance calls for massive psychic energy, which is not always available.

Theorists of consociation have shown how dependent it is on political leadership which is experienced, confident, and flexible; conscious not only of its own constituency but also of a plural public sphere (Lijphart 1977). James O'Connell's comparative analysis underlines this point. Northern Ireland's political parties have undeniably failed so far to meet these demanding criteria, and no linear progress towards such norms can be assumed. In the absence of such a civic culture it would be dangerous for governments to seek to replace party politics, but they need not therefore be paralysed. As with many public policy issues, governments have some freedom of choice about what they regard as public opinion. In the past, governments have been inclined to put great stress on the need to eliminate violence—a requirement which gives gunmen an effective power of veto over political processes. The security of life and property is unquestionably a primary public issue, but within certain limits governments can exaggerate or downplay political violence. If they conspire with the press to play up its extent and significance, they are wittingly or unwittingly closing off their own policy options.

The outstanding question for Northern Ireland is whether the paramilitary organizations, which have now reached an unprecedented depth of entrenchment in the social and economic structure of their communities, remain marginal to the political process (Adams 1986; Nelson 1984).* So far both republican and loyalist paramilitaries have proved unable to develop a politics to replace the established representative system, but it is not impossible that they could do so (Aughey and McIlheney 1981). The parallels with vigilantism or fascist militia activism are not wholly far-fetched. At the very least, as long as the issue of security is made a test of the effectiveness of consultative procedures like the Agreement, paramilitaries will retain their capacity to interdict political development.

---

* Adams's account of the entrenchment is useful, if sensational. Nelson's work is one of the most honest efforts to explore paramilitary attitudes. The difficulty of getting them right is shown in the vague use of different terminology: paramilitaries, paramilitarists, paramilitants—each could give a substantially altered edge to the notion of 'paramilitarism'.

SYNERGY AND POLARITY IN IRELAND
Historical Elements of the Problem of Consensus
Charles Townshend

To raise the issue of consensus in Ireland is necessarily to focus on the weaknesses of 'government without consensus'. These weaknesses were vividly detailed in a classic work of modern political science published at the onset of the present crisis in Northern Ireland, Richard Rose's *Governing Without Consensus* (1971). It has always been a sobering throught that the pathbreaking research into public attitudes which formed the basis of Rose's analysis was conducted in a period of comparative, if not absolute, tranquillity; a period, indeed, when the prospects of political synergy were reckoned by many to be better than they had been for over a hundred years.

What, though, is political consensus? It is rarely, in even the most homogeneous societies, a truly harmonious coordination of effort, a synergy of the sort implied in the organic metaphors beloved of conservative political scientists. The image of the 'body politic' is as profoundly misleading as it is revealing of human aspirations—or of the sophistry of governors. Tom Paulin's grim reformulation 'cadaver politic' may well be more accurate, not only for Northern Ireland. Even where total harmony appears to be spontaneously generated, as in some 'just' wars or revolutions, closer analysis will always reveal discordances. The French revolutionary *levée en masse*, the Nazi *Gleichschaltung* alike manifested political rhetoric rather than reality.

Yet the profound aspiration to harmony in civil society, such as the *Burgfrieden* of Germany in August 1914, is a force to be reckoned with. Even Anglo-Saxon society, which has self-consciously turned its face against the more febrile forms of political rhetoric, enshrines—less ostentatiously but no less fervently—the ideal of civil peace. The composite 'law and order', however much it may smack of Machiavellian manipulation (*legge e ordini*), flowers in its English form into an expression of communal responsibility. Order, the 'king's peace', is not merely an absence of disorder, but a positive acting-out of shared values.

To some extent the existence of such peace is not merely an ideal, but a functional precondition of a political system. The question is, to what extent? How closely must the attitudes and aspirations of society match? Clearly a degree of approximation is possible. Indeed, it may be thought that the more ambiguity a society can tolerate, the better. In polarized societies, ambiguities are apt to be stripped bare and inconsistencies brutally revealed. An instance might be the word 'community'. The characteristic vagueness with which the term is employed in Britain says much about the tolerances of the British system; transferred to Ulster it becomes vacuous or dangerously obfuscatory, as when the Prior White Paper spoke of 'the two sides of the community' (1982).

The limited usefulness of the term is luminously conveyed in another classic study of Ulster attitudes based on research carried out in the pre-1969 period. The small border town of 'Ballybeg', where the anthropologist Rosemary Harris did her fieldwork in the 1950s, was a community at one level: it was a coherent economic entity. (Although its astonishingly—to British eyes—diverse economy rested on a complex set of kin and sectarian loyalties, utterly different from an open or 'free market'.) It shared the same physical space, and an outwardly similar pattern of life. On one occasion during Harris's research, civic consciousness appeared—when a slur was cast by the County Health Department on the cleanliness of the town's water supply. But this occasion was unique: apart from it, she could discover 'no situation in which it could be said that a majority of the inhabitants shared a common viewpoint, still less that they acted together for a common end, no matter how trifling' (1972, p. 9).

The difficulty of building political consensus on such foundations is obvious. Less obvious, perhaps, is the fact that the structures of separate socialization registered by Harris and many others have been created by, as much as they have created, polarized political identities. Consensus may not require unanimity about ends—in practice a rough approximation of means probably suffices—but it seems to require agreement about the limits of the possible. The stark fact about political debate over Ireland in the last hundred years has been the polarity of ultimate objectives, which has fed back into all intermediate political activity. Thus, as has so often been pointed out, the alignments associated with modernizing societies, the primacy of social and economic issues, have remained subordinate to the 'constitutional' issue, the nature and symbols of political allegiance, identity, and territory. The aim of Protestant workers has consistently been to preserve the 'Protestant ascendancy'—however defined—rather than to pursue social and economic power through working-class mobilization.

The historical problem is to determine how this came to be; what 'loyalism' means and how it has survived a number of drastic changes in historical context. It has, of course, not done so in isolation, but as part of a triangular relationship of direct reciprocal action. In what follows I shall try to outline two sides of the relationship—the persistence of loyalism and the persistence of what may be labelled 'republican' nationalism, and deal with the third through a more specific analysis of British political decision-making: the evolution of the partition concept between 1911 and 1925: in other words, the origins of Northern Ireland.

One sure guarantee of infuriation to the string of British statesmen —Lloyd George, Ramsay and Malcolm MacDonald, Austen and Neville Chamberlain—who had to negotiate with Eamon de Valera, was that the crimes of Oliver Cromwell invariably formed the starting-point, and often the terminal point, of all discussions. De Valera's vision of Irish history is itself of vital importance to the issue, as will appear shortly, but there are other reasons for looking back at least as far as the seventeenth century. These reasons are so compelling that many historical introductions to the 'Irish problem' find themselves trapped in a routine narrative scanning several centuries. I hope to avoid this here, but my starting-point is that the very force and coherence of the loyalist outlook suggests deep rootedness in history. The Ulster Protestant sense of identity has been so marked as to lead many analysts to characterize it as, in the weakest (and currently preferred) term, a separate 'tradition', in the strongest, a separate nationality. The more moderate term is 'culture', which is less demanding in its political implications, and has been widely accepted (FitzGerald 1972). But is there really an Ulster Protestant culture?

Answers to this question may vary according to definitions of culture, and the comparatively undeveloped state of cultural history as an analytical technique leaves many interpretative uncertainties (MacDonagh 1983; Moxon-Browne 1983, esp. chs. 1, 7; Prager 1986). But it is possible to say that by the strictest canons, Ulster Protestants are not a separate historical culture. By the criteria of house-types, social pattern, and economic activity, the mass of the 'Scots-Irish' people introduced by the seventeenth-century plantations were broadly homogeneous with the 'native' population (Buchanan 1982). The exceptions were the English planters, but it was they who became assimilated—in a strictly cultural sense. Thus to an anthropologist observing a border town in the 1950s it remained evident that, on the basis of such things as patterns of address, this was 'an area that despite all its social divisions had a kind of common culture' (Harris 1972, p. 123).

But if it is not cultural distinctness, it must be some form of identity that accounts for the universally attested persistence of a feeling of apartness. It is at this point that the matter of religion is usually introduced to resolve the analytical problem (Wright 1973). Undoubtedly, religion was the primary distinguishing characteristic of the planters, and the equation of Protestantism with 'loyalty' was the political motive of the plantation. But to imply, as many writers have done, that the continuing civil crisis in Ulster is some sort of throwback, a time warp, a freakish persistence of the wars of religion, is a manifestly inadequate explanation. To the extent that armed conflict over routes to salvation does persist, it has become inextricably merged in a set of attitudes which must be defined as political, or, more precisely, constitutional. This set is certainly unusual, perhaps unique in the modern world, but it is not inexplicable.

The principal task is to situate the notion of the constitution in the context of popular perceptions, and to grasp the mechanisms by which it adapted to—and in a way subverted—the general process of modernization. Any attempt to do this here can only be an impoverished borrowing from David Miller's brilliant study *Queen's Rebels*, which has a good claim to be the most important single contribution to any understanding of the Ulster problem (1978). The essential point to isolate is the vibrancy of the Ulster Protestant idea of the constitution, far from the dry legal concept which constitutional lawyers would make of it, and more akin to the vital force of Hayek's 'constitution of liberty'. This is an element in the daily lives of ordinary people—a 'way of life' which is a dynamic compound of 'freedom, religion and laws'. The contingent place of law in this compound is illuminated by one of Professor Miller's many telling quotations (1978, p. 35), from 'A Lawyer Volunteer' in 1779 (*Hibernian Journal*, 24–6 November 1779):

It has been the invariable custom of Formalists and Hirelings to confound the *Constitution* and the *Law*, and to call that the *only* support of the Constitution which is but *one* support, and is, at certain Times, insufficient;—I mean perfect Obedience to *positive Law*.

As must by now be well understood, 'loyalty' was loyalty to this constitution, not to any specific institution; to an indefinable essence (such as the 'British empire') rather than a concrete substance (such as the British parliament). Loyalty to the British Crown was conditional on the Crown's support of the Protestant constitution; it was, in other words, a reciprocal or contractarian loyalty.

But words, however vibrant, tend not to subsist *in vacuo*. In this case there existed a remarkable vehicle for the transmission of this contractarian concept through time. This was the tradition—one might be tempted to say 'institution'—of public banding. The frontier impulse to territorial domination, originally expressed in bands under the leadership of the landed élite, persisted as a manifestation of Protestant solidarity. A crucial aspect of the quasi-military ritual displays was their unique capacity to transcend the sectarian rivalry that has always been a marked feature of Ulster Protestantism. This point was registered by Rosemary Harris in the 1950s, along with the far from trivial observation that the atmosphere surrounding grand marches like those on the twelfth of July acted as a communal catharsis. 'Such a demonstration was a mixture of colour, gold and purple and scarlet, and a unique cacophony that trumpeted forth not only hostility to foes, but local pride in this climax to long, hard work, and the release of jubilant, bacchanalian carnival.' (1972, p. 165). Likewise the dominant organization, the Orange Order, was the sole means of articulating an overall Protestant self-consciousness, the central impulse of which was its fraternalism, its egalitarian spirit.

According to Miller's persuasive thesis, it was this function that carried the institution across the threshold of modernity. The image of Ulster Protestant society as an 'idealized feudal arrangement', in which reciprocal gentry–tenant relations remained more important than free-market capitalism, had powerful attractions for those pushed to the margins of the modernizing economy (Miller 1978, p. 50). Hence, while modernization drastically altered the social structure of Ulster, 'Orangeism sustained for Protestant workers in town and country the sense that the most important feature of the old structure—a special relationship between them and their Protestant betters—still obtained'. Specifically, the symbolism and pageantry of Orangeism 'gave to its humbler members a sense of having a more direct relationship to authority, in the person of the monarch, than they had enjoyed in the public bandings of the eighteenth century' (1978, pp. 56, 63). The polarizing effect of this sublimation was actually increased rather than diminished by urban growth in the nineteenth century. Premodern agrarian attitudes were sucked by rapid urbanization into the epicentres of the modernizing process (Stewart 1977, p. 140).* The most spectacular example was, of course, Belfast, where intensifying communal riots indicated the compression of territoriality, to the evident puzzlement of successive governmental commissions of inquiry (*Report of the Belfast Riots Commission*, HC 1887 (C. 4925), xviii. 1):

The extremity to which party and religious feeling has grown in Belfast is shown strikingly by the fact that the people of the artisan and labouring class, disregarding the ordinary considerations of convenience, dwell to a large extent in separate quarters, each of which is almost entirely given up to persons of one particular faith, and the boundaries of which are sharply defined.

These were the words of the commission investigating the outbreak of June 1886, whose centenary fell recently. In these 'sermons in stones' 32 people died and 371 were wounded: Belfast went beyond disorder and into civil war. The riots were a direct response to the first Home Rule Bill; the fact that the second and third bills in 1893 and 1912 did not provoke greater bloodshed was due simply to the channelling of popular Protestant energy into large-scale quasi-military organizations —no source of comfort to the authorities.

By the 1880s the direct polarity of loyalism and nationalism was apparent. In the circumstances it was hardly surprising that Irish nationalists, long subjected to the public triumphalism of the loyalists, should have found it hard to project a sense of brotherhood with their oppressors. And in any case it seems likely that loyalists would have set their faces against nationalism in whatever guise. But it was none the less unfortunate that at this time Irish nationalism, conforming in this respect to shifts in Europe generally, was losing its liberal cast of mind and becoming increasingly 'integral' and exclusive. William O'Brien's United Irish League of 1898, for all its remarkable qualities, was a jejune echo of its namesake a century before (Bew, 1987; Bull 1972; West 1986).† Thomas Davis was the last representative of the

* 'Patterns of Conflict' is perhaps the most valuable section of this outstandingly valuable study.

† The best analysis of the UIL so far published is that of Bew, though it permits some

nonsectarian 'United Irish' idea to have a chance of directing the national movement. His humiliation on the issue of secular education by O'Connell was a decisive moment. Thenceforth Irish nationalism was unapologetically Catholic in outlook; in the supremely ironic words of a modern republican nationalist, Wolfe Tone's political separatism was 'purified' of its irreligion (Moody 1966; Cronin 1980). The impact of such a shift on Protestant loyalism scarcely requires emphasis. Catholic nationalist triumphalism began with 'the invasion of Ulster', launched by T. M. Healey's election victory in Monaghan in 1883. Integral nationalism amplified its cultural repertoire through the creation of the Gaelic Athletic Association in 1884 and the Gaelic League in 1893. Between these dates, Parnell carried the Home Rule movement to its zenith. His crash, and the subsequent nationalist infighting, did nothing to temper Unionist hostility—the strife merely confirmed their belief in the political incapacity of Catholics, at the same time that Irish-Irelanders were making ever more exacting claims on outsiders to submit to the dominant 'Gaelic' culture. A truly integral nationalism was reached in the pungent writings of D. P. Moran: from the loyalist standpoint it is hard to imagine a more sinister or hostile formula than Moran's assertion that 'the foundation of Ireland is the Gael and the Gael must be the element that absorbs' (1905, p. 37; Lyons 1979, p. 60). At one level the reasoning behind this is accessible enough—Moran was concerned to avoid failure and consequent ridicule, and as he put it in more homely style, 'when we look out on Ireland we see that those who believe, or may immediately be induced to believe, in Ireland as a nation are, as a matter of fact, Catholics' (*Leader*, 27 April 1901; Boyce 1982, p. 243). But there is more to it than this. Like all nationalism, Irish nationalism was rooted in irrational, aesthetic, or mystical ideas of a 'natural' world order, and of the inner community of the nation (*Volksgemeinschaft* in the terminology derived from Herder and Fichte).

Irrationality is a quality not exclusive to nationalists; as M. W. Heslinga has wryly observed, many a professional geographer, 'while no longer prejudiced against "artificial" land boundaries, still has a weakness for sea boundaries' (1971, p. 12). The irrationality of this proclivity can be simply demonstrated, as Heslinga does—'a sea not only keeps peoples apart: it also binds them together'. This was clearly

---

slippage between two distinct conflict dimensions, landlord/tenant and Protestant/ Catholic. The clearest defence of the 'lost opportunity' of O'Brien's assimilation is contained in Bull.

the function of the sea between north-west Ireland and south-west
Scotland in an age when water was an incomparably more efficient
medium than land. But the fusion of aesthetic and political ideas can
generate an extraordinarily powerful imagery, as John Bowman argues
at the start of his remorseless exposition of de Valera's attitude to
Ulster (Bowman 1982; O'Halloran 1987). The political independence
and unity of the whole island of Ireland seemed a self-evident, natural,
if not actually divinely-ordained, outcome. De Valera's nationalism
was simultaneously inclusive and exclusive, recognizing no contradiction between these modes. 'Do you think', he demanded rhetorically
of an Irish-American audience in 1927, 'that the Irish people are so
mean that after all this fighting for seven and a half centuries they are
now going to be content to have six counties of their ancient territory
cut off?' (*Irish World*, 26 March 1927; Bowman 1982, p. 103).

Yet how were the inhabitants of those six counties to be persuaded
to embrace the national outlook and tradition they had so far
repudiated? De Valera always disavowed the use of force, in principle.
Verbally, however, the aura of force—force deriving from the abstract
justice of the national claim, or real force of numbers—always
suffused his public utterances on Ulster. In his view loyalists had no
right to their political attitude; they must learn to 'think nationally';
they had no proprietory rights—they were like 'the robber coming into
another man's house and claiming a room as his'; in another metaphor
they had 'wilfully assisted in mutilating their motherland', and could
'justly be made to suffer for their crime' (Bowman 1982, p. 99).

Loyalists may well be forgiven for failure to recognize the boundary
between metaphor and reality in an assertion such as (*Irish World*, 26
May 1927; Bowman 1982, p. 103):

We have a point in front of us that the enemy cannot strengthen. We are strong
enough in Ireland to break it down [applause] and when we have broken it
down are you going to tell me that the conquering army is going to stop at that
point? It is not!

and for seeing it as an all but limitless threat. What is significant about
de Valera's views is not just that they were those of a politically
dominant figure, but that they were not idiosyncratic. Although Kevin
O'Higgins might allege that 'Mr de Valera hates facts as a cat hates
water', the tendency to ignore disagreeable realities—or rather, to
regard them as unreal—was a characteristic of the national movement
long before his time. It was particularly noticeable in the Home Rule

leaders' insistence that Ulster Protestant threats of organized resistance to Dublin government were mere bluff. Again, as with de Valera, such attitudes were not simply foisted by leaders upon followers. Nationalists were imprisoned by the implications of their own rhetoric. If they had compromised their demands, they would have lost their constituency. This was nowhere clearer—or perhaps more disastrous in the long run—than in Redmond's vacillating response to the 1907 Irish Council Bill, shifting from acceptance to condemnation (Bew 1987, pp. 130–3).

These sketches of the loyalist and nationalist psychological-political claims indicate, albeit cursorily, the constellation of forces amongst which the British government manœuvred. It may of course be argued that Britain had itself largely determined the balance of this constellation. The contention that 'loyalism' was a direct creature of British policy has certainly been a major feature of nationalist attitudes until quite recently. Arthur Griffith put it as well as anyone, during the Anglo-Irish Treaty negotiations: 'Undoubtedly the British Government has created this position. Like all Empires it divides and conquers' (Conference, 14 October 1921; Jones 1971, p. 131). Analysis of this argument would require extended historical treatment; here I shall limit my concern to the issues facing one single government, the Liberal administration of 1905–15, and its extension via coalitions under Asquith and Lloyd George through to 1922.

Looking at this government from the standpoint of its responsibility under the Act of Union to govern Ireland, it must be said to have shared the ignorance and indifference towards Irish affairs which have been a feature of the British political structure as a whole. It is difficult to quantify or evaluate the impact of this unconcern, but its effects can be registered not only during periods of obvious drift, but also during (much rarer) periods of coherent action. The Liberal government did have an Irish policy. It was committed to developing the infrastructure (local government, education, agriculture, trade and industry that was non-injurious to British interests); it was further committed to constitutional reform in the shape of Home Rule. This commitment was accepted with varying degrees of enthusiasm across the Liberal party, but nowhere—beyond the embers of John Morley's youthful Gladstonian passion—did the enthusiasm burn brightly. Rather Home Rule was faced, as a recent historian puts it, in a 'stoical spirit of obligation' (Jalland 1980, p. 25). The progressive sections of the party saw it as an encumbrance, an electoral liability which imperilled the programme of social reform. The imperialist wing, to which Asquith belonged, was sceptical on more traditional political grounds (Koss 1976, p. 50). The sheer force of A. V. Dicey's (1886) argument that Home Rule was an unstable hybrid concept, and that there was no real resting-place between dependence and independence, was not lost on them. The Gladstonian contention that Home Rule would strengthen rather than weaken the Empire, by turning Ireland from a discontented and disloyal liability into a satisfied and loyal asset, required a good deal of wishful thinking.

Uncertainty about the viability of Home Rule accounts for the sequence of weaker modes of autonomy proposed, from Joseph Chamberlain's 'Central Board Scheme', through the Liberal proposal of 1906–7, the Irish Council Bill, to Lloyd George's 'Grand Committees', and the wider notion of United Kingdom federalism or 'home rule all round' (Jalland 1979). But uncertainty was confined to the issue of relations between Ireland and Britain; there was little awareness, in spite of the occurrences of 1886 and 1893, of any substantial intra-Irish problem. Thus, when Asquith's government finally turned to the drafting of a third Home Rule Bill it saw no need for either urgency or originality of approach. The 1893 Bill was adopted as the drafting model, right down to its references to Queen Victoria (some of which survived into the seventh month of draft printing). A Cabinet committee began work on the Bill in January 1911; in December the current draft was shown for the first time to the nationalist parliamentary leaders with the casual remark that it 'was not the result of serious consideration, but had been thrown hurriedly together'—a damning indictment, as Patricia Jalland observes, of the supposed labours of the committee over the previous year (Jalland 1980, p. 41).

The feeble apologia was perhaps a symptom of guilt that the Cabinet had, at last, begun to cosider the need for some form of special treatment for Ulster, or those parts of it which were most fiercely hostile to Home Rule. Lloyd George's 'Grand Committees' had already entered and left the Cabinet drafts; federal devolution had been extensively aired in the committee. More significantly, perhaps, the first suggestion of outright partition had been made, in the shape of 'county option'. Though there is no evidence to support Churchill's claim that he advocated exclusion on this basis as early as 1909, it is clear that some discussion took place in August 1911, apparently at the instance of the Chief Secretary for Ireland, Birrell (who was otherwise a loyal supporter of the full nationalist claim.) The suggestion was that 'were the question referred to Ulster county by county' it might turn out that only Antrim and Down would reject Home Rule. They could then 'stand out' for five years, after which 'there should be a fresh referendum to settle their fate' (Birrell to Churchill, 20 August 1911, quoted in Jalland (1980), p. 59).

For a mixture of reasons, none of these proposals, not even the relatively innocuous idea of special status for Ulster (in the form of overrepresentation and/or veto powers in the Dublin parliament, often misleadingly referred to as 'Home Rule within Home Rule'), was built into the new legislation. Drift was undoubtedly one factor, but it was magnified by Asquith's deliberate strategy of reserving concessions until the last moment, in the hope of thereby minimizing them (Jenkins 1964, pp. 278–82). Churchill found this strategy 'baffling', and it undoubtedly helped to foster an appearance of weakness as concessions were wrung from an apparently reluctant government. It seemed all the more unnecessary in that Asquith was convinced two or three months before the Bill was introduced that 'we should probably have to make some sort of bargain about Ulster as the price of Home Rule' (Asquith to Churchill, 19 September 1913; Jalland 1980, p. 67). It was as if he simply could not face Redmond and the Nationalist Party with the fact. But those who argue that he should have done so are apt to forget that what was a 'fact' to a British politician would not have been automatically accepted as such by Irish nationalists. It may well be that nothing short of the Ulster crisis could have generated such acceptance. The implication that the Nationalists were bound to accept a Home Rule Bill in whatever form the government deemed suitable ignores their earlier rejection of the Irish Council Bill.

Nor is it clear that an early concession would have achieved Birrell's object, that 'there could be no Civil War'. 'Home Rule within Home Rule' would have cut very little ground from under the loyalists' feet, since the whole justification for their position was that they should not be 'driven out' of the United Kingdom. Unless Home Rule meant nothing at all—in which case it would be rejected by Nationalists—it would deprive Ulster of British government. Temporary exclusion by county option might have stood some chance if it had been built into the original Bill, but it would more likely have been rejected by both loyalists and nationalists. Only the 'clean cut' for at least four counties offered Unionists the prospect of rescuing something acceptable from the disaster of Home Rule.

With hindsight, partition takes on an air of inevitability—not least from the frequency with which British administrations resorted to it in other parts of the world. This is tacitly conceded by speaking of the need to make a 'bargain about Ulster' as a 'fact'. Was it? The only alternative to partition was that the British government should cleave to the Nationalist Party, refuse to concede the necessity of placating Ulster, and, in Churchill's words, 'go forth together and put these grave matters to the proof'. At one or two points during the tortured negotiations of 1912–14 it looked as if this might happen. The most spectacular instance was the botched instructions which produced the so-called 'Curragh mutiny' in March 1914. Here, it is clear, definite preparations were being made to frustrate a military coup by the Ulster Volunteer Force (Townshend 1983, pp. 249–55, 268–73; Stewart 1967). But, as events showed, the government was unable to manage its public relations so as to prevent such defensive measures from being perceived as 'coercion' of Ulster. This indicates how heavily the odds were stacked against any successful 'calling the Ulster bluff'.

Ulster bluffs have run an up-and-down course in the past century. The threat of mobilization in 1893 was treated with open derision by the government (Harcourt to Saunderson, 29 May 1892; Saunderson MSS, T. 2996/3 19). The actual mobilization of 1912–14 produced an unstable compound of fear and scepticism. Was 'Civil War' really in prospect? While 1974 was widely seen as retrospective confirmation that the 1914 rebels had the power to win—if not by military coup, then by civil resistance—1978 and 1986 have tended to encourage a return to more sanguine evaluations. The question of what the UVF was up to in 1914 remains important. Even if it was a 'stage army', reluctantly armed by the Unionist leadership in order to divert grassroots enthusiasm away from more catastrophic pursuits, the need to accept the arming of the people was significant. Loyalism achieved that subtle balance between the threat of violence and the promise of control which had powered the successes of O'Connell and Parnell in the past (as it would, incidentally, those of Hitler in the future). But the mass-armament of the UVF through the Larne gunrunning in April 1914 raised the consciousness of the role of force in politics to a new level. The Gaelic Leaguer Eoin MacNeill saw the Ulstermen (with whom he identified by descent) as striking, through their military organization, a major blow for Irish self-determination. Though this logic seemed paradoxical, Patrick Pearse reinforced the point more rhetorically—'it is a goodly thing to see arms in Irish hands' (1913).

The nationalist response to the UVF, the Irish Volunteers, was to have enduring influence; the organization provided the musculature of the Easter Rebellion and later, as the Irish Republican Army, of the guerrilla campaign which confronted Lloyd George's government at the end of the World War; and later still, of the unending struggle against partition.

The World War itself played a pivotal part in expanding the role of force in Irish politics. Two moments stand out with particular clarity: the British reaction to the 1916 rebellion, and the 'conscription crisis' of 1918. In 1916 the impact of war psychology was very evident in the automatic instinct of the politicians to leave the suppression of the rising to the soldiers. The results are too well known to require cataloguing here. The need to give priority to British rather than Irish public opinion produced, if possible, even more serious effects in 1918. Resistance to the principle of conscription created a formidable *ralliement* of moderate nationalists and the Catholic church with the advanced nationalists—both violent and nonviolent—of Sinn Féin (Townshend 1983, pp. 318–19). Overall, loyalists could have hoped for no more persuasive confirmation, in the arena of British opinion, of their contention that the Catholic Irish were disloyal.

This was not necessarily a barrier to Home Rule, but it surely delivered the decisive validation of partition. When Lloyd George's government at last sat down in 1919 (with even less alacrity than Asquith's in 1911) to address the Home Rule question, it started from the legislation of 1914. Home Rule was indeed on the statute book, but suspended until the end of the war—an event originally expected in five months rather than five years—and until special provision had been made for Ulster. Such provision made no sense unless the Unionists were offered enough to ensure that, if they rejected the offer, British opinion would cease to support them. In the circumstances this meant the option of permanent exclusion, exercised not by counties but *en bloc* by whatever area was deemed suitable.

Discussions over the fourth Home Rule Bill (the first to be known to history by its proper style, the Government of Ireland Bill) centred on two issues: the size of the excluded area, and the status to be accorded to it. Nicholas Mansergh (1974) has argued skilfully that these two issues were directly connected, though this does not seem to have been fully recognized at the time. The Unionist demand in 1914 had been for six counties, with full administrative autonomy but no legislative powers. The Cabinet committee of 1919 preferred the separation of all nine counties of the 'historic province' of Ulster—then as now an odd mixture of terminology, since the counties are not 'historic' units in this sense, and 'Ulster' had never been an administrative unit—with legislative powers parallel to those of the proposed Dublin parliament. (In effect, dual Home Rule.) Substantial additional powers were to be available through a joint Council of Ireland, as an incentive to unity.

The explicit intention of the committee in recommending a nine-county area was to avoid the appearance of a sectarian partition, and to make eventual unity more likely. Even Bonar Law, the pre-war diehard, seems to have gone along with this pious window-dressing, with an eye firmly on overseas opinion. The decisive Unionist voice now proved to be that of Law's old leader Balfour, who turned the committee's logic on its head (or, as he might have said, set it on its feet). This *was* a sectarian partition, and its whole object was to avoid unity. Balfour followed the brutal reasoning of the Ulster Unionist chiefs, that a six-county area was the biggest they could expect to control in perpetuity. At the same time, he was alert enough to the prevailing diplomatic *mores* of the Versailles epoch to assume that the exact delimitation of the area would be based on plebiscites, to minimize friction as far as possible (Lord President of the Council to Prime Minister, 19 February 1920. C.P. 681. Public Record Office, CAB. 24 98).

This, of course, is notoriously what did not happen when the border was established. During the Anglo-Irish treaty negotiations of 1921 the Sinn Féin emissaries were confronted by the existence of the six-county Northern Ireland as a *fait accompli*. Their efforts to secure reversion to 'county option' (Birrell's 'referendum'), let alone any more sensitive register of popular opinion, got nowhere (Jones 1971). What they got was a 'boundary commission', a device with a meaning even less clear than 'plebiscite' or 'referendum', and one which seems to have originated from the Unionist camp. As is well known, the approach of the Boundary Commission which eventually sat under the chairmanship of judge Feetham was almost a caricature of conservative adhesion to the status quo. The outcome was a Northern Ireland substate with major inbuilt, and quite predictable, flaws. This was a polity born, as it were, in a terminal condition.

A brief survey of the history of the six-county system between 1925 and 1972 reveals the working-out of these inherent defects. The point has often been made—and is no less valid for that—that Lloyd George's achievement was not to solve the Irish problem but to remove it from Westminster for fifty years. Once that was done, British indifference could reassert itself with a clean conscience. The degree of supervision implied in the 1920 Act was never applied after 1922; the government of Northern Ireland was left to place its own stamp on the conduct of public life. When allegations of oppression or discrimination were laid before the London government, as happened with increased regularity after de Valera's return to power in 1932, they were subjected to ineffectual scrutiny. On one such occasion the Home Office, after claiming to be unable to secure unprejudiced evidence, observed baldly that in any case 'it is of course obvious that Northern Ireland is, and must be, a Protestant "state", otherwise it would not have come into being and would certainly not continue to exist' (Townshend 1986, p. 124).

The problem was that such naked sectarian character ran increasingly into collision with public standards in the wider world. While it would be an exaggeration to say that the Northern Ireland state was founded on the denial of political rights to Catholics, it was certainly based on the assumption that as long as Catholics remained 'disloyal' they excluded themselves from political rights. (Hence, for instance, the 'gerrymandering' of constituencies was defended in part by reference to the fact that nationalists had boycotted the machinery for drawing up boundaries.) So to argue that there could be a legitimate political role for nationalists within the Northern Ireland system was an absurdity. And while it is clear that many Protestant Ulstermen, as Lord Dufferin reported in 1938, deplored the treatment of Catholics as 'a minority to be kept under rather than as part of the nation to be incorporated', and were 'uneasy about the attitude of their government which had the effect of perpetuating a division which a more enlightened policy might close' (Townshend 1986, p. 124), such a policy did not recommend itself, on grounds either of principle or of expediency, to those in power.

2

INTERPRETATIONS OF THE
NORTHERN IRELAND PROBLEM*
John Whyte

SINCE the current troubles began in 1968, an enormous literature on Northern Ireland has been accumulated. This paper is designed to survey the literature, in order to ascertain what common ground, if any, exists among the various authorities. The sources will be grouped into four categories, according to where the authors see the primary conflict in Northern Ireland to lie, as follows:

Interpretation	Perceived Primary Source of Conflict
nationalist	Britain v. Ireland
unionist	South v. North
Marxist	capitalist v. workers
internal-conflict	Protestant v. Catholic (within Northern Ireland)

True, these various interpretations are not mutually exclusive, and it is rare to find an author who holds any one of them in pure form. However, in practice there has seldom been any difficulty in deciding where a given author sees the most important conflict to lie, and in classifying him/her accordingly. This paper is therefore organized into four sections, one for each of the interpretations just listed. Under each heading I shall start with the literature available in the 1960s and trace developments since then.

---

* In 1978 I published a paper entitled 'Interpretations of the Northern Ireland Problem: An Appraisal' (Whyte 1978). The present paper is designed to replace that one. Although I have retained a few phrases and sentences, it represents a total rewriting. There are four reasons why a complete revision was necessary: (*a*) An enormous amount of fresh material has come out, some of it of high quality. Indeed, its volume is so great as to be embarrassing. In my 1978 article I was able to devote space to expounding some of the more interesting theories; in this paper, if I am to keep it within reasonable bounds, I can do no more than allude briefly to one theory before hurrying on to the next; (*b*) I am no longer satisfied with the classification I adopted in 1978; (*c*) My opinion of some of the works I discussed in 1978 has since altered; (*d*) Slightly more common ground is detectable now than then.

I. THE NATIONALIST INTERPRETATION

The nationalist view of Northern Ireland is as old as Northern Ireland itself. Among early statements of it are the North-Eastern Boundary Bureau's *Handbook of the Ulster Question* (1923), Harrison (1939), and, with some deviations peculiar to the author, George O'Brien (1936). The tradition was continued after the war by Denis Gwynn (1950) and by the various publications of the All-Party Anti-Partition League in the late 1940s and early 1950s. The most comprehensive statement of the case was presented in Frank Gallagher's *The Indivisible Island* (1957), which subsumed and amplified the publications of the Anti-Partition League.

This interpretation can be summarized in two propositions: (*a*) The people of Ireland form one nation. The unionists of Northern Ireland do not belong to a different nation: while they have some regional peculiarities, these are not greater than are to be found within the confines of many other nations, and, if foreign interference did not stir them up, they could easily adjust their differences with their fellow-Irishmen; (*b*) The fault for keeping Ireland divided lies with Britain. It is she who has encouraged the unionists to make unreasonable claims, and has then propped up their position by financial and military aid. The case is summed up by Gallagher (1957, p. 88):

Britain based her partition policy on divergences she herself created and fostered among the Irish people. Other democratic nations have had similar problems to those of Ireland. These have been solved, with justice to all concerned and within the framework of the national units in question, because no powerful neighbour set out to prevent a settlement by exploiting internal differences.

The evidence for this view is largely historical. Much of Gallagher's book is a survey of the mischievous role played by British politicians in fomenting Irish differences during the nineteenth and early twentieth centuries. It is argued that partition was not wanted by either nationalist or unionist within Ireland, and that it would not have come about had not British politicians engineered it for party advantage. The possibility that unionists might have had good reasons for not wanting to join an all-Ireland state is not even discussed.

Even in its heyday, however, this interpretation was not unanimously held by those in the nationalist tradition. A thin dissident stream of literature existed (Sheehy 1957; Barrington 1959) which argued that the unionist tradition had a strength of its own which could not be explained away as the result of British manipulation, and that nationalists would have to come to terms with it if they were ever to attain a united Ireland.

Since the current troubles began, the nationalist interpretation in its traditional form has come under increasing fire. Unionists have shown a strength of feeling which goes beyond what could be explained as a result of British manipulation, while the British role has been to restrain the unionists rather than stir them up. The reforms of 1968–73 were put through under British pressure, and British troops were introduced on the streets of Belfast and Derry in 1969 in order to protect the Catholics from the unionists. The British constructed the power-sharing executive of 1974, and much more recently have signed the Anglo-Irish Agreement with Dublin in November 1985. Unionists on the other hand have shown overwhelming opposition even to these compromises, and have used every instrument in their grasp—elections, strikes, even assassinations—to show that they oppose any change that could conceivably be regarded as a move in the direction of a united Ireland. True, many nationalists would accuse the British of not standing up to the unionists sufficiently, especially during the collapse of the power-sharing executive in 1974—but that is a long way from saying that they actually provoked the unionists to resist.

Another factor which has helped the re-examination of traditional nationalist attitudes has been the progress of historical scholarship. The development of scholarly history in Ireland has occurred only in the last few decades, and it was to be the 1970s before historians examined nineteenth- and early twentieth-century Ulster in any detail. When this was done, it emerged that the Ulster Protestant community had a distinct consciousness long before the Home Rule issue became salient, and that when it did become salient, Ulster Protestants of all classes felt they had good reason for opposing it (Buckland 1973; Gibbon 1975; Miller 1978; Akenson 1979; Patterson 1980; Laffan 1983). There was not much ground here for claiming that a basically minor cleavage had been inflamed by British politicians for their own ends.

Faced by such considerations, there has been a far-reaching reappraisal within the nationalist camp. The beginning of the change can be illustrated by two books published in 1972. The first, *Towards a New Ireland*, by the future Taoiseach Garret FitzGerald, maintained part of the traditional nationalist interpretation: the author argued that

Ireland was still 'one nation' (p. 175), despite the existence in it of different cultures. But he conceded that British interference in Irish affairs was no longer the crucial problem (p. 91), and that unionist objections to a united Ireland had an autonomy which required recognition.

The other book published in 1972, Conor Cruise O'Brien's *States of Ireland*, went further. O'Brien argued that Irish nationalists had never really believed their own dogma: by countless unguarded words and actions they showed that they did not consider the unionists to be one nation with themselves. Recent events had brought the contradiction into the open (p. 297): 'what has been coming across to ordinary people is that our problem is *not* "how to get unity" but how to share an island in conditions of peace and reasonable fairness, and that such conditions *preclude* unity as long as the Ulster Protestants reject that'. The point has since been put even more strongly by the political scientist John Coakley (1983, p. 129): 'The people of Ireland do not constitute a nation not only because most Protestants do not give their loyalty to this group (i.e. the people of Ireland as a whole) but, in particular, because *most Catholics do not give their primary loyalty to this group either*' (original italics).

The most authoritative restatement of the nationalist view can be found in the *Report* of the New Ireland Forum (1984a). The Forum represented the three major parties in the Republic (Fianna Fáil, Fine Gael, and Labour), and also the main constitutional nationalist party in Northern Ireland, the SDLP. It could thus claim to speak for the overwhelming majority of Irish nationalists, north and south. It is traditionally nationalist in that it looks to a unitary Irish state as the best denouement to the current problem (para. 5. 7). But in its analysis of the problem it is, apart from a few stray phrases, predominantly revisionist. It acknowledges that there is a unionist identity and ethos distinct from the nationalist one, and that 'both these identities must have equally satisfactory, secure and durable, political, administrative and symbolic expression and protection' (para. 5. 2 (4)). The change from, say, Gallagher (1957), who dismissed the unionist identity as a fabrication by the British, is so extensive that the Forum *Report* can hardly be said to belong to the same tradition. It is more appropriately classified under another heading, and I shall come back to it when I discuss the community-conflict approach.

It is true that traditional nationalism has not died. A trickle of publications continues to appear which show little change from the attitudes of the 1950s. Among them Kelley (1982), MacBride (1985), and the various books of Kevin Boland (1972, 1977, 1982, 1984) are the most uncompromising. Tom Collins (1983) flirts with the idea of an independent Northern Ireland as a possible solution, but in his analysis of the problem is as critical of British policy as the most dedicated nationalist could wish. Seán Cronin's *Irish Nationalism* (1980) is a book that hovers on the margin between revisionism and traditionalism; some sharp criticism of traditional attitudes is meted out in the course of the book, though the conclusions are traditional. On the whole, however, literature from the nationalist viewpoint has undergone a major change in the last twenty years, from ignoring the autonomy of the unionist viewpoint to giving it ample recognition.

When I say that traditional nationalism has now shrunk to the status of a minority stream in the literature, it is important to stress the limits of what is being stated. This does not mean that the British and/or the unionists are now conceded to have been in the right. In particular: (*a*) It does not mean saying that the 1920 settlement was just. Granted that there were two distinct communities in Ireland, the Government of Ireland Act of 1920 did not hold the balance fairly between them. It gave the unionists much more territory than they were entitled to on a head-count, and failed to provide effective safeguards against the oppression of minorities; (*b*) It does not mean exonerating subsequent British policy from charges of neglect or pusillanimity; (*c*) Most of all, it does not mean giving up the ideal of a united Ireland. Even if we agree that Ireland is not one nation, that does not mean that it should not be one state. It could be argued that the two communities are so intermingled that it is impossible to divide them into two uni-national states, and that the healthiest arrangement might be a single bi-national state. This, however, is to put the case for a united Ireland on a quite different footing from that traditionally employed.

2. THE UNIONIST INTERPRETATION

The nationalist interpretation has always been opposed by the unionist view. Among the presentations of it made down to the early 1960s were a book by Ronald McNeill (1922), two works by Hugh Shearman (1942, 1948), a pamphlet by W. A. Carson (1956), and, probably the fullest presentation, *The Irish Border as a Cultural Divide*, by the Dutch geographer M. W. Heslinga (1962).

The traditional unionist view, to a greater degree than the traditional nationalist one, has continued to be rearticulated throughout the current troubles (Shearman 1970, 1982; New Ulster Movement 1972; Paisley 1972; Smyth 1972, 1975; Stewart 1977; Allister 1981; McCartney *et al.* 1981; Paisley *et al.* 1982; Cielou 1983). This can perhaps be explained on the ground that the case for a united Ireland continues to be made, and therefore in unionist eyes needs to be rebutted, even though the argument for unity has, in many minds, profoundly changed.

The arguments against a united Ireland to be found in unionist literature can be put under three main headings: religious, national, and economic. I shall discuss them in what seems to be their ascending order of importance.

The *economic* argument is, quite simply, that Northern Ireland is far better off as part of the United Kingdom than it would be as part of a united Ireland. The Republic of Ireland is portrayed as a weak economy, kept from collaopse by high emigration, to join which 'would be to join economic hopelessness and a huge debt' (Paisley *et al.* 1982, pp. 50–2). A southern Irish economist is cited who calculated in 1972 that the national income of the Republic would have been between 25 and 40 per cent higher if it had remained within the United Kingdom (Shearman 1982, p. 183, citing Raymond Crotty in *The Times*, 3 July 1972). However, it would be a mistake to put too much emphasis on the economic argument. Some authors stress that it is only a subordinate aspect of the unionist case (New Ulster Movement 1972, p. 3; Smyth 1975, p. 26). Others do not mention it at all (McCartney *et al.* 1981). The main stress in unionist literature is put on the other two factors.

The *national* argument asserts that unionists feel themselves to be of British nationality (New Ulster Movement 1972, p. 5):

To a large minority in Northern Ireland, British nationality seems as natural as the air they breathe. They travel on British passports, join the British armed forces or civil services, use the term 'our' when they are talking about things British. They erect memorials in their towns, schools, and institutions to those who have died in the British forces during the two world wars.

They would therefore feel ill at ease in a state founded on an anti-British nationalism. To the argument that they should accept the will of the Irish people as a whole, they reply that Ireland has never been united except under British rule, and that there is no reason why, when the southern Irish left the United Kingdom, the northern Irish should have followed them (Paisley *et al.* 1982, p. 39).

The argument which most authors develop at greatest length is the *religious* one. Some specifically state that it is the most important: 'the one decisive factor in partition is . . . the simple determination of Protestants in north-east Ireland not to become a minority in a Catholic Ireland' (Stewart 1977, p. 162). The objections have been partly to specific items of law, such as the prohibition of divorce, the difficulties in the way of obtaining contraceptives, church control of education, and the existence of a literary censorship (McCartney *et al.* 1981, p. 5; Paisley *et al.* 1982, p. 50). But it should not be thought that legislative change in these areas would dissolve the difficulty—indeed restrictions on the sale of contraceptives were removed in 1985, without making any detectible difference to unionist attitudes. Those attitudes are based more on perceptions of an atmosphere, than on particular grievances. The Catholic church in the Republic is seen as being 'in such a position of entrenched power because of the control it exercises indirectly through the minds and attitudes of the faithful, as to be able to dictate policy to the State on matters which the Church considers essential to the maintenance of its position' (McCartney *et al.* 1981, p. 3).

A point made in almost all the unionist literature is that the Protestant population of the Republic has halved since independence. Some writers put this down to discrimination (e.g. Paisley *et al.* 1982, p. 50); Allister 1981, p. 16; Shearman 1970, p. 45), but even a relatively restrained writer concludes from it that 'the Republic is not a country in which the average Protestant thrives' (Smyth 1975, p. 29).

Much of this unionist argument derives from a particular view of the Republic, and it therefore needs to be checked against research actually done on the Republic. When this is done, not all of it survives unscathed. Studies of the Protestant community in the south do not give the impression of a downtrodden group (Viney 1965; White 1975; Bowen 1983—though for a partially divergent view see Akenson 1975, pp. 109–34). Discrimination against Protestants is specifically denied (Viney 1965, p. 10), or seen as a minor and vanishing phenomenon (White 1975, p. 169). All authorities stress that Protestants continue to be overrepresented in the higher strata of society.

The decline in Protestant numbers in the period 1946–71 has been examined by Brendan Walsh (1970, 1975). He found one reason for decline which may be attributed to pressure from the majority—

namely, the loss of a number of children to the Protestant community in each generation because of Catholic insistence that children of mixed marriages be brought up as Catholics. But the two main factors were a high death rate (due to an unfavourable age structure) and a low birth rate, for neither of which could Catholics be blamed. Walsh found that the Protestant emigration rate was much lower than the Catholic, which does not suggest that Protestants felt the Republic to be a country in which they were unable to thrive.

On the national issue the unionists have a stronger case. It is a fact that the twenty-six-county state has progressively broken all the symbolic links that formerly joined it to the United Kingdom, and that the state celebrates as heroes the leaders of anti-British rebellions. Indeed the New Ireland Forum *Report* (1984*a*, paras. 4. 9, 5. 1 (10)) recognizes that a sense of Britishness is an essential part of the unionist identity, which nationalists have hitherto underestimated.

The unionists' economic case seems also to be well founded. The Northern Ireland economy is now in such deep crisis that it requires a major power like the United Kingdom to shore it up. A small country like the Republic would be quite unable to do so, particularly in view of its own economic difficulties. A forecast prepared for the New Ireland Forum concluded that, in a united Ireland without foreign subvention, there would be 'exploding and unsustainable deficits' (New Ireland Forum 1984*b*, p. 87). Indeed, if unionists were to read more of the careful and unsentimental research being done on society in the Republic by southern Irish scholars, they would find additional ammunition for their case. Some of this research shows the Republic to be, not just a poorer society than the United Kingdom, but also a more unequal one. A study of social mobility in the Dublin area showed that it was markedly more limited than in England (Whelan and Whelan 1984). Education and housing policies perpetuate these inequalities (McCashin 1982, p. 216). A comparison of the position of women in the two parts of Ireland found that 'overwhelmingly the differences are to the advantage of the North' (New Ireland Forum 1983, p. 2).

The unionists' view of the south, then, receives at least partial confirmation from independent research. Although not every charge is supported, quite enough survives to validate their central point—that they are in important ways distinct from the Irish majority, and that they have good reasons for not wishing to be absorbed into a united Ireland. This indeed has been widely conceded, as we saw in the last section, and the 'one-nation theory' is now almost dead among those who have devoted study to the Northern Ireland problem.

Nevertheless, the unionists' view is not widely accepted. The reason seems to lie, not in their basic contention, but in the deduction which they would seek to draw. Unionists see as the heart of the problem the refusal of Irish nationalists to accept their right to self-determination. Particular offence is taken at the territorial claim in Articles 2 and 3 of the Republic's constitution (Shearman 1970, 1982; McCartney et al. 1981; Paisley et al. 1982). This claim is not only resented in itself; it is seen as legitimizing the IRA campaign (McCartney et al. 1981, p. 2; Paisley et al. 1982, p. 41).

These conclusions take no account of the contribution which the unionists' own behaviour has made to the current problem. Northern Ireland is not a homogeneous community under threat from outside; it is a deeply divided community whose problems stem at least in part from the treatment which the unionist majority has meted out to the nationalist minority. In the eyes of many observers, this mistreatment must be taken into account as well.

Support for such a view can be found in recent studies of the unionist regime. The unionists have long been criticized for discrimination, gerrymandering, and a biased security system (e.g. in the later chapters of Gallagher 1957). The government files are now (with some exceptions) open for the early decades of the Northern Ireland state, and researchers have been able to check on the truth or falsity of these claims. Almost without exception they are upheld. Local government boundaries were indeed deliberately gerrymandered (Buckland 1979, pp. 231–46). Discrimination was indeed rife against Catholics in the civil service (Bew et al. 1979, p. 77; Buckland 1979, pp. 20–3). The B Specials were indeed a sectarian force (Farrell 1983), which a Westminster civil servant described in 1922 as 'purely partisan and insufficiently disciplined' (1983, p. 153). I said in the last section that research into nineteenth and early twentieth-century Ulster has not helped the nationalist case. It can also be said that research into Northern Ireland since 1920 has not helped the unionist case.

The archives for the later years of the unionist state are not yet open, but enough is available from other sources to permit an appraisal of its performance. The spectrum of opinion runs from writers who present a generally benign picture of the regime (Hewitt 1981), through to others who present a highly critical one (CSJ 1969). I do not wish to survey this material here, particularly as I have already done so in another paper (Whyte 1983a). Suffice it to say that, even when the wilder charges are discounted, enough remains to show that there was substantial ground for complaint. I agree with the conclusions reached by John Darby (1976 pp. 77–8), who has made a similar appraisal of the literature: 'There is no doubt that some of the allegations of discrimination against the Unionist government are not supported by evidence and that others have been exaggerated . . . [but] there is a consistent and irrefutable pattern of deliberate discrimination against Catholics'.

The clearest evidence of unionist reluctance to deal fairly can be seen in the location of the boundary of Northern Ireland. Granted that there is a distinct community in the north-east of Ireland, and granted that it has a right to self-determination, that right cannot be used to justify the border where it now stands. For the border was drawn so as to corral within it not only almost all areas with unionist majorities, but also considerable areas with nationalist ones. If the county is taken as the unit, there were at the time of partition unionist majorities in only four of the six counties in Northern Ireland. If some smaller unit had been chosen, then parts of Tyrone and Fermanagh might have been reclaimed for unionism but considerable parts of other counties would have been lost to nationalism.

The anomaly worried the British. With the opening of archives in the 1970s the inside story became available of how the Government of Ireland Act 1920, the measure which partitioned the country, was framed (Mansergh 1974, pp. 41–8). The British government saw the partition of Ireland as a temporary measure, pending reunification, and in that case the fact that the boundary did not closely fit the area of unionist majority mattered less, because it made the whole arrangement more provisional. It meant that the proportion of the population that nationalists would have to win over in order to achieve unity was less than it would have been in a smaller Northern Ireland. As Lloyd George said to Griffith during the treaty negotiations of 1921, when the latter complained of the number of nationalists included in Northern Ireland against their will, 'in order to persuade Ulster to come in there is an advantage in her having a Catholic population' (Jones 1971, p. 131).

I have come across no comparable agonizing among unionists. Their only worry was how much territory they would be able to control. The idea that it might be unjust to ask for more territory than was actually unionist apparently never entered their heads.

That does not mean that the problem could now be solved by redrawing the boundary of Northern Ireland. The two communities live so intermingled that it would be impossible to find a boundary which divides them neatly. In any case, Northern Ireland has now existed as a unit for sixty-five years and has developed its own structure and atmosphere. Most observers assume that it must be dealt with as a unit. But it does mean that there is a disagreeable supremacist streak in unionist ideology which repels many who are unconvinced by the nationalist case. For such observers, the only satisfactory analysis of the Northern Ireland problem is one which recognizes that unionists have indeed valid grounds of complaint against nationalists, but that the converse is also true. However, before examining such theories, we must look at the class-based interpretations of Marxist writers.

3. MARXIST INTERPRETATIONS*

Twenty years ago one could have used the singular—'the Marxist interpretation'. For at that time there was one dominant view of Ireland in the Marxist world, derived from James Connolly, the martyr-hero of 1916, who had pioneered the application of Marxist theory to Ireland. I shall use the three-volume collection of his writings edited by Desmond Ryan, which was first published in 1949–51 and reprinted in the 1960s, and in particular the second volume, entitled *Socialism and Nationalism* (1948).

For Connolly, the fundamental conflict in Ireland as everywhere else in the capitalist world was between employer and worker, and his overriding aim was a workers' victory. In the Irish context, that entailed national independence. The British empire was 'the most aggressive type and resolute defender' of capitalism (Ryan 1948, p. 9), and socialism could not be built in Ireland without a total break from Britain. It was hopeless to look, as some Belfast socialists did, for salvation from the British labour movement—the backgrounds of the British and Irish movements were 'so essentially different' (1948, p. 105). True, the Protestant workers of the Belfast area seemed to wish to maintain British rule. This was because the master class, 'with devilish

---

* A difficulty in dealing with this group of interpretations is to decide who is a Marxist. Much mutual excommunication takes place among Marxists, and some of them would deny to others listed here a place in the Marxist camp. I have adopted the policy of accepting as a Marxist anyone who claims to be one either explicitly, or, by the use of a certain kind of vocabulary, implicitly.

ingenuity' (1948, p. 102), had succeeded in fomenting divisions between Protestant and Catholic. But their opposition need not be taken too seriously: with Home Rule once established, 'the old relation of Protestant and Catholic begins to melt and dissolve' (1948, p. 73). The partition of Ireland must, however, be opposed at all costs, because it would keep alive the national issue. 'All hopes of uniting the workers, irrespective of religion or old political battle cries will be shattered, and through North and South the issue of Home Rule will be still used to cover the iniquities of the capitalist and landlord class' (1948, p. 114).

For forty years Connolly's ideas were hardly challenged on the left. True, Strauss (1951), in a history of Ireland written from a Marxist point of view, suggested that northern Protestant workers' opposition to Home Rule could not solely be attributed to ruling-class manipulation (p. 234), and that unionist attitudes were nourished by 'solid interests' (p. 290). But these were only passing remarks in a book whose focus did not lie in Ulster. It was not until the troubles erupted that the traditional Marxist interpretation—for the same reasons as the traditional nationalist one—attracted increasing criticism. The intensity of feeling shown by unionists was such that the arguments used to account for it—manipulation by the British (the traditional nationalist view) or manipulation by the capitalist class (the traditional Marxist one)—just did not seem sufficient to explain it.

The first Marxist grouping to break away from the traditional view was a body, small in numbers but prolific in publications, called the British and Irish Communist Organisation. It used Marxist terminology to reach conclusions almost diametrically opposed to Connolly's (e.g. BICO 1970, 1971). It argued that differential economic development had produced two nations in Ireland: the Protestants of the north-east, and the Catholics of the rest of the island. In these circumstances, to claim that the Protestant or British bourgeoisies were dividing the working class was the reverse of the truth. It was the Catholic nationalists of the South who played this role, by stirring up the Catholic minority in the North against acceptance of the state in which they lived, and thus preventing the development of working-class unity in Northern Ireland (BICO 1971, p. 7). BICO buttressed its case with a number of carefully researched historical pamphlets (BICO 1972a, 1972b, 1973, 1974b, 1984), showing that the separate identity of the northern Protestants had deep historic roots, and could not be explained away as the result of manipulation by a cunning bourgeoisie. If Connollyite Marxism can be seen as a red variant of traditional nationalism, BICO's Marxism can be seen as a red variant of unionism.

For this reason, perhaps, its thesis has not found universal approval. As we saw in the last section, the unionist interpretation has failed to win general acceptance, not because its claim to a separate identity is denied, but because it takes insufficient account of the seamy side of unionism. The same charge can be made against BICO. Nevertheless, BICO raised sufficient doubts about the traditional interpretation to start a torrent of questioning within the Marxist camp. Over the last fifteen years a number of other revisionist analyses have appeared. I shall list them roughly in chronological order.

1. A Danish socialist, Anders Boserup (1972), accepted, like BICO, the reality of the unionists' separate identity. However, he saw the most important clash within Northern Ireland as being not between unionist and nationalist, but between moderate and extreme unionist. (At the time he was writing this clash was indeed more evident than it is today.) He saw this conflict as based on the conflict between two different kinds of capital, one locally based and conservative, the other multi-national and relatively progressive. Moderate unionists such as Brian Faulkner articulated the interests of the latter. Boserup urged socialists to give them tactical support.

2. Two writers in a french Marxist periodical, Van der Straeten and Daufouy (1972), argued that Ireland was too small to be an independent economy, that the great mistake made by the Irish working class was to separate itself from the English working class, and that its interest lay in an alliance with Britain.

3. A Scottish nationalist who was also a Marxist, Tom Nairn, argued in his book *The Break-up of Britain* (1977) that the United Kingdom was disintegrating anyway, that an independent Northern Ireland was the likeliest outcome of the conflict there, and that the best course to adopt was to accept that probability and work within it.

4. A somewhat similar position was adopted by Belinda Probert in her work *Beyond Orange and Green* (1978). She accepted the reality of the distinct Protestant identity, and sought ways of developing class politics within that. Her message to her fellow-socialists appeared to be that they should support the more class-conscious elements within the Protestant paramilitaries.

5. Bew *et al.* (1979) offered a detailed investigation of class relations

within the Protestant community. While admitting more readily than BICO the seamy side of the unionist record, they concluded that 'there is nothing inherently reactionary about the Protestant working class' (p. 221). In a more recent book, two of these authors (Bew and Patterson 1985) have argued that there is nothing inherently reactionary either about the British presence in Northern Ireland—'the problem of the involvement of the British state in Northern Ireland lies not in its existence but in its specific forms' (Bew and Patterson, 1985, p. 144). They conclude (1985, pp. 147–50) that Britain should stay in Northern Ireland but undertake a more vigorous programme of structural reforms than it has so far done.

The authors discussed in the last five paragraphs differ from each other in important ways, but they all agree in rejecting the Connollyite view that the British presence was the root cause of working-class weakness in Ireland. They can, with BICO, be loosely grouped together as a 'revisionist Marxist' school. The disarray in Irish Marxism brought about by the rise of this school is illustrated by the papers from a seminar of Marxists interested in Ireland held at the University of Warwick in 1978 (Morgan and Purdie 1980). Of the ten contributions, four can be described as traditional and six as in varying degrees revisionist.

This does not mean that the traditional Marxist perspective has been eclipsed. Books which more or less adhere to it have continued to pour from the presses—Devlin (1969), de Paor (1970), Dudley Edwards (1970), Greaves (1972), *The Sunday Times'* Insight Team (1972), Boulton (1973), McCann (1974, 1980), Farrell (1976, 1983), Bell (1976, 1982, 1984), O'Dowd *et al.* (1980), Reed (1984), and most of the contributions in Collins (1985). Some of these are of high quality. Farrell's two historical works are exhaustively researched and show how Connolly's interpretation can be applied to the developments of Northern Ireland in the decades after Connolly's death. O'Dowd *et al.* (1980) lent weight to the traditional Marxist view that Northern Ireland is irreformable by documenting how little has been changed by the reforms introduced between 1968 and 1973. Among articles, I would single out Martin's (1982) survey of the two schools of Marxism, in which, despite accepting the force of some revisionist views, he none the less comes down in favour of the traditional interpretation.

Nevertheless, such works have not proved sufficiently persuasive to re-establish the unity of Marxism. Even those attracted by Marxist analysis will no longer find there a generally agreed interpretation of the Northern Ireland problem. And of course the majority of writers on Northern Ireland are not Marxists at all.

Some have shown this by explicitly attacking the Marxist approach. The theoretical sections of Richard Rose's *Governing without Consensus* (1971) can be taken as a sustained attack on Marxist and other economic interpretations of the Northern Ireland problem. Rose's key claim is that the conflict is so intractable because it is *not* economic. Economic conflicts, about the share-out of material benefits, are bargainable: conflicts about religion and nationality are non-bargainable and therefore much harder to resolve. It is Northern Ireland's misfortune that its conflicts are about religion and nationality (Rose 1971, esp. pp. 300–1, 397–407). More recently, Hickey (1984) has written a book arguing, with copious quotations from Protestant journals, that religion is of autonomous importance and that religious feeling cannot be accounted for as a by-product of economic forces. Other writers who have expressed reservations about Marxist analyses include Wright (1973) and Burton (1978, pp. 156–62).

These writers can, no doubt, be attacked in their turn. Rose, for instance, has been criticized for underplaying the importance of economic forces (Gibson 1972), and his data have been reanalysed to show that he understated the extent of Catholic economic grievances (Covello and Ashby 1980). But wherever the final balance may lie in the argument between Marxists and non-Marxists, the weight of publications shows that the Marxist interpretation is far from the dominant one. Like the nationalist and unionist approaches, it currently secures the allegiance of only a minority of students of Northern Ireland.

4. THE INTERNAL-CONFLICT APPROACH

Brendan O'Leary (1985, p. 36) has made a useful distinction between exogenous and endogenous explanations of the Northern Ireland conflict:

Exogeneous explanations situate NI in the network of Anglo-Irish state relations and/or imperialism. 'Solutions' require international transformations. *Endogenous* explanations analyse Northern Ireland as largely autonomous of exogenous influences. 'Solutions' may employ exogenous instruments but the 'problems' are endogenous.

The nationalist, unionist, and many of the Marxist interpretations can be labelled 'exogenous'. We now come to a school of thought which emphasizes the endogenous factors. This does not mean that all the authors in this school dismiss the existence of exogenous factors: some criticize quite sharply the actions of British (or Irish) governments. But it does mean that they concede to such factors only a secondary importance.

This school of thought was surprisingly late in emerging. Until the 1960s all the literature that I know of on the Northern Ireland problem could be classified under one of the three preceding headings. The first book to be organized round the principle that the root of the difficulty lay within Northern Ireland was Barritt and Carter's *The Northern Ireland Problem* (1962). This book carefully examined different areas of contention—social relations, education, discrimination, civil rights, and so on—drawing on information collected from both communities. Reread in the light of later events, it seems unduly complaisant towards the unionists, extenuating practices such as gerrymandering, which have long since been abandoned as untenable. The authors implicitly accepted this criticism when in the 1972 reissue of their book they added a preface and postscript which were distinctly more acerbic. This bias does not however destroy the pioneering quality of the book.

The approach which seemed innovating in 1962 has become widespread since. The bulk of academic writing on Northern Ireland has adopted the internal-conflict interpretation, either implicitly by its choice of subject, or very often explicitly. As examples we can list the following:

1. Two major attitude surveys, conducted in 1968 and 1978 respectively, and presented in Rose (1971) and Moxon-Browne (1983). These are largely structured round an exploration of the differences between Protestant and Catholic.

2. The work of social psychologists, many of whom are also concerned to explore the extent and nature of community differences. Among books we can point to Fraser (1973), O'Donnell (1977), Harbison (1980, 1983), and Heskin (1981). Among articles, there are numerous papers by Ed Cairns, Liz McWhirter, and Karen Trew (e.g. 1982, 1983, 1983 respectively).

3. Social anthropologists and sociologists have produced a number of local studies exploring community relations in particular areas

(Harris 1972; Leyton 1975; Burton 1978; Larsen 1982*a*; Jenkins 1982, 1983; Buckley 1982; Nelson 1984; and a number of unpublished theses). Dervla Murphy's (1978) account of her travels in Northern Ireland can perhaps be mentioned here.

4. Geographers have examined the spatial distribution of the two communities—e.g. Boal (1969, 1982) in Belfast, and Poole (1982) in the smaller towns.

5. A group of researchers have explored the economic gap between the Protestant and Catholic communities. Many, though not all, of these studies were commissioned by the Fair Employment Agency and have been collected by Cormack and Osborne (1983).

6. Some writers have offered general studies of the Northern Ireland problem from an internal-conflict perspective: for instance, Jackson (1971), Darby (1976), Rose (1976), Aunger (1981), Watt (1981), O'Malley (1983), Fennell (1983), Hickey (1984), and Boyle and Hadden (1985).

7. Along with these can be listed a number of reports from official or unofficial bodies, all of whom coincide in seeing the problem primarily as a conflict of traditions within Northern Ireland: Nils Haagerup's report (1984) for the European Parliament; the Ulster Unionist Party's *The Way Forward* (1984); the report of the New Ireland Forum (1984*a*); the Kilbrandon report commissioned by the British–Irish Association (1984); and, perhaps, the most closely argued of all, the report produced by a commission of the SDP/ Liberal Alliance in Britain (Alliance 1985).

While these authors differ widely among themselves, a number of points can be noted on which there is a fair degree of convergence between them:

1. The two communities in Northern Ireland are best labelled Protestant and Catholic. Not every authority agrees with this categorization: some have preferred to talk of unionist and nationalist (e.g. New Ireland Forum 1984*a*), or even of Ulster British and Ulster Irish (Pickvance 1975). The choice of labels makes a difference, because not every Protestant thinks of himself as unionist or British, and not every Catholic sees himself as nationalist or Irish. However, the great majority of writers prefer the religious labels. The reason seems to be that social organization in Northern Ireland revolves to a great extent round the religious divide. An academic literature is growing up on how people distinguish Protestant from Catholic

(Burton 1978, pp. 37–67; Cairns 1982; Jenkins 1982, pp. 30–1). There is no literature on how to distinguish unionist from nationalist. The religious divide is somehow seen as more fundamental. Indeed, even where it appears to be transcended it may be present beneath the surface. Moxon-Browne (1983, pp. 64–80), reporting on the results of his attitude survey, includes an interesting chapter on those of his sample who claimed to support the Alliance party. The Alliance party claims to draw support from both communities, and Moxon-Browne's data support this conclusion, showing that Alliance party supporters split five to four between Protestant and Catholic (Moxon-Browne 1983, p. 65). But detailed analysis of their opinions showed a considerable divergence between Protestant and Catholic Alliance supporters.

2. There is a high degree of segregation between the two communities. Intermarriage is rare—a factor whose importance was first expounded by Harris (1972, pp. 143–6). The schools systems are almost wholly separate (Darby et al. 1977). In some parts of the province, notably Belfast (Boal 1982), there is residential segregation. Leisure activities and voluntary organizations are often segregated (Darby 1976, pp. 151–60). The Orange Order plays an important part in the lives of many Protestants (Harris 1972, pp. 162–7, 192–7; Wright 1973, pp. 249–50; Larsen 1982b), while Catholics are excluded from membership. The churches themselves are the centre of much social activity (Barritt and Carter 1962, p. 175; Larsen 1982a, p. 152).

3. Segregation has been accompanied by a high degree of stereotyping (O'Donnell 1977), prejudice, and the maintenance of social distance (Fraser 1973; Doob and Foltz 1973; Jahoda and Harrison 1975). Though there are exceptions (O'Donnell 1977), most such studies show a somewhat higher degree of prejudice and social distance among Protestants than among Catholics (Fraser 1973; Jahoda and Harrison 1975; Hickey 1984, p. 139).

4. Despite this degree of segregation and mutual suspicion, the two communities to a great extent share common values. This point is most stressed by the anthropologists. Harris (1972) devotes three chapters to the common culture before spending five on the differences between Protestant and Catholic. Leyton (1974), Larsen (1982a), and Buckley (1982) also stress the similarities. But exponents of other disciplines make the same point. Rose (1971) showed that in many areas of life Protestant and Catholic had similar outlooks. They had

much the same reasons for liking and disliking Northern Ireland, much the same attitudes to trade unions and big business, to family life, authority, and to social class. It was only on strictly political issues, and on a cluster of questions relating to ecumenism, that their attitudes varied widely. Hickey (1984, p. 139), presenting a small-scale survey of Limavady, concluded from it that the separateness of the two groups is far from complete. McKernan (1980, p. 139), studying a group of Protestant and Catholic school pupils, found that they had highly similar value systems. Trew (1983) and McWhirter (1983) have shown, in surveys of recent research by psychologists and others, that religion is not salient in every situation in Northern Ireland. The common culture even extends to segregated institutions: Dominic Murray (1985) has conducted a participant-observation study of two primary schools, one Protestant and one Catholic, and has concluded that the ethos which they convey is in many ways similar.

5. The common culture is insufficient to counteract important differences. The Catholic community suffers from multiple disadvantages compared with the Protestant one. This was most obvious under the Stormont regime, when the Protestants controlled the government, but it has continued under direct rule. Catholics are economically worse off than Protestants (Cormack and Osborne 1983). Their unemployment rate remains persistently higher, despite the depression which has affected both communities (FEA 1985, pp. 23–30). Although in the general service grades of the civil service they are now, in proportion to their share of the population, over-represented among recent recruits (FEA 1983, p. 41), they are under-represented in the higher ranks (1983, p. 51) and are still under-represented in recruits to higher grades (1983, p. 33). Security policy appears to be weighted against the minority. Though much of the evidence for this claim comes from biased sources, it is backed up by academic research (Hadden and Hillyard 1973; Boyle et al. 1975, 1980; Dermot Walsh 1983). Indeed even official reports contain a number of disquieting admissions: on excesses by the RUC in the early days of the troubles (Cameron 1969, pp. 73–4; Scarman 1972, pp. 15–16); on ill-treatment of detainees (Compton 1971), and of suspects in police custody (Bennett 1979).

Finally, Catholics, in so far as they are nationalists, can claim that the institutions of the state take inadequate account of their identity (Boyle and Hadden 1985, pp. 79–80).

6. The reality of Catholic grievances does not mean that Northern

Ireland can be seen as a society neatly divided into oppressor and oppressed. Protestants have their own acute anxieties. Some of the reasons for their state of mind are brought out in the unionist literature surveyed in a previous section. The nature of their fears is described by several of the community studies (Harris 1972; Nelson 1984), in survey data (Rose 1971; Moxon-Browne 1983), and in reports of discussions with representative Protestants (Murphy 1978; Galliher and DeGregory 1985). Northern Ireland can be seen, in the words of Harold Jackson (1971, p. 4), as a 'double-minority' situation, in which each group feels itself beleagured. The object of statesmanship must be to find some framework whereby the fears of *both* groups are assuaged.

Unfortunately, it is at this point that consensus within the community-conflict school of thought breaks down. Even those who agree that the root of the problem lies within Northern Ireland offer the most diverse remedies for that fact. Some have seen a united Ireland as the best framework for a solution (New Ireland Forum 1984*a*). Others have proposed total integration of Northern Ireland with Great Britain (Campaign for Labour Representation in Northern Ireland 1982; Institute for European Defence and Strategic Studies 1984). Others again have proposed an independent Northern Ireland (New Ulster Political Research Group 1979; Dervla Murphy 1984). Yet others have recommended repartition (Critchley 1972, and, more tentatively, Compton 1981, pp. 80–4). A majority of the Kilbrandon Committee recommended a form of joint authority between the United Kingdom and Ireland (Kilbrandon 1984). The Alliance commission on Northern Ireland suggested as a long-term aim a confederation of the British Isles (1985, p. 122). I have no space in a short paper to discuss the merits and demerits of all these options. Anyone who wishes to explore further will find most of them discussed in the chapter entitled 'The Simple Solutions: Why they will not work', in Boyle and Hadden (1985). Suffice it to say that none has achieved anything approaching general approval.

In these circumstances, it is not surprising that some authors have gone to the other extreme and concluded that no solution to the Northern Ireland problem is practicable. Rose (1976, p. 139) surveys various possible settlements, finds that none is workable, and concludes: 'the problem is that there is no solution'. Frank Wright has brought out a fatal dilemma in Northern Ireland. Some argue that a

British withdrawal is essential because otherwise the two sides will
never have the incentive to work out a compromise. Others argue that
it would be disastrous because it would lead to civil war. Wright (1981,
p. 200) suggests that both propositions are true at the same time.
Moxon-Browne (1983, p. 178) points out that there is not just one but
a cluster of problems, and that a solution addressed to one may
exacerbate another. I have myself argued in a paper entitled 'Why is
the Northern Ireland Problem so Intractable?' (Whyte 1981) that all
parties to the conflict pursue policies which exacerbate it, but that they
are constrained to do so by the political and psychological pressures on
them.

However, there is not even a consensus in pessimism. An emerging
school of thought among adherents of the internal-conflict interpretation
holds that, while no generally acceptable solution exists at present, it
should be possible at least to ameliorate the situation. As Moxon-
Browne (1983, p. 178) puts it, 'to seek a solution to *the* Northern
Ireland problem is to pursue a mirage in the desert: a better ploy would
be to irrigate the desert until the landscape looks more inviting'.
O'Malley (1983), Boyle and Hadden (1985), and the Alliance
Commission on Northern Ireland (1985) have suggested a number of
steps that can be taken which, while not satisfying everyone, would at
least reduce the degree of alienation felt on all sides. The Anglo-Irish
Agreement of November 1985 appears to be based on similar
assumptions. The risk in this strategy is that it leaves ultimate
objectives ambiguous. The Anglo-Irish Agreement was signed by
people who hope that it will lead towards a united Ireland, and by
people who hope that it will strengthen the position of Northern
Ireland within the United Kingdom. The trouble with this is that it
arouses the fears of those to whom either of these long-term objectives
is of overriding importance. Mr Haughey has attacked the Agreement
because it strengthens partition; the unionists, because it does not.

CONCLUSION

We have surveyed four different approaches to the Northern Ireland
problem. The most popular is clearly the internal-conflict interpretation.
The traditional Marxist approach probably comes second, but a long
way behind. Revisionist Marxists, nationalists, and unionists contribute
relatively little to the literature.

The emergence of a dominant interpretation could be seen as an advantage. There can be no agreement on the solution to the Northern Ireland conflict until there is agreement on where the problem lies. However, there are two limits to the advance. The first is that, as we have just seen, even those who agree to this definition of the problem still do not agree on the solution. The second is that a consensus among those who have put themselves to the trouble of sustained research into the problem is not matched by consensus in the wider population. The traditional nationalist and traditional unionist viewpoints may have meagre support among the specialists; they still win widespread support among the Irish electorate, north and south. If consensus is to be attainable, the experts will have to get their views across to a wider public.

APPENDIX

The above paper is printed as it was presented to the Keele conference in April 1986. At the conference it was followed by a long and constructive discussion which—at least for me as the author—proved most helpful. I shall outline some of the points made, and my reactions to them.

   1. The nationalist and unionist interpretations are, despite their apparently opposite conclusions, closer to each other than to the other interpretations. In the language of R. S. Kuhn, they apply the same paradigm. They both portray the conflict as being primarily about whether Ireland should or should not be united; they devote little attention to the divide between the two communities in the north-east, which has to be faced regardless of what constitutional status that part of Ireland may have. They should therefore be classified as variants of the same interpretation, rather than as different interpretations. My response is that they do indeed share some presuppositions, but that, since they define the principal antagonists in different ways, they can still justifiably be classified as distinct interpretations.

   2. A Marxist critic chided me for oversimplifying the Marxist view. It is not necessarily true that Marxists see the conflict as one of capitalist versus worker, but rather that they see class as constraining the choices which ethnic groups can make. My response is that this may have been true of the work of my particular critic, but that many Marxists do see things in just the stark terms I described.

   3. Marxists differ so widely in their conclusions that they are best distributed among the other three categories—traditional Marxists going to the nationalists, BICO to the unionists, and other revisionists to the internal-conflict school. There is much in this criticism, and in some cases I had found

it difficult to decide whether to classify a particular author as Marxist or nationalist. Nevertheless, I still prefer on balance to corral the Marxists together. However much they vary in their conclusions, they still share a perception of what is important. They also share a universe of discourse: they argue with each other, while some of them do not even seem to read much of what is produced by non-Marxists.

4. The very concept of a primary conflict is dangerous—in other parts of the world what makes a situation explosive is the admixture of several conflicts, and perhaps that is true in Northern Ireland as well. This is a point well taken, and I would agree that the situation in Northern Ireland is exacerbated by the fact that more than one conflict is going on. But there can be a hierarchy of importance among conflicts. Writers do differ markedly about where they see the principal conflict to lie, and it is helpful to classify them accordingly.

5. The paper takes insufficient account of the wider context. Northern Ireland is not an entity on its own: it is part of an island, which in turn is part of an archipelago, and both these facts affect the conflict. I would accept that my paper shows a real deficiency here. Even those authors who put most stress on the conflict *within* Northern Ireland often recognize that that conflict is partly about the wider context. The clash between the two different communities in part arises because they relate differently to (*a*) the rest of Ireland, and (*b*) Great Britain. This point is in fact made by a number of the authorities I cited under the internal conflict interpretation (e.g. Jackson 1971; Watt 1981; O'Malley 1983; New Ireland Forum 1984*a*; Kilbrandon 1984; Boyle and Hadden 1985), and I should have noted it.

3

INITIATIVES FOR CONSENSUS
Power-sharing
John Darby

THE concept of power-sharing was spawned by the violence of the late 1960s in Northern Ireland, and the gestation period was remarkably short. As late as 1969 it is accurate to describe minority demands in Northern Ireland as liberal-democratic—effectively requests for concessions from a Unionist government. The initial demands of the Northern Ireland Civil Rights Association not only envisaged a reformed Northern Ireland rather than a united Ireland, but did not even investigate possible routes for minority involvement in executive power within Northern Ireland. Within three years, however, the minority demand for power-sharing had become so insistent that the British government, exercising Direct Rule from Westminster, had become convinced that no solid settlement could be reached without it (Discussion Paper 1972):

There are strong arguments that the objective of real participation should be achieved by giving minority interests a share in the exercise of executive power if this can be achieved by means which are not unduly complex or artificial, and which do not represent an obstacle to effective government.

Civil protest is a powerful yeast. The emphasis had shifted from content to process, from seeking concessions on civil rights to demanding involvement in the machinery through which concessions were granted.

The principle of power-sharing—that the minority population should have a significant and genuine involvement in the administration of Northern Ireland—has remained a bi-partisan principle of British policy since its adoption by the Heath government in 1972. Since then, therefore, debate has focused on the definition of what constituted genuine involvement, and on the various methods of implementing it. It is possible to identify four major attempts to break the deadlock of Direct Rule, all unsuccessful and all insisting on power-sharing between nationalists and unionists (for a good account of this process, see Birrell 1981). The first was the most productive. Following the Northern Ireland Constitution Act in 1973, the only power-sharing devolved administration in Northern Ireland's history took office in January 1974. It comprised the Social Democratic and Labour Party (SDLP), the Alliance party, and part of the Official Unionist Party (OUP) under Brian Faulkner. By May it had been forced to resign as a result of a political strike organized by the Ulster Workers' Council (UWC), supported by the Democratic Unionist Party (DUP) and the majority of the Official Unionists.

The two years following the fall of the Executive saw a second attempt by the government to move to another political accommodation in Northern Ireland. Following a Review Paper on the Northern Ireland Constitution, a Constitutional Convention was set up, failed to agree on a form of devolved government, and was dissolved in 1976. The disagreement was between the Unionist parties and the SDLP over power-sharing at executive level. This phase teased out the elements of power-sharing, introducing to the concept such alternative devices as executive committees, directly elected ministers, and guaranteed minority-weighting in possible administrations. The reason for the Convention's dismissal was the refusal of the Unionist-sponsored report to satisfy the British government's requirement that any devolved executive should have 'widespread support' (Review Paper 1974).

The attempt by Humphrey Atkins to launch another initiative in 1980 to devolve power to Northern Ireland was even less successful. This Discussion Paper (1980), *The Government of Northern Ireland: Proposals For Further Discussion*, suggested two ways in which a 'positive role' might be achieved for the minority community. One was an Executive which reflected electoral ratios—power-sharing; the other was the formation of a Council of the Assembly, formed from departmental committees. This effectively led to the policy of 'rolling devolution', where the local parties would be given power in a phased way, each step depending on the success of the previous one. In practice the boycott of the Assembly by the SDLP meant that it never became more than a consultative body, and never had any real prospect of assuming executive responsibilities.

The fourth attempt to tackle the problem of power-sharing occurred, of course, during the build-up to the Anglo-Irish Agreement in 1985. First the Official Unionists, the DUP, and Alliance—the three parties attending the Assembly—offered to share power with the SDLP for an initial five-year period, after which an arrangement might be reached which required minority agreement on all matters of special communal concern. This initiative, known as the Catherwood Proposals, was designed to undercut the more radical changes anticipated in the Anglo-Irish Agreement. In fact, although both governments clearly desired devolution, the agreement made no provision for it. By implication, therefore, power-sharing continued to represent the policy of the British government, as it had since 1972.

1. PUBLIC OPINION

There is an impressive array of evidence that people in Northern Ireland share this preference for power-sharing. Since public opinion polls began to offer power-sharing as an option it has commanded high levels of support from both Catholic and Protestant communities. A survey by the BBC and the *Belfast Telegraph* in 1975 found 70 per cent in support of it, made up to 60 per cent Protestant and 93 per cent Catholic. The most recent *Belfast Telegraph* survey, in January 1986, found surprisingly similar results. Some 68.4 per cent supported power-sharing, comprising 61 per cent of Protestant and 78 per cent of Catholic respondents; Protestants were also more likely than Catholics to oppose it (33 per cent v. 13 per cent).

In those surveys which approached the question by presenting respondents with a list of options, including power-sharing, the findings are more difficult to analyse. In 1974, when the power-sharing Executive was the main topic of political debate, power-sharing was the favourite option for Catholics (88 per cent), and third for Protestants (52 per cent). By 1976 its popularity was replaced by a resigned acceptance of Direct Rule in both communities, and it ranked fourth for Protestants (20 per cent) and third for Catholics (45 per cent). By 1978, however, it was again the preferred choice of seven options, acceptable to 35 per cent of Protestants and 39.3 per cent of Catholics (Moxon-Browne 1979). This was confirmed by the *Fortnight/ RTE* poll in 1980 in which 44 per cent chose power-sharing and 42 per cent a continuation of Direct Rule; preference for power-sharing was greater among Catholics (79 per cent) than among Protestants (36 per cent); further, 67 per cent of Protestants said that they would try hard to make power-sharing work, while only 17 per cent said that they would work to make it fail (*Fortnight* 178, October-December 1980). Even during the hunger strike in July 1981 it was the only course which found support from both communities; in a *Sunday Times* poll the principle of power-sharing was accepted by 57 per cent of Protestants and 77 per cent of Catholics, with 27 per cent and 10 per cent respectively opposed.

The form of question posed in the *Belfast Telegraph* survey in January 1986 is similar to many of the other polls. Respondents were presented with eight options, and the question, options, and responses were as shown in Table 1.

TABLE 1. Over the next five years, what do you think would be the best form of government for Northern Ireland?

	Catholic	Protestant	All
Devolved government with power-sharing	27.8	20.9	24.1
Complete integration with GB	5.7	35.4	23.0
Devolved government with majority rule	2.4	17.7	11.4
Direct Rule	6.0	11.7	9.6
United Ireland	21.2	0.5	8.6
Joint authority (London–Dublin)	16.9	1.6	7.9
Independence	5.3	6.2	5.6
Federal Ireland	5.0	1.0	2.8

Certainly this poll was conducted during a period of considerable political agitation, especially for Protestants. Nevertheless, its main findings are consistent with almost all other surveys over the last decade: that the only two options which command significant support in both communities are power-sharing and Direct Rule. As Birrell pointed out, in reference to the 1980 poll, there was 'a much greater readiness among rank-and-file supporters than party leaders to contemplate some form of partnership in a devolved assembly' (1981, p. 199).

2. PARTY POSITIONS

It has often been observed that the most notable characteristic of Northern Irish politics is its constancy and immobility. Since the introduction of the principle of power-sharing by the British government, however, there have been considerable changes in the positions of all the parties.

The Alliance party has been perhaps the most constant supporter of power-sharing, but its views on what constitutes an acceptable minimum have been more variable. It was a partner in the 1974 Executive and, until 1980, regarded minority involvement at executive level as a prerequisite for proper power-sharing. In 1980, although its preferred option was a power-sharing Cabinet, it was prepared to accept a system of departmental committees which reflected electoral strength but did not require SDLP membership of the Cabinet.

The SDLP has refused to consider any scheme of devolved government which did not involve them, as the largest party representing minority views, in executive power. In 1980, for example, they rejected two schemes short of Cabinet membership—a Council of the Assembly which could block legislation and a system of weighted voting which would require more than a straight majority. Quite apart from this wrangling about parliamentary devices, however, it is important to remember that power-sharing within Northern Ireland was only one of the two main strings to the SDLP's bow. The recognition of an 'Irish dimension' to the Northern Ireland problem was the other. During the period of the power-sharing Executive in 1974, the 'Irish dimension' was secondary to the party's aim of sharing executive power within Northern Ireland. After the fall of the Executive and the failure of all parties to reach an accommodation on power-sharing, the SDLP increasingly looked towards Anglo-Irish negotiation at government level to secure its objectives. In that sense the Anglo-Irish Agreement in 1985 was a victory for the SDLP. In its wake the party's interest in devolved power-sharing appears to have diminished, or at least receded.

The records of the two main unionist parties have been even more variable. The Official Unionist Party, having split on the issue when some of its members joined the 1974 Executive, joined with other unionist groupings in the United Ulster Unionist Coalition (UUUC) to press for devolved government with majority rule. In 1980 they split again when the OUP refused to participate in the Constitutional Conference proposed by the Secretary of State Mr Atkins, insisting on a devolved government determined by a straight majority. Indeed, some leading members of the party went further, and advocated total integration with Britain. By 1986, however, they were generally in harness with the DUP in opposition to the Anglo-Irish Agreement.

The DUP has been the most consistent and the most vocal opponent of power-sharing, but showed greater willingness than the

Official Unionists to explore options which involved the minority at a second tier of control. They did not boycott the 1980 Conference and, while insisting on an Executive comprising the majority parties, did not reject the concept of departmental committees.

At one level an objective analysis of the competing party positions might suggest that the differences on the issue of power-sharing were not insurmountable. It is the very *raison d'être* of the Alliance Party. The DUP had shown some willingness to examine devices of control at committee level. The Official Unionist Party, perhaps pushed by the Anglo-Irish Agreement towards concessions on power-sharing, made offers in early 1986 which would have been unthinkable in 1985. The SDLP, which might have accepted them incredulously in 1985, showed little interest in 1986.

And therein lies the problem. The same objective analysis would recognize that the more conciliatory positions of the parties never coincided. The SDLP's willingness to play down the 'Irish dimension' in favour of power-sharing found little sympathy among unionists, and was terminated by the UWC strike. The new flexibility of the Official Unionists in 1986 has so far been greeted by silence from the SDLP, flushed by its coup in the Anglo-Irish Agreement. This failure to make concessions at the same time was not coincidental. It is in the nature of politics in Northern Ireland. The position of either side on the issue was not determined by negotiation, or by material benefit, or by the attraction of executive power. It was determined essentially by the position of one's opponents.

Nevertheless, the positions of the parties have not been as intransigent as they appeared at first sight. They are situational, not absolute. Consequently, it is difficult to see any patterns to them. They are determined by *ad hoc* criteria—jockeying for position rather than moving logically towards intransigence or accord. This is an optimistic conclusion. It is one of the few signs of what might be described as honest, decent politics, based on greed, self-interest, and bargaining. It is a process to be encouraged. While people are motivated by venality, they will behave reasonably. It is when they believe that they are motivated by principles that the trouble starts.

3. THE GOVERNMENTS' RATIONALE

The arguments which have been advanced in favour of and in oppositon to power-sharing are illuminating. The position of British governments since 1972 rests on two main premisses. The first is the peculiar nature of Northern Irish politics, where, as McCracken put it, 'there is no floating vote on the constitutional issue'. Each election is effectively a battle within the two communities for control—currently between the SDLP and Sinn Féin on the nationalist side, and between the OUP and the DUP among unionists. Far from attempting to entice converts from across the sectarian divide, these parallel contests pull the more moderate parties away from compromise and towards policies which will dissuade voters from defecting towards more extreme parties in their communities. Compromise, the very stuff of politics, is universally used as a synonym for treason. In a society riddled with suspicion, the heretic, who is prepared to contest the orthodox sectarianism while remaining within the community, is a greater threat than the renegade, who has left the fold and can easily be dismissed as a traitor. This process diminishes the potential influence of the middle ground, as the Northern Ireland Labour Party found in the 1960s and the Alliance Party in the 1970s. In the light of these features, majority rule would simply place power in the hands of the majority community for the foreseeable future. The result would be that 'a large permanent majority—if it represents not just a party or a political view but a whole community—is likely, if it sees no prospect of a general opportunity to share in the direction of affairs, to oppose not just the government of the day, but the whole system of government itself' (Discussion Paper 1974). Apart from the likely effect of permanent opposition on the Northern Irish minority, there was concern that majority rule may not be implemented impartially. The experiences of the old Stormont regime and the recent behaviour of unionist-controlled councils have been cited as examples of the incipient triumphalism of unionism.

The second concern which pushed the British government towards power-sharing was a perceived relationship between minority alienation and republican violence. The argument is that failure to allow legitimate expression of minority views will validate illegitimate violence and sanction the activities of the IRA. In political terms, the most effective means of eroding support for Sinn Féin and the IRA was to involve the SDLP directly in the exercise of power. Their enthusiastic participation in a campaign against IRA violence would rapidly improve the security situation and encourage many Catholics to accept the instruments of the state.

4. POLITICAL POSITIONS AND PUBLIC OPINION

On the face of things the contradiction between public opinion and political positions is puzzling. There are two likely explanations: first, that the opinion polls measure only vague low-priority views which do not indicate a willingness to do anything about it—rather like asking people if they favour the reduction of famine; the other explanation is that political leaders have failed to grasp this possible compromise either from fear of losing their constituencies or from conviction.

This latter view finds some academic support. Lijphart, for example, has examined the Northern Irish conflict from the viewpoint of consociational democracy—a system which rejects majoritarianism in favour of accommodative practices at élite level, allowing each of the competing groups considerable control over their own social, economic, administrative, and political affairs (Lijphart 1975). Comparing Holland and Northern Ireland, Lijphart identified three major obstacles to power-sharing in Northern Ireland: the absence of a multiple balance of power, which meant that unionists could exercise hegemonic control; insufficient support for the idea of a grand coalition; and insufficient basic national solidarity. The introduction of a proportional representation system of voting, while encouraging some fragmentation, has not led to a greater search for cross-sectarian accommodation.

Other academics have suggested that there are a number of ways in which highly fragmented societies have evolved systems for accommodating their differences. Aunger, too, has examined Northern Ireland as a case study in consociational theory. Comparing it to New Brunswick, another divided society but one which had evolved a workable political system, he concluded that neither of the main strategies which had led to success in New Brunswick applied in Northern Ireland. The first was cross-cutting cleavages, which weakened cohesion and predisposed parties towards compromise. The other was co-opeartive élites—leaders who were prepared to deal with each other and deliver agreements to their followers. As Lijphart had put it, 'overarching cooperation at the élite level can be a substitute for cross-cutting affiliations at the mass level' (1981, p. 200). Aunger blamed the latter as much as the former for Northern Ireland's continuing impasse, arguing that not only were leaders unwilling to negotiate secretly or seek a bipartisan consensus, but that they actually encouraged attitudes of confrontation and discord.

What then is the best way ahead? Public opinion polls indicate consistently that the only two approaches which attract substantial support from both communities are power-sharing and the continuation of Direct Rule from Westminster. Aunger considered that Direct Rule was the most likely outcome. The problem is that it is a deferral of a settlement rather than a settlement. This leaves power-sharing as both the likely prerequisite for a solution, and the major obstacle to one. It seems sensible, then, to tease out this no man's land and to examine whether there is sufficient flexibility in the concept of power-sharing to suggest ways forward.

5. A PACKAGE OF IMPURITIES

The Anglo-Irish Agreement has had a considerable effect on this impasse, although it is difficult to gauge whether or not it was the intended effect. The main obstacle to change before its signature came from the unionist side. It arose from the fear that any change would diminish their position, and from the realization that the penalties for advocating reform were high, and the possible rewards elusive. Since the Agreement this position has no longer been tenable. Changes had been effected, and above their heads. Further, Dublin had not only been involved in introducing the changes, but had been given a role in the future administration of Northern Ireland. The symbolic rather than the real meaning of this was more profound than has been appreciated outside Northern Ireland. But, behind the clamour and the braggadocio of the 'day of action', it has produced an outburst of compromise proposals from unionists which is quite unprecedented. In addition to an official proposal from the party leaders for a constitutional convention followed by tripartite talks between London, Dublin, and Belfast, there have been different proposals from Harold McCusker, John Taylor, even William Craig. All demanded as a prerequisite the dismantling, or at least the postponement, of the Agreement. In a political environment starved of movement, this amounts to an earthquake. The explanation is clear. The bitter pill of power-sharing had suddenly become more palatable when the alternative seemed the infinitely more bitter pill of 'Dublin Rule'. The two are increasingly being seen, by unionists if not by the SDLP, as alternatives. Power-sharing has been effectively put back on to the agenda.

One factor seems indisputable: it is difficult to see a solution emerging which represents a total victory for one or other side in the conflict—either a unionist-controlled devolved executive or a unitary united Ireland. The last fourteen years indicate that unionists have not been sufficiently attracted by the prospect of power to trim the purity of their position. Similarly, the SDLP have steadfastly refused to become involved in any devolved executive or legislature unless their two main demands of power-sharing and acknowledgement of an Irish dimension are met. The result has been stalemate. It is likely to continue unless some new ground can be identified. If the 'pure' solutions are not compatible, the time has come to put together a package of impurities.

The first part of the package is to examine seriously alternative forms of power-sharing, other than involvement in a devolved executive. Many of these have been suggested, and not all rejected out of hand by the SDLP (see e.g. Rose 1976). They include weighted voting, separate electoral rolls, designated Cabinet posts, executive committees, and government through centralized boards. Unionists have declared themselves willing to negotiate on some of these options, short of sitting on the same executive. Indeed, before the Anglo-Irish Agreement was signed, the parties attending the Northern Ireland Assembly agreed to the Catherwood Proposals which, in the opinion of one commentator, 'offered in effect to share power with the SDLP' (*Fortnight*, December 1985). More emotional, but equally revealing, was the remark made by the deputy leader of the Official Unionist Party Harold McCusker, following publication of the Anglo-Irish Agreement, that he would rather be ruled by a Northern Irish Catholic nationalist than Dublin. It has become more difficult to assess the SDLP's reaction to this, since their satisfaction with the Anglo-Irish Agreement has not yet produced concessions towards the Unionists; however, the informal talks between some members of the SDLP and the Official Unionist Party, although condemned by John Hume, suggests that there are some members of the party to whom an internal accommodation may be more important than the Irish dimension.

The other half of the package of impurities is an acknowledgement of an Irish dimension in Northern Ireland, short of direct Dublin involvement in executive power. As with power-sharing, there are a number of alternatives here, not the subject of this paper. It is worth mentioning, however, that all the plethora of individual and official initiatives from unionists since the Anglo-Irish Agreement have expressed a willingness to acknowledge an Irish dimension, if the

Agreement itself were scrapped. Of course, intentions are one thing, delivery another. Kind words butter no parsnips. But the unionist suggestion that the Agreement should be suspended—not abolished —during the talks offers room for negotiation.

The premiss of this package is that, of the two main planks which have supported the SDLP position since 1974, power-sharing within Northern Ireland is more important than the Dublin connection if both could not be achieved. This is by no means certain, especially when the alternatives are expressed so starkly. Both have been part of the SDLP's policy for more than a decade. There is a difference between them, however. While involvement in power has been a consistent and unnegotiable demand, the commitment to the Irish dimension has varied from lukewarm to hot. The heat has increased through time, and been further fanned by the Agreement. It remains to be seen which would be regarded as negotiable by the SDLP if the two were expressed as alternatives.

Westminster plays the critical role in trying to move towards an internal accommodation. The attempt to build up the political middle ground, through proportional representation and general support, has failed. In political terms the middle ground is insignificant. In other ways, however, its role is critical. It will obviously form one of the elements of any settlement; it remains an essential conduit acceptable to the two adversarial groups; its influence is greater outside Northern Ireland˙than within; its emphasis on the need for reconciliation through social, economic, and educational reform is critical. The role of the middle ground will be to make the case that any solution must have two levels—not only political agreement at the macro level, but support for the social mechanisms which have kept the violence under control. Little attention has been paid to the latter in recent years, as political dissension has dominated public interest.

In political terms, however, it would be better to acknowledge a number of realities, perhaps distasteful ones. Over the last fifteen years politics have become even more polarized in Northern Ireland. It is not possible to make major advances through buttressing or expanding the middle ground, but through negotiations between the main antagonists. This is not only the key strategy, but the only strategy. Bridge-building is a common metaphor in Northern Ireland. It makes sense if the two banks are widely separated, and if there is a convenient and substantial island between the two which can be used to hold an arch. If there is not, then alternative technology will be required to span the banks. To continue the analogy, it is important to resist the temptation to erode the banks, but rather to acknowledge their existence, no matter how unreliable they seem.

If it is not possible to deliver a settlement through a strong middle ground, or through an Anglo-Irish agreement, the main strategy remaining, and the core of any process, is cross-sectarian negotiation. The language is that of the market-place, not the church; that of bargaining, not fellowship. It does not require that we love our enemies. But it insists that they are respected, if not for their views, then for their ability to frustrate our aims. When the word 'pragmatism' is regarded by both sides as a praiseworthy objective, we will be well away towards a solution.

4

INITIATIVES FOR CONSENSUS
Minority Perceptions
Paul Arthur

'MINORITY' is a trickier concept than is generally acknowledged (van Amersfoort 1978). It varies according to the political environment and can be especially troublesome where there is a dispute about the boundaries of the political unit. Hence in his celebrated study of the Northern Ireland problem the journalist Harold Jackson (1971, p. 4), refers to the 'problem of the double minority', where he found 'the disastrous advent of a ruling establishment with the reins of power irremovably in its hands but acting under the stresses of a besieged minority'. To complicate matters further Conor Cruise O'Brien described the problem as that of a double majority, that is two minorities acting as though they were majorities because they believed they could call on their respective guarantors (1973, p. 434).

In the wake of the Anglo-Irish Agreement, signed at Hillsborough Castle on 15 November 1985, the role of the external guarantors very much came into play to establish a new asymmetry within Northern Ireland involving a divided and demoralized unionist 'majority' and a more self-confident nationalist minority. 'Nationalists can now raise their heads knowing their position is, and is seen to be, on an equal footing with that of members of the unionist community', the Taoiseach Dr FitzGerald announced at the Hillsborough press conference. Events since then would suggest that there was a degree of hyperbole in that statement, but for the most part the new asymmetry is still in place.

This chapter will take as its point of departure the Hillsborough Agreement for several reasons. It is the new reality. Its signatories perceive it as a process and not as a solution. In that respect they were recognizing that ethnic conflict is not static but that it produces its own dynamic. That is a matter of the utmost import in the evolving Northern Ireland question. Secondly, the new reality places constitutional nationalism in the driving seat . . . at least in the short term.

Article 2 (*a*) of the Agreement establishes an Intergovernmental Conference 'concerned with Northern Ireland and with relations between the two parts of the island of Ireland, to deal, as set out in this Agreement, on a regular basis with (*i*) political matters, (*ii*) security and related matters, (*iii*) legal matters, including the administration of justice, (*iv*) the promotion of cross-border co-operation'. These were the matters which had most concerned the nationalist minority, and to reinforce the *symbolic* significance of the Conference it was to be serviced by a permanent Secretariat with officials from both sides of the border meeting at Maryfield outside Belfast. Hence the majority perception was that Dublin had its foot very firmly in the door and even occupied a piece of Northern Ireland territory. Thirdly, the Agreement was launched with a fund of international goodwill calling into play the significance of the Irish diaspora: in other words it raised further questions about the territorial boundaries of the 'Northern Ireland problem' (Pocock 1982).

I. FACTIONALISM AND POLITICAL UNDERDEVELOPMENT

Cynthia Enloe has stressed the importance of political underdevelopment in understanding the nature of the problem: 'The glaring evidence of their underdevelopment is not their inability to dominate rival ethnic communities but their common vulnerability to internal factionalism, which undermines communal leaders' capacity to govern' (1973, p. 171). Following the Northern Ireland general election in 1925 the unionist leaders were conscious of the threat of factionalism and took immediate action to remove the proportional representation system of voting which encouraged it. The history of Northern Ireland elections between 1929–69 is a story of maintaining an artificial communal solidarity around the constitutional issue. What appeared to be a monolith rapidly diminished when the unionist leadership was challenged with fundamental questions about minority and human rights.

The degree of factionalism became apparent following the prorogation of Stormont in 1972 and the reintroduction of proportional representation elections. Even in this period, however, there was a degree of solidarity based on what unionists were *against*. Since Hillsborough, however, while they remain united in their opposition to Irish unity, fissiparous tendencies have arisen around tactics and options. The Democratic Unionist Party, led by Dr Ian Paisley, have taken a more militant lead in their use of extra-parliamentary means, including forms of civil disobedience, while the Ulster Unionist Party (UUP), led by James Molyneaux, have reacted in a diversity of ways to these tactics. Additionally, a fundamental debate centring on the merits of devolution versus integration has been widely canvassed. Variants of these two themes, including Ulster independence, have been thrown into the ring to add further confusion. Interestingly, the most insightful document, *Common Sense*, appears under the paramilitary Ulster Defence Association (UDA) banner and advocates a devolved system of government based on power-sharing (Ulster Political Research Group 1987). The relevance of the above to (nationalist) minority politics may not be readily apparent but several points can be made. In order to avoid a 'snapshot' and checklist approach to the problem one needs to be conscious of the changing patterns of majority/minority relationships. Again the theoretical literature is useful. Enloe has developed a situational interpretation of ethnicity which 'allows for changing collective definitions and fluctuating emotional intensities' whereby 'the saliency that an ethnic group member assigns his or her own ethnicity can wax and wane'. She adds that 'politics can shape as well as simply mirror ethnic pluralism' (1980, pp. 2, 4, *et passim*).

Secondly, it illustrates that there was a perception of a besieged majority which enabled the minority to have trust in the future: 'We had a holding position' was the obituary pronounced by the leader of the Nationalist Party on the demise of that party following the 1969 general election. There was in short a belief in manifest destiny—nature had made Ireland an island which God would unite some day.

But thirdly, factionalism was not necessarily a unionist trait. Numerous election results highlight the degree of fragmentation in opposition politics in Northern Ireland. If we look at parties of the Left which contested the 1945 election, for example, we discover no less than seven groupings: Labour, Independent Labour, Federation of Labour, Commonwealth Labour, Communist Party, Socialist Republican, Derry Labour. The one-man party was an Ulster phenomenon, and Cornelius O'Leary records that before the 1964 Westminster election two one-man parties came together to form one two-man party, Republican Labour, led by Gerry Fitt. Opposition fragmentation was not really relevant to the political process in the years of Unionist Party dominance. It is only when it becomes conscious of the scent of power that it becomes a real issue. So long as nationalists believed in being an opposition of principle intent on destroying the system on which government rested it could afford the luxury of irresponsible and narrow opposition. Once the civil rights movement changed the nature of the debate it also changed the rules of the game. 'Civil' rights may have been a misnomer. The original demand of the Northern Ireland Civil Rights Association (NICRA), 'One Man, One Vote', was for a political right, but the demands were stepped up by the radical People's Democracy to encompass social rights, especially employment and housing. It was only when the question of the administration of justice became prevalent that the civil rights aspect entered. It remains, however, a major issue and is recognized as such in the Agreement and the subsequent work of the Conference. For the most part political and social rights are no longer on the agenda, although the latter will continue to be a problem so long as Northern Ireland remains a scarcity society. Nevertheless, the civil rights movement remains central to a discussion of minority perceptions and, just as importantly, majority perceptions of the minority. Its emergence heralded the end of nationalist quiescence and a more positive seeking after justice. Its initial demands created a crisis pertaining to participation and distribution but when these demands were not met the crisis became a more fundamental one of identity and legitimacy (Rudolph and Thompson 1985). Finally, its leadership represented a new generation much better educated and aware of the importance of organization and mobilization. These were to be the qualities which were to guide minority politics after 1970.

2. MINORITY AND HUMAN RIGHTS

The majority population was disorientated by the civil rights movement. After all, it was led by children of the welfare state, many of them educated to university level and beyond. They sought 'British' rights, not the end of partition. They attempted to conduct their campaign in a non-violent manner—and in that respect they managed to wrongfoot the republican movement as well. There were those, even in government, who acknowledged the justice of the civil rights case; the Prime Minister Terence O'Neill recorded in his *Autobiography* (1972, p. 111), 'Any liberal-minded person must admit that the Civil Rights movements brought about reforms which would otherwise have taken years to wring from a reluctant Government'. And yet it cost him his premiership to persuade his party to accept the principle of 'one man, one vote'.

Perhaps the most devastating aspect of the civil rights campaign was that it complicated politics in Northern Ireland. In the past unionists had little or no trouble understanding the minority—they were disloyal: 'There are only two classes in Northern Ireland, the loyal and the disloyal', a unionist backbencher is alleged to have said in the 1950s. The latter was composed of socialists, communists, and nationalists/republicans. Now, here was a minority seeking British rights in a world which was becoming attuned to the vocabulary of minority and human rights. Their pleas may have fallen on deaf ears at Stormont, but they were being picked up in London and Washington. At the very least the Northern Ireland government needed to re-evaluate its attitude towards the minority.

Part of the difficulty arose in defining the type of minority it confronted. In her outstanding study of 'Ballybeg', Rosemary Harris follows Louis Wirth in attempting to classify minorities in their competitive relationship with majorities. She distinguishes between the pluralistic, the assimilative, the secessionist, and the militant. The pluralistic trys 'to preserve its own identity and culture upon a basis of tolerance of differences and equality of opportunity', whereas the assimilative seeks 'to merge with dominant group'. At the other end of the continuum the secessionist seeks to achieve political separation from the dominant group, and the militant desires political domination over the majority. She summarizes thus (1972, p. 208) '. . . competition between groups has to be considered to relate to the object of the competition, the terms under which the minority competes and the political aims of the minority'. The early days of the civil rights campaign suggests that such rigid distinctions were not possible. Indeed we shall see that as the conflict developed its own dynamic, minority perceptions changed. At this stage all we need to note is that the wider perception of the civil rights campaign was that it was seeking only a greater sense of participation and share of distribution within the Northern Ireland political system.

So much seemed evident in the Constitution of the Social Democratic and Labour Party (SDLP), formed in August 1970 from the remnants of the Nationalist Party and the mainstream of the civil rights campaign. Clause 2 referred to the principles and objects of the Party, the first of which was 'to organise and maintain in Northern Ireland a Socialist Party'; and the fourth was to 'promote the cause of Irish unity based on the consent of the majority of people in Northern Ireland'. The remainder of Clause 2 would suggest that the SDLP was unexceptional in the West European democratic socialist tradition, a fact reinforced by its membership of the Socialist International and the Confederation of Socialist Parties of the European Community. But, of course, the local political environment did make it an exception in the European tradition, and the self-imposed constraints of its own constitution ensured that it did not fit the usual parameters of minority political practice in the province.

In the first place the acceptance of majority consent meant that the party had to have a 'catchmore appeal' extending its party programme beyond the traditionally narrow (and sterile) demand for Irish unity. It needed a manifesto based on reason (and not manifest destiny) and an organizational base strong enough to withstand the prospect of permanent opposition. Such a prospect did not appeal to those in the republican movement who scorned the compromises of the political process in favour of what Burke calls the 'degenerate fondness of tricking shortcuts'. This fundamental clash about means and ends created a dialectic which is currently operating inside the minority community.

Secondly, the minority's apparent lack of political success since the 1970s has had a paradoxical effect: 'Not only are we not in government, we aren't even in opposition' was how John Hume put it at the 1985 SDLP Annual Conference. Limbo has certain advantages. Minorities feed on both 'adversity and denial', as well as concessions. Their lack of progress can be blamed on discrimination rather than poor leadership. The removal of executive power from the SDLP after the UWC strike in 1974 reinforced its view that it could never expect fair play and that the majority community would change the rules of the game to suit itself. The collapse of power-sharing had two additional 'bonuses'. The exigiencies of power produce their own responsibilities. That short period between January–May 1974 demonstrated that in taking unpopular decisions a party will discard some of its potential support. (The Scottish National Party realized this with a vengeance after 1974 when it had to decide whether to adopt a gradualistic approach to independence in return for winning concessions from a minority Labour Government in London or to insist on a purist dogma at the cost of frightening away more moderate support. The Parti Quebecois discovered the same lesson in 1976, when it took over outright control of the Province).

The second advantage was that loss of power concentrated the mind wonderfully. It had an energizing effect. Why, party strategists argued, could power be removed from us so effectively by a small body of the United Kingdom electorate employing dubious means when we were led to believe that we had the might of the British government (including its army) behind us? It led them to question the possibility of a purely internal settlement and that, in turn, forced them to establish a much higher international profile. In short, they made use of the Irish diaspora at a period when the human rights issue was high on the political agenda.

The post-war period has seen a shift in international law from minority to human rights because of a change in the political climate induced by the United States' dominant role in the United Nations. The US reflected its melting-pot traditions to the detriment of separate rights for minorities in its public proposals. Besides, it was conscious that the Soviet Union expounded a pro-minorities view (Thornberry 1980). None of this is of direct relevance to the nationalist minority in Northern Ireland. It did not have a tradition of seeking redress in the courts, and even after the advent of the civil rights movement it used the international courts rarely. But it was tuned into the language of rights and it possessed enough examples of adversity and denial to elicit considerable international sympathy. Moreover, one segment of the minority appealed for justice on the fundamental human right of self-determination, an appeal which, we shall see, was doomed. The other segment rested its case on the more modest request for the benefits emanating from the general human rights provisions in international law. The modest approach was to be more rewarding, but the combination of both persuaded the majority that the nationalist minority was becoming more militant.

In one sense they were correct to make that assumption. The state of political pathology in Northern Ireland was a vivid illustration of the breakdown of order. It was easy to assume that in nationalism the line between constitutional and physical force was a very narrow one; after all, there has always been an ambivalence about political violence in the Irish tradition. What such critics ignored, however, was the intensity of disagreement among the nationalist factions and the extent to which nationalists generally still perceived themselves to be reacting to majority intransigence. If republicanism represented the militant minority, constitutional nationalism hovered somewhere between the pluralistic and secessionist brand. It shared with republicanism a crisis of identity but did not reject fully the legitimacy of the political processes governing it. Rather than be quiescent it set out to use the political process to shape rather than mirror the ethnic conflict.

3. MOBILIZATION

In an analysis of the factors which persuade a majority to share power with a minority Morton Deutsch (1973, p. 393) asserts that 'if Bolt (the majority) has no concern whatsoever for Acme's (the minority) needs and no belief that Acme's pressure will be sufficiently strong to be disturbing, Acme must attempt to develop, mobilise and publicise its power sufficiently to convince Bolt that negotiation would be a prudent course of action'. The SDLP, playing the role of Acme, did precisely that in the years following the collapse of power-sharing. The Hillsborough Agreement may be seen as the first historic landmark on the road towards mobilization. The journey to Hillsborough was arduous and debilitating and underscored the fragility of minority solidarity.

SDLP strategy was first enunciated by party leader John Hume in an article in *Foreign Affairs* in 1979. Hindsight enables us to realize just how significant this article was to be. Hume sought two goals, both of which are now accepted as part of the common vocabulary of the Northern Ireland problem (1979, pp. 309–10):

The time has come for a positive and decisive initiative. It must be taken by both Dublin and London acting together. They should first make it clear that there are no longer any unconditional guarantees for any section of the northern community. There is only a commitment to achieving a situation in which there are guarantees for all. Second, they should make it clear that there is in fact no pat solution as such, but only a process that will lead to a solution. They should declare themselves committed to such a process, a process designed to lead to an agreed Ireland with positive roles for all. They should invite all parties to participate in this process, the process of building a new Ireland.

With the creation of the Anglo-Irish process beginning with a summit in May 1980 and culminating in the signing of the Agreement in November 1985 the Hume scenario came into play. In his *Foreign Affairs* article he invoked both sentiment and strategic considerations in his appeal for assistance from the Irish diaspora and from the North American and European communities. He made his appeal, too, based on reason—an unusual commodity in the Northern Ireland question

—and on morality (with á strong denunciation of the Provisional IRA's actions).

A skilful diagnosis of the parameters of the problem was only the beginning: motivating the actors was to be much more difficult. The international dimension did not present too many problems, as was evident in Article 10 (*a*) of the Agreement, which established an International Fund to promote economic and social development to regenerate the beleaguered Northern Irish economy; and in the fund of goodwill emanating from President Reagan and the US Congress, from the Secretary General to the United Nations, from all major West European states and the EEC, from Canada, Australia, and New Zealand. In the European context substantial groundwork had been undertaken already in a Report drawn up on behalf of the Political Affairs Committee of the European Parliament by Neils Haagerup on the situation in Northern Ireland and tabled on 2 March 1984.

The major stumbling blocks were to be found in London, Dublin, and Belfast. Everyone was conscious of the unionist veto within Northern Ireland—hence the failure of internal settlements attempted by various Secretaries of State from William Whitelaw through Merlyn Rees and Humphrey Atkins to James Prior. Little progress could be expected by pouring all of one's effort into that particular quarry. Priority was given to engaging the sustained attention of Dublin and London. In many respects Dublin proves to be a more intractable problem, a fact acknowledged by Hume in 1979: '. . . there is an important sense in which the principal source of Irish nationalist sentiment, i.e., Dublin, has not yet fully clarified its intentions. Unionists will not be able to bring themselves to entertain seriously the notion of Irish unity unless Dublin unambiguously spells out what it understands by unity and gives clear evidence of its commitments' (1979, pp. 308–9).

The New Ireland Forum was to be Dublin's attempt at removing the ambiguity. It was composed of the three major constitutional parties in the Republic (Fianna Fáil, Fine Gael, and Irish Labour) and of the SDLP, and set itself the task of reinterpreting Irish nationalism for the end of the century. It held its first public meeting on 30 May 1983 and completed its work with the publication of a Report on 2 May 1984 after a total of 28 private sessions, 13 public sessions, 56 meetings of a Steering Group, and numerous meetings of subgroups, which examined economic issues and alternative constitutional structures in detail. Judged on the evidence of the final *Report* (1984*a*) it might be asserted that Irish nationalism retained its ambiguity towards unity. Certainly that was the primary aspiration of the Forum parties, although they considered sympathetically and in detail models of federalism/confederalism and of joint authority. In addition, para. 5. 10 of the Report provided the authors with a fail-safe mechanism when it stated that the 'Parties in the Forum also remain open to discuss other views which may contribute to political development'.

The publication of the *Report* was greeted with some dismay, and for that reason many missed the significance of the total Forum exercise. It was evident that it was a *nationalist* report replete with a nationalist interpretation of Irish history; and that in moving from the centrifugal (as was clear in the different aspirations expressed by the party leaders in the first public session of the Forum) to the somewhat bland centripetal final Report the exercise had lost a little of its dynamism. But that was to miss the central thrust of the Forum exercise which was established (*a*) to have an edifying and educative effect on the new generation of Irish nationalists, and (*b*) to appeal to the responsibilities and role of the British in fashioning a solution.

Since partition Irish nationalism has been noted for its rhetoric, the aspirational rather than the operational. The New Ireland Forum forced them to look at the expensive and uncongenial realities which Irish unity would impose. It highlighted the uncomfortable fact, confirmed by public opinion polls, that the population is generally not too discontented with partition. The Forum was aimed first and foremost at the political élite. It was conscious that there might be (to paraphrase W. Harvey Cox) the basis for an *Irish* case against Irish unity: 'Uniting the *territory* will disrupt the *nation* and endanger, not fulfil, the state; and it will do so because it will incorporate into the state a large minority who adamantly refuse to regard themselves as part of the nation' (Cox 1985*b*, p. 453). They are aware that 'the old de Valeran, Catholic, Gaelic, republican consensus on Irish unity' is dead. They are confronted with something much more intangible: 'The politics of Irish unification in the Irish Republic now presents itself not solely or even principally as the politics of verbal affirmation of assumptions held to be self-evident, but as the politics of engagement in a series of conundrums' (Cox 1985*a*, p. 45).

Among the components of the Irish nation confronting these realities none is more relevant than that of the Catholic church. Through its attitude to the violent conflict in the North and demands for modifications of church–state relations in the Republic one can witness all the ambiguities, all the self-doubt inherent in paying the price of Irish unity. All of this became abundantly clear when the New Ireland Forum met an Irish Episcopal Conference Delegation in public session on 9 February 1984. With only a slight, but understandable, degree of hyperbole, the Fine Gael TD John Kelly pronounced it 'as probably the first time since St Patrick arrived that the representatives of the Hierarchy were asked to think on their feet' (New Ireland Forum 1984a, p. 46). Much of the debate centred on the issue of minority rights, but the minority being addressed was that of the Protestant minority in the Republic. And while the Church representatives were able to give satisfactory answers as to how they would insist on the protection of the Northern Protestants' interests in a new Ireland they were hesitant and uncertain about the minority they had already within the boundaries of the Republic. Senator Mary Robinson could not receive a satisfactory answer to her rhetorical question: 'The question is why are you not raising your voices now in relation to the Protestants and others who are not of the Catholic faith in this part of the country? Surely they too are entitled to full civil and religious liberties'.

One captures a similar degree of ambiguity among certain churchmen in relation to the 'armed struggle'. In a brilliant piece of historiography Oliver MacDonagh has analysed the systematic political ambivalence of the Irish church in an earlier age and concludes with a commonplace which is profound: 'The priests were but the populace writ large'. He traces a triple ambiguity which enabled the Church to hold an uneasy balance when the republican and revolutionary secret society was rising or dominant in Irish nationalism, the first of which he termed recessional—as 'nationalistic violence receded in time so might it be safely sanctioned'. The second was the gestural—'the gestures which carried no dangerous consequences within themselves . . . the rank-and-file clergy . . . [giving] vent to their inherent anglophobia and [participating] in national posturing in complete security'. The third he describes uneasily as humanitariansm—'what one really needs is a compound embracing sympathy with suffering, the distinction between a man and his beliefs, and elemental tribal identification' (MacDonagh 1983, pp. 97–101).

MacDonagh's ambiguities, especially the third, can be adapted to contemporary conditions. One sees ambiguity, for example, in the emotional reaction of Cardinal Ó Fiaich after a visit to protesting prisoners in the Maze prison in 1978. One sees it, too, in his flock following the coffins of the ten dead hunger-strikers, and one realizes the extent to which the church is a pastoral church in Ireland. As such, it was highly conscious of the drift from the church by many of the younger generation inspired by revolutionary rhetoric and action. And in the Republic the pastoral church has reacted to what Tom Garvin calls the 'erosion of the liturgical edifice' by appealing to the old, more doctrinal, values. Both of these make the task of persuading unionists of the advantages of Irish unity more difficult, and do little to lighten the load of those constitutional spokespeople of the minority who base their case for unity on the doctrine of consent.

Surprisingly, the task of persuading the British government of the advantages in the Anglo-Irish process proved more straightforward. Neither the Prime Minister nor her Secretary of State for Northern Ireland was unduly impressed by the New Ireland Forum *Report* (1984*a*). Following an Anglo-Irish summit in November 1984 Mrs Thatcher did brusquely reject the three preferred Forum options. But that left her in the position of having to present a viable policy in its place, a circumstance foreseen by John Hume in a Commons debate on 2 July 1984: '. . . the most important aspect of the report is not the three options, but the views of Irish Nationalists about the ways in which realities must be faced if there is to be a solution'. The Hillsborough Agreement was the joint Dublin/London response.

CONCLUSION

One of the factors which encouraged Dublin and London to co-operate was an awareness of a growing sense of nationalist alienation. It manifested itself during the hunger strikes and was converted into votes when Sinn Féin adapted its policy of the armalite and the ballot-box. In the local government elections of May 1985 Sinn Féin had established itself as the fourth largest party in the province with 11.8 per cent of the first preference votes and the capacity to produce a nationalist majority (with the SDLP) in six of the twenty-six local councils. In addition, Gerry Adams had raised Sinn Féin's international profile when he won the Belfast West seat at the 1983 Westminster general election. Following the signing of the Agreement there has been a significant slippage in Sinn Féin's electoral support. In a series of fifteen by-elections following the resignations of Unionist MPs in protest at the Agreement SDLP support increased in those four constituencies in which it stood from 54 per cent to 65 per cent, whereas Sinn Féin diminished from 46 per cent to 35 per cent in the same constituencies. In the Republic Sinn Féin could secure only 1.9 per cent of the popular vote in the 1987 Dáil elections. One should not read too much into this simple comparison. After all, the theme of this chapter has been the dynamics of ethnic consciousness, and the fluidity of the ballot-box has been one barometer of intra-ethnic competition. The SDLP cannot be certain that the electoral pendulum will continue to swing in its direction. If Hillsborough cannot be seen to be relieving nationalist alienation, then SDLP strategy is in deep trouble. One of the factors which has sustained the momentum of the Agreement has been the growth in majority alienation; the minority surmises that if it is not to the liking of the majority then there must be something in it for them. Clearly the package cannot be sustained on such a humble diet. In the meantime unemployment in Northern Ireland remains above twenty per cent and, notwithstanding a plethora of fair employment legislation, the minority is twice as likely to be unemployed as the majority. Eighteen years of incessant violence has damaged the social fabric, some would say irrevocably. It is in this context that we must examine majority/ minority relations and minority perceptions.

In a very real sense the minority is governed by a conflict of the armalite *versus* the ballot-box. The ambivalence towards political violence which has been a feature of both communities has been brought into sharp relief by the events of the past eighteen years. If unity by consent genuinely represents *the* minority policy, then certain uncongenial realities have to be faced by the components which make up that minority. The church has to recognize its schizophrenia— favouring unity but not the pluralism which might attract the majority. Republicans (of the Provisional variant) have to weigh up the costs of their campaign, not simply in terms of whether it has set back the date of Irish unity, but the sheer physical cost it has imposed on a community which it purports to protect. And the SDLP has to recognize that it has undertaken a high-risk strategy, because it is dependent upon the goodwill of so many other actors, both endogenous and exogenous.

All of this illustrates the complexity of minority politics. This much can be asserted on its behalf. It has displayed an amazing resilience (like the majority) and in inauspicious circumstances has managed to place the 'political' at the top of the agenda. This has been achieved at some cost to communal solidarity—unity on the issue of identity but disunity on the means to reach it—but the alternative (the cynical strategy of the armalite *and* the ballot-box) holds out the prospect of the communal graveyard. The 'political' offers tremendous challenges, but it holds out the potential of some form of peace:

> . . . And when Peace here does
> house
> He comes with work to do, he does not come to coo,
> He comes to brood and sit.

> (Gerard Manley Hopkins, *Peace*, 1879.)

5

INITIATIVES FOR CONSENSUS
A Unionist Perspective
David Trimble

T HIS paper is written by a lawyer who dabbles in politics. As it is for a gathering of political scientists it is, perhaps, appropriate to avoid those matters which would reflect the interest of a lawyer. The object is to consider the feasibility of consensus. In my view that, if applied strictly, would exclude consideration of the Anglo-Irish Agreement of 1985, as it has manifestly failed to create any consensus, except among unionists, who are united in their loathing of it.

It has been said that the immediate objects of the Anglo-Irish Agreement are, among other things, to provide for better cross-border co-operation and to encourage the acceptance of power-sharing within Northern Ireland. In considering the prospects for consensus it is proposed to consider, first, unionist attitudes to these two issues, some aspects of the Anglo-Irish Agreement, and then to attempt to see, from a unionist perspective, if there is any prospect of consensus.

I. POWER-SHARING

The first point to make concerns definition, for the phrase power-sharing is used as if its meaning were obvious to all, yet it is rarely defined. Almost anyone involved in the political process has the prospect of exercising, or influencing the exercise of, power. As a result even a back-bench opposition member of parliament could be said to have a modest share of power. If this is true within a parliamentary body of some 650 members, then it must have been equally true of the opposition members of a parliament of 52 members. But the point is made that it is not just any share of power that is sought by the nationalist minority in Northern Ireland. The use of the term in that context goes back to the early seventies when it was the declared object of the British government to provide for a permanent and guaranteed role in government for the minority, although the identification of that minority as either Catholics or nationalists seems to have varied over the years. Unionists, when they define power-sharing, usually do so as meaning a system of government in which Irish nationalists are to be permanently guaranteed a place in government, irrespective of the outcome of an election. Unfortunately unionists themselves are not always consistent in using that definition, for sometimes the meaning of power-sharing is contracted to 'having nationalists in government' and, more embarrassingly, in the mouths of some unionists the term 'nationalist' is replaced by the terms 'Roman Catholic'. However, this paper will endeavour to be consistent in its usage. It has in more recent years become common for the term 'partnership' to be used instead of 'power-sharing'. This is an even vaguer term and no attempt will be made to define it, as it is suspected that it is a euphemism for power-sharing.

It should be remembered that in the early seventies a significant body of unionist opinion was prepared to countenance power-sharing. In the 1973 Assembly elections 26.5 per cent of voters (or 42 per cent of unionist voters to use the fashionable way of presenting these statistics) voted for candidates who later supported the power-sharing executive. Whether this was a true measure of support for power-sharing at that time is debatable, as hard-line unionists believed the power-sharing unionists had obtained their support on a false basis, and indeed support for power-sharing evaporated quickly once their intention became clear. (By February 1974 their support was down to 13.1 per cent of voters: this decline is often attributed to the creation of the Council of Ireland, but at least one local government by-election held after the agreement to form a power-sharing executive, but before the conclusion of the Sunningdale Agreement, displayed a significant fall in support for the Faulkner unionists.)

In addition to the electoral support for power-sharing in the early 1970s there is also a consistently high level of support for power-sharing in opinion polls and surveys. For example, Moxon-Browne (1983) found that 36.5 per cent of all those surveyed (35 per cent of Protestants, 34.5 per cent of Ulster Unionist, 12.3 per cent of Democratic Unionist, but, surprisingly, only 52.8 per cent of Alliance supporters) gave power-sharing as their favoured solution. However, the survey evidence gives rise to difficulty, for the attitudes expressed in the surveys are not put into practice in electoral terms. This may be a result of interviewees telling interviewers what they think the latter would like to hear, or to the failure to define power-sharing—so that people are assenting to their notion of power-sharing but then voting against the forms actually on offer at any time—or it may just be a reflection on the way the electoral process works.

It is not proposed to rehearse the reasons why unionists reject power-sharing. For this the reader is referred to paras. 74 to 96 of the Report of the Northern Ireland Convention (1975). In the late 1970s it seemed that government policy was moving away from power-sharing. This may be attributed to the change of government, but the commitment to power-sharing seems to have been in decline even before 1979. This may have been caused by the simple problem that if a majority of the electorate oppose power-sharing, and return to an elected body a majority of members opposed to it, then that body can scarcely function. If, on the other hand, a majority will support power-sharing, there is no need to create an elaborate constitutional structure designed to bring a power-sharing executive into existence. In the original agenda published for the Atkins Conference (Cmnd. 7763), the government set out a range of options. These were narrowed to two in the second Atkins White Paper (Cmnd. 7950), one of which was of a power-sharing nature and the other was for a majority rule Cabinet balanced by an elaborate committee structure with, potentially, blocking powers on some or all legislation and policy decisions. It is interesting to note that at the time both options were said to be equally adequate to meet the need for minority participation and equally acceptable to the government. Unfortunately, neither option was acceptable to all the parties at the Conference, and in the years immediately following the demise of the Atkins Conference the parties have concentrated, not on trying to achieve a consensus, but on trying to capture the support of the government in order to use that support as a weapon against their opponents.

The stated positions of the two unionist parties before the Anglo-Irish Agreement derive in a large measure from their experience of the Atkins talks. The Democratic Unionists are still very attached to Atkins's option 2, although they seem prepared to experiment with weighted majorities for certain purposes. The Ulster Unionists did not attend the Atkins Conference, mainly because it represented a departure from the integrationist policy contained in the 1979 Conservative manifesto. This was Mr Molyneaux's preferred position. They have tried to return to that position indirectly in 'The Way Forward' (1984), in which it was suggested that the difficulties of Cabinet formation could be avoided by concentrating on the administrative devolution of what were essentially local government matters which would be administered by committees, probably formed on a proportional basis. (Thus introducing a form of power-sharing at the lower level.) There was some reason to believe that this proposal was not unacceptable to the Democratic Unionists. The future development of this proposal was left shrouded in ambiguity, but if it had developed by the addition of legislative powers it would have probably resulted in a position virtually indistinguishable from the stated policy of the Alliance Party. For the proportionality of committee membership would also have been carried into the allocation of committee chairmanships, and this would have provided the embryo of a proportional executive. Indeed, it is suspected that this was the intention of some of the authors of the proposal. The proposals of the two Unionist parties were contained in the second report of the Devolution Report Committee of the NI Assembly, which also contains the proposals of the Alliance Party (NIA 182, 19 February 1985).

The third report of that Committee was prepared with the assistance of Sir Frederick Catherwood MEP, and endorsed as a basis for negotiation by all three parties participating in the Assembly. The key proposal in that report (NIA 225, 29 October 1985) was:

that the initial administration in a new Assembly with devolved powers should require a vote of confidence of two-thirds of the members of the Assembly. This is slightly less than the 70% mentioned in paragraph 53 [of the Prior White Paper, Cmnd. 8541] but it is considered that the 70% should apply only to constitutional changes and that the very slightly lower figure is appropriate for the establishment of the first administration. The Committee considers that the establishment of the first administration with devolved powers is exceptionally important and requires the exceptional two-thirds majority. It is accepted that, for the establishment of a long term method of devolved government, the second administration also has some importance and it is recommended that a figure of 55% should operate for the establishment of the second administration. . . . Thereafter a simple majority would operate and the committee believes that by then the experience of parties working together would enable the normal democratic processes to operate.

It should be stressed that this proposal was only endorsed as a basis for discussion, and in the aftermath of the Anglo-Irish Agreement the unionist parties have withdrawn their support for the 'Catherwood Plan'. This was probably only a tactical move, for the Catherwood Plan has been included in a collection of policy positions published by the

Ulster Unionist Party during the 1987 election. However, it may be that the qualified endorsement of the plan is itself a tactical move, but this has not been put to the test.

The weighted majority proposed by Catherwood for the formation of the first administration would have created a position where the parties would have had to bargain. It would not have guaranteed the SDLP a position in government. Nor would it have allowed the unionist parties to form their own administration. Since the emergence of Alliance it is virtually impossible for the unionists to reach 66 per cent, unless there is a nationalist boycott of the elections (a much more unlikely event than a boycott of the Assembly). The position of Alliance would have been crucial and their position is clear. They would insist on an offer being made by unionists to include the SDLP in the administration on terms that the Alliance consider to be reasonable. Then if the SDLP refuse that offer Alliance will no longer feel bound to stand by the SDLP and would enter an administration which excluded them.

It is fascinating to speculate on what would happen if such a situation were to occur. Most unionists, and not a few Alliance, are of the opinion that the SDLP would refuse any offer of participation in the government of Northern Ireland; that the SDLP now regard the 'Irish Dimension' as more important. On the other hand, it is very doubtful if the Democratic Unionists could bring themselves to make any offer to the SDLP (unless that party radically changed its stance). The DUP position seems to be that they would support a system of government based on 'Catherwood', but that they would not participate in a government involving nationalists. The DUP would, it is thought, revel in the opportunity of becoming the loyal opposition. The position of the Ulster Unionists would then be crucial. They would probably want to make an offer, but whether they would make one on suitable terms and whether their nerve would hold would depend on the circumstances and the personalities involved.

It is difficult to speak with confidence about the position of unionism at the moment. The unionist leaders have asked Mrs Thatcher to set aside or suspend the Agreement and to consider alternatives. These have not been stated. Some have hinted at a greater willingness to consider options hitherto considered unacceptable. For example Mr McCusker in the debate in the House on 27 November 1985 said that had he known twelve years ago that he would never be treated equally, his attitude would have been different and he 'would have looked at

political developments in Northern Ireland differently'. Mr Millar, the
Party Secretary, has talked of the need for flexibility if any talks occur,
and in a policy statement adopted by the Unionist Executive on 28
February 1986, in which the party proposed a two-stage conference,
one on devolution and the other on London–Dublin–Belfast relations,
it is said:

> We appreciate that the success of this proposal would require agreement at
> both conferences but we warn that if agreement is to be achieved the process
> of compromise and barter must be a two-way street.
>
> Specifically we believe it must be made plain to nationalists that they must
> be expected to give as well as to take and that we have no intention of entering
> into negotiations on the basis of abject surrender. In order that our position be
> understood, and to alleviate any possibility of subsequent confusion or
> misunderstanding, we wish it to be understood that the requirements made of
> unionism at one conference would have a direct bearing on our capacity for
> manœuvre and accommodation at the other. This is to say we will expect
> nationalists to consider which is the more important—a new relationship with
> the Irish Republic or a role in the internal government of Northern Ireland.

This document contains what Mr Millar has called a commitment to
negotiation and compromise and is clearly trying to hint at a flexible
approach. Its final sentence could be read as an invitation for the
SDLP to choose between power-sharing or an Irish dimension, but
neither of these options is explicitly offered by the document, and in
view of the discussion above it may be doubted if either would be
offered at any conference or if the offer would be sustained by unionist
public opinion.

2. CROSS-BORDER CO-OPERATION

It is invariably assumed that cross-border co-operation is a good thing
and that the unionist attitude to such co-operation is negative. This
latter view is wrong. The most recent statement of the unionist attitude
to cross-border co-operation was set out by Mr Molyneaux and Dr
Paisley in their letter to Mrs Thatcher on 28 August 1985 as follows:

> PROVIDED United Kingdom sovereignty remains undiminished, and
> provided the Republic's territorial claim is withdrawn, we are willing to
> contribute to a process of British/Irish discussion and co-operation
>
> (a) as members of a newly formed government of Northern Ireland meeting
> with opposite numbers in the government of the Irish Republic to consider

matters of mutual interest and concern within the purview of respective departmental responsibilities, and

(*b*) as members of a devolved government comprising part of a United Kingdom delegation to talks with the government of the Irish Republic about matters of mutual interest and concern to both states exclusive of those matters referred to in (*a*) above, and those touching upon United Kingdom sovereignty over Northern Ireland.

These proposals from the two unionist party leaders were clearly intended to influence the talks then proceeding between London and Dublin, and the proposal in (*b*) appears to be new. Obviously the unionist leaders were trying to project themselves as reasonable men who were prepared to take a positive attitude to cross-border matters, and who were trying to meet the desire of Whitehall for a closer relationship with Dublin. But lest it be thought that their proposals were made simply to create a better image, it should be recalled that previous Stormont governments did engage in a significant amount of practical co-operation with Dublin, and that proposal (*a*) in the Molyneaux/Paisley letter was merely a description of past practice. It may be useful to illustrate that practice.

Unionist willingness to develop a relationship with Dublin governments can be traced right back to the creation of Northern Ireland. Sir James Craig seems to have been particularly anxious to create some *modus vivendi*. Evidence of this can be seen in his meeting with de Valera, before the truce in 1921, and, probably more significantly, his meetings with Collins in January and March 1922. These meetings took place at a time when the new administration in the South was reluctant to accord recognition to the North and indeed was encouraging nationalists in the North to refuse to recognize the Northern authorities. Indeed, Collins himself was deeply involved at this time in supporting paramilitary operations by the IRA against Craig's government. The March 1922 meeting produced the well-known 'Craig-Collins Pact', which has recently been referred to as creating a joint security authority (Kennedy 1984). The following comment from Buckland (1979, p. 203), however, contains an interesting comment on these agreements.

. . . such agreements with Collins strengthened the position of the more uncompromising nationalists . . . There were indications . . . that some nationalists would be prepared to recognise and co-operate with the northern government, and there had been discussions between Craig and certain Belfast Catholics, who reported to the local bishop, as to what the government could do to encourage such recognition. However, they complained unceasingly that their influence was undermined by the virtual recognition of Collins as the leader of the northern minority. By making representations to the imperial government, and having both it and the northern government responding, Collins was able to appear to be supervising affairs in the north, thus increasing the influence of the Sinn Fein party there.

The Craig–Collins pact broke down for a variety of reasons, and relations with Dublin over the next few years were affected by the Boundary Commission, to which unionists objected. However, a new relationship seemed possible after the tripartite agreement of 1925, in which the Free State recognized Northern Ireland and its existing boundaries. That agreement was embodied in the Ireland (Confirmation of Agreement) Act 1925. Article 5 of the agreement is of interest in the present context: it reads as follows—

The powers in relation to Northern Ireland which by the Government of Ireland Act 1820, are made powers of the Council of Ireland, shall be and are hereby transferred to and shall become powers of the Parliament and the Government of Northern Ireland; and the Governments of the Irish Free State and of Northern Ireland shall meet together as and when necessary for the purpose of considering matters of common interest arising out of or connected with the exercise and administration of the said powers.

Apparently a couple of meetings did take place in 1926, one involved the two agriculture ministers and the other a trip by the Southern executive council's parliamentary secretary to the Northern Cabinet at ministerial level. It appears, however, that the Southern authorities were not keen to develop a relationship with their Northern counterparts, partly because they were not prepared to treat them as equals, and partly because, as Cosgrave, the Prime Minister, said to the Dáil in 1926, the bitterness aroused by the conflict was such that 'Things could be done much better without advertising them.' (quoted in O'Halloran 1987, p. 120). In any event the atmosphere changed with the election of Fianna Fáil in 1932, and then after the adoption of the 1937 Constitution, with its declaration that the national territory consisted of all of Ireland, co-operation became very difficult.

In the post-war period there are many examples of positive and successful co-operation. These, however, did not involve direct ministerial contact. The unionist position was that there could not be co-operation on that level unless the Republic recognized Northern Ireland. This position was an attempt to return to the position of the

1925 Act, and it was his disregard of this unionist policy that helped to cause O'Neill's problems within the unionist party after his meeting with Lemass.

It is proposed to set out some examples of the post-war co-operation in order to give a fairer picture of the attitude of unionist administrations. The survey will avoid security matters for the simple reason that police co-operation, which did sometimes occur, was done very quietly. (There was, for example, an unofficial, and illegal, form of extradition of 'ordinary' criminals practiced before the 1965 legislation.)

Some co-operation was on an informal basis; for example, there was a considerable amount of administrative co-operation between the two Ministries of Agriculture, particularly with regard to the eradication of disease among animals, which was successfully tackled on an all-Ireland basis. Other notable examples are the Erne drainage scheme and the electricity supply scheme, which was to connect the electricity grids of Northern Ireland and the Republic. However, the inter-connector between the two grids was blown up by the IRA in the early 1970s and has been kept out of action since. This may seem like an Irish joke, that a group passionately in favour of uniting Ireland should destroy the all-Ireland electricity system. But it is not as silly as it seems, for it prevents Northern Ireland, which has spare generating capacity, selling electricity to the Republic and the effect is to increase the cost of electricity in Northern Ireland and so further weaken its economy. Then in 1965 there was an agreement on the construction of a Belfast–Dublin road link which was to be of motorway or dual-carriage-way standard. Work in Northern Ireland is almost complete but that in the Republic has scarcely been started.

There were two schemes which involved an element of joint authority. These were the Great Northern Railway Board (wound up in 1958 after line closures) and the Foyle Fisheries Commission. The history of the former is given by Robb (1982, p. 10):

> By the end of 1950 the company's financial resources were exhausted . . . Faced with such a crisis the two governments had no option but to take immediate action . . . agreement was reached with the company to buy the entire undertaking . . . paid in equal shares by North and South . . . and it was placed in charge of a new body . . . consisting of ten members appointed half by each government.

The Foyle Fisheries Commission was established in 1952 after a High Court decision in the Republic affecting the ownership of fishing rights in a branch stream of the Foyle in the Republic. As this decision, together with a high level of poaching from the southern side, threatened the management of the valuable salmon fisheries in the Foyle, the government of Northern Ireland approached the authorities in the Republic to try and achieve a solution. The result was parallel legislation in both jurisdictions establishing the Commission, which consists of four members (two from the North and two from the South). After the previous fishing rights were bought out, these rights and the management of the fisheries in the entire Foyle basin were vested in the Commission. The legislation creates a number of criminal offences, which are treated in an interesting manner. Officers of the Commission are given powers of search and arrest. If within Northern Ireland they arrest a resident of the Irish Republic the offence is not pursued in the Northern courts, instead the offender is delivered to the Republic and prosecuted there and vice versa.

These matters have been set out at some length to show that co-operation on matters of mutual concern should present no difficulty. Problems arise, however, when co-operation is proposed for political reasons, or without regard for the practicalities of the matter, or when some institutional relationship is proposed. An example of impracticality concerns co-operation on economic development. In the debate on the Forum report, Mr Peter Archer MP said, 'I find it hard to see advantages in having two competing authorities concerned with attracting overseas investment into Ireland.' The impracticality of a single authority can be appreciated when questions such as 'Where is the plant financed by the investment going to be located?' are asked, and when it is realized that the fiscal regime is a matter of vital concern to an inward investor. A single development authority is possible only within a single country. Indeed it has been said that the Anglo-Irish Agreement is itself an obstacle to overseas investment, for investors interpret it as a signal that Northern Ireland may soon cease to be part of the UK and so the fiscal and marketing context of their investment might radically change before that investment is recovered.

When formalized relationships such as that contained in the 1985 Agreement are proposed, unionists may object on one or both of two grounds. First, they will want to know what the ultimate object of the relationship is to be, and they will want to be sure in their own minds that the relationship will not be prejudicial to the continued existence of Northern Ireland. The second objection is closely related to the first. Unionists say that they cannot enter into such relationships with a state that maintains a claim to sovereignty over them. Consequently, they see the replacement of Articles 2 and 3 of the Republic's constitution as a necessary prerequisite to such a relationship.

Some people may think that the reference to changes in the Republic's constitution are just a smokescreen and that unionists have no intention of dealing with the Republic. However, such suspicion is unfair. The above examples show that unionists are prepared to co-operate on an *ad hoc* basis, even with the claims in Articles 2 and 3 intact. If those claims were gone, and there was a greater equality of esteem as between Belfast and Dublin, then the situation would be different. To put it another way, a certain level of trust is necessary before there can be a good relationship between the two parts of the island. Trust is impossible while Dublin still proclaims the object of absorbing one part within the other. If that claim were to go a new relationship is possible. The recent policy statement of the Ulster Unionist Party (28 February 1986) contains evidence of this. In it a willingness, subject to certain preconditions, is expressed to have discussions between:

London and Dublin and a newly constituted Government of Northern Ireland to agree a new British/Irish framework within which genuine friendship, co-operation and consultation may be developed and encouraged

Reference could also be made to the paper 'Community of the British Isles' (Vanguard 1973), which sets out a unionist vision of the possible relationship within the British Isles to contrast with the Anglo-Irish Agreement.

Those who negotiated the Anglo-Irish Agreement do not seem to have fully appreciated the need to persuade the Republic to change its constitution and its attitude to Northern Ireland. If they had succeeded in forcing such changes then the story would be very different. Perhaps they tried and failed, or what is worse, perhaps they do not realize that they have failed. Some of the pro-Agreement propaganda assumes that the anodyne statement in Article 1 of the Agreement constitutes a recognition by the Republic of Northern Ireland, and that the *Report* of the New Ireland Forum (1984*a*) marks a new approach to the rights of unionists. It is submitted that neither of these assumptions can in fact be sustained.

3. THE ANGLO-IRISH AGREEMENT

From a unionist viewpoint the Agreement has clearly failed to achieve consent. As evidence of this one can refer first to the demonstration called immediately after the signing of the Agreement. This was not adequately reported in Great Britain, but the response to it clearly exceeded the expectations of the unionist leadership. We are told that the army estimate of the attendance was 203,000. Second, reference can be made to the mini-election arranged following the resignation of the unionist members of parliament and held on 23 January 1986. It is difficult to argue that the vote was not a test of opinion on the Agreement. There was probably a measure of tactical voting in the four marginal constituencies, and this also affected the way the nationalist vote split in those constituencies. But in the other eleven constituencies the issues were clear, and pro-Agreement unionists could have voted for the Agreement without the danger that they would be letting in a nationalist. The result was a clear verdict on the Agreement. It may be noted in passing that the unionist anti-Agreement vote in 1986 (418,000), while slightly down on the unionist vote in those constituencies in the 1983 general election, comfortably exceeds the anti-Sunningdale vote in all constituencies in the February 1974 election (366,000), and the total unionist vote in the October 1974 and 1979 elections. Third, it is clear that unionist opposition has not diminished by the lapse of time. The demonstration called for on the anniversary of the Agreement drew what was generally agreed to be a larger crowd than the first. Newspaper estimates of 250,000 have been made. Interestingly, this time the army estimate was not leaked, which has been taken as confirmation of the belief that the attendance was in excess of 203,000.

However, the government has claimed that the requirement of consent, generally recognized as applicable to constitutional change in Northern Ireland, should not be applied to the Agreement. The justification for this appears to be that the Agreement comes within the area of international relations, which are exclusively a matter for government, and also that the Agreement does not involve any constitutional change that would invoke the 'guarantee'. But unionists are emphatic in their opinion that the Agreement changes the status of Northern Ireland in that it affects the structures and processes of government in the province and, because it affects these internal matters, it cannot be treated as ordinary exercise of the treaty-making power. Unionists find the present stance of the government to be in conflict with its policy at the time of the 1984 summit, when its position appeared to be that changes to the structures and processes of Northern Ireland would have to be 'acceptable to both Communities' (Communiqué, 19 November 1984), and in conflict with the Agreement itself, which purports to contain an agreement that there can be no change in the status of Northern Ireland without consent.

Not only has there been no consent to this Agreement, but the Agreement also fails to meet the criterion of 'widespread acceptance'. This is demonstrated by the withdrawal of unionists from parliament, local government, and the Assembly. This withdrawal was never complete. One, occasionally two, members regularly took part in proceedings at Westminster, and all the unionist members have returned on certain occasions for particular debates or where there was an opportunity of embarrassing the government. The Assembly was also used occasionally as a platform for anti-Agreement propaganda, until it was dissolved by the government in 1986 before it had run its full term. No elections have been held for a new Assembly, apparently because they are unlikely to produce the 'right' result. At district council level the withdrawal was initially quite striking. The eighteen councils dominated by unionists consistently adjourned meetings without transacting business for over a year and failed to strike a rate for 1986. These councils contained some 240 councillors, of whom all were aware of the possible legal and financial penalties they are exposed to, yet at that time only four councillors deliberately failed to vote against striking a rate.

However, it has proved impossible to sustain the policy of adjourning council meetings for legal reasons. Actions have been brought, largely by members of the Alliance Party, which have resulted in the courts declaring that the adjournments were unlawful. It should be noted that the courts held that it was legitimate for councils to discuss the Agreement, as it clearly impinges on the work of district councils, and for councils to express their opposition to the Agreement by resolution and even the expenditure of money on anti-Agreement publicity, an option that has since been taken up. However, the courts said that to do no business was, in the local government context, an unreasonable decision within the meaning of *Associated Provincial Picture Houses* v. *Wednesbury Corp.* [1948] 1 KB 223 (see *In re* Cook and Other's Application [1986] 1 NIJB 43). At first the unionist councils sought to defy the courts, and this resulted in contempt proceedings against Belfast City Council. In these proceedings no attempt was made to seek the committal of the defiant councillors or to fine them. Instead, a fine was levied on the council in the expectation that the amount of the fine would later be surcharged on the responsible members (see *In re* Cook and Others Application (No. 2) [1986] 3 NIJB 64). This resulted in the council abandoning the adjournments and initially deciding to comply with the court's order to conduct 'normal business'. This example has gradually been followed by other councils, as actions have now been taken against virtually all the protesting councils. While these actions were in train there were signs of disunity among the councillors, and at one point the Ulster Unionist councillors rejected the advice from Mr Molyneaux that there should be mass resignations. During this period a number of councillors decided to defy the party's policy, and a small number of resignations and expulsions occurred. But it would be wrong to see these difficulties as a sign that unionists might abandon their opposition to the Agreement.

The unionist hope that government might be forced to appoint commissioners to run local government was frustrated partly by the powers taken by the government in the Local Government (Temporary Provisions) (Northern Ireland) Order 1986 and partly by the fact that district councils have so few functions that they do not now require a full-time commissioner to execute them.

The courts, when they ordered a return to 'normal business', did not define this concept. Since then the unionist-controlled councils have generally done what they have considered to be the minimum business that they are required by statute to do, and have also, in some cases, revised their procedures to reduce the participation of minority councillors in committees. The legality of the former course is questionable, and there is dicta in one case indicating that those councils could still be in contempt. The doubt stems from the fact that district councils have very few actual functions: most of their time in the past had been spent on their purely consultative role. As to the latter course, while litigation has been threatened it may not be successful, for a survey conducted by Belfast City Council revealed that the pre-1987 practice with regard to the composition of committees had been much more generous to minority parties than the modern practice in many English councils.

Other forms of action were also adopted to demonstrate the withdrawal of consent. There was a 'day of action' on 3 March 1986, which was a success in all unionist areas, and, so far as the author could see, involved a lower level of intimidation than any of the four previous political strikes since 1972. There are threats of further civil disobedience, but these have not resulted in any major action. There was a campaign to temporarily withhold rates and some other payments, and continuing tension over marches and demonstrations. But the protests generally have been restrained. This results in the danger for unionists that government will simply continue to ignore the protests and treat the absence of a violent uprising as tacit consent.

It is not proposed to pursue the issue of consent further, nor to examine in detail the arguments against the Agreement. These can be seen in the *First Report* of the NI Assembly Committee on the Government of Northern Ireland, in 'Why Unionists say No' (Joint Unionist Working Party, March 1986), and in the part of the Assembly *Report* dealing with consent and the issue of parliamentary sovereignty. Here it is only proposed to look briefly at some other issues, namely the status of Northern Ireland and the Intergovernmental Conference.

In article 1 (*c*) of the Agreement the two governments:

affirm that any change in the status of Northern Ireland would only come about with the consent of a majority of the people of Northern Ireland . . .

This should be contrasted with the declaration of the Republic at Sunningdale:

that there could be no change in the status of Northern Ireland until a majority of the people desired a change . . .

The two are virtually the same except that 'could' with its normative undertones is replaced in 1985 with the more descriptive 'would'.

In 1973 the British declaration identified Northern Ireland as being part of the United Kingdom, and declared that it was the policy of the British government to support the wishes of the majority of the people of Northern Ireland. Both these statements are missing from the 1985 Agreement. The omissions are significant. The latter is interpreted by unionist as being a broad hint as to the British government's current policy. The former means that the Agreement does not identify the present status of Northern Ireland. It may be felt that the facts speak for themselves, but in the constitutional law of the Republic of Ireland, Northern Ireland is part of the Republic, and as a result of the Boland case ([1974] IR 338) it is clear that the Republic's government is constitutionally incapable of recognizing the status of Northern Ireland as part of the UK. The Agreement does not therefore reinforce the 'guarantee'. It is also silent on an important point, namely whether the parties are free to follow a policy of seeking change in the present position of Northern Ireland with or without consent, or whether there is an undertaking not to pursue such a policy. This is a matter of no little importance, for this Agreement, at the very least, gives the Republic an input into policy-making, and it would be reasonable to expect some indication of the way the Republic will exercise its new rights. In the meantime unionists have listened to the speeches of government ministers in the Republic and concluded that they will use their new position in a sectarian manner.

The issue of status could be pursued at greater length, but just two further aspects of it will be mentioned. The first is the question of the so-called guarantee. It should be understood that the status of Northern Ireland does not derive from or depend on the 1973 Constitution Act which contains the so-called guarantee, nor even the Government of Ireland Act 1920; but from the Treaty and Acts of Union. Article 1 of the latter states that 'the said kingdoms of Great Britain and Ireland shall . . . and for ever be united into one kingdom . . .'. The secession of 26 of the counties of Ireland did not give the remainder of the kingdom of Ireland a new status. The 1973 Act is not simply an affirmation of the status created by the Acts of Union, rather it contains a procedure whereby that status can be changed and so, in a sense, weakens the real guarantee which is the 1801 Acts and the 1800 treaty. In theory, therefore, repeal of section 1 of the 1973 Act would strengthen the union.

The second point is that the Acts of Union intended to create one kingdom. That supposes a degree of uniformity, or at least equal treatment, within the kingdom. Not anticipating the issues of the 1980s, the Acts contain little detail on this point, although there is the reference in Article 6 to Britain and Ireland being, for certain purposes, on the same footing. This was one of the points that unionists relied on in their abortive legal action against the Agreement. The failure of that litigation does not deprive the point of validity. Can you speak of there being a united kingdom when one part is being treated, against its will, in a radically different way? Some unionists take the position that the union they supported was broken by the government when it signed this Agreement and that the question now at issue is whether the union can be restored.

The position of the Intergovernmental Conference will be dealt with more briefly. The British government asserts that it is merely consultative. This assertion lacks credibility even for those unionists who would like to believe it. The assertion is undermined partly by statements from the Republic that the Agreement goes beyond a consultative role (FitzGerald), gives the Republic a major and substantial role in the day-to-day running of Northern Ireland (Noonan, while Minister of Justice), and is the foot in the door (John Kelly, a prominent Fine Gael TD). Parts of the Agreement clearly go beyond a consultative role, and at no point does the Agreement say that the Republic's role is limited to consultation. The government has relied on the concluding words of Article 2 (*b*), that each government 'retains responsibility for the decisions and administration of government within its own jurisdiction'. But this does not identify how those decisions are made, and in view of the obligation that the government has undertaken to make 'determined efforts . . . through the conference to resolve any differences' (also Art. 2 (*b*)) there can be no doubt that some decisions will be taken by the government within the Conference or as a result of the Conference's deliberations. Indeed, it has been the practice to announce in the communiqués issued after Conference meetings that one government has 'reported' to the other that certain policy decisions have been taken or legislation is to be made or amended. The minister concerned will then be responsible for that decision to parliament, and thus the proper constitutional form will be observed, though that form will have been drained of content.

4. PROSPECTS

The position of the government in 1986 appeared to be to sit tight on the Agreement and try and encourage the growth of unionist acquiesence. However, the government started off from a weak position in that no unionist of a representative character is even prepared to 'give the agreement a chance'. Considerable efforts have reputedly been made to encourage unionist support—many moderate unionists have been invited to private functions at Hillsborough Castle, though it is said that after being hectored for a couple of hours by Northern Ireland Office ministers most of these moderates left in a rather immoderate frame of mind. Still, no doubt the government remembers that immediately after the imposition of Direct Rule unionist opposition was virtually total, with Mr Faulkner making angry speeches about 'Herr Heath', but a few months later he agreed to fall in with government plans.

While there is very little prospect of unionist support for the Agreement at the moment, there may be more encouragement for the government in the possibility that divisions within unionism can be created and exploited. In particular there seemed to be a hope on the government's part as the summer of 1986 approached that some unionists would engage in, or be provoked into, violent attacks on the police and others, and that there would then be a revulsion from this within the unionist community which would, in some unspecified way, lead to acceptance of the Agreement. Government statements continually harped on this theme, and there is in some quarters a suspicion that government decisions were influenced by a desire to provoke a reaction (e.g. the decision to ban the 1986 Easter Monday parade in Portadown, and the decision to hold a meeting of the Conference at Belfast immediately after the unionist 'day of action'). These actions did result in a spate of attacks by unionists on the police. But they were minor attacks compared with republican violence and they soon petered out. When the summer actually came matters passed peacefully, as there was a compromise concerning the major flash-point (Portadown), which compromise was acceptable to unionists, although it provoked public protests from Dublin.

At first the government approached the issues that the Conference was intended to deal with in a cautious manner. As a result it was slow to deliver anything to nationalists except its own existence and the prospect of conflict between unionists and the government that, according to such theory as underlies the Agreement, is supposed to be the representative and guardian of their interests. Some minor changes have occurred, notably the repeal of the Flags and Emblems Act and the enactment of new public order legislation which is more stringent than the recent English Act and which appears to be aimed at unionists. The more far-reaching changes to the police and the judicial process, hinted at in the Agreement, have yet to occur.

On the unionist side there appears to be a three-way division of opinion emerging. First, there are those who after 'withdrawing' from active participation in the political process would prefer to confine their action to token gestures or other non-violent action. Their hope is that the Agreement will eventually break down as a result of nationalist frustration or as a result of a change in British politics after the next general election. Secondly, there are those who are less sanguine and who want to escalate the protest action. A few of these publicly advocate violence, more refer to it in coded language or in private. The third group contains those who have reacted to an Agreement that distances them from the rest of the Kingdom by trying to become even more British than before. These are sometimes referred to as integrationists, and their number probably goes beyond the active supporters of the campaign for equal citizenship.

What is unknown is how many rank-and-file unionists will support the more vigorous measures wanted by the second group and how far they will be prepared to go. At the moment those endorsing violent action are a minority within unionism and do not seem to have mobilized sufficient support. But it does not follow that they will continue to be inactive or that their action will be unsuccessful. The first and third groups of unionists may be reluctant to work actively against the Ultras within unionism, and even if there is a revulsion from the Ultras' actions, that recoil will not necessarily lead to support of the Agreement. Instead, a more passive attitude will probably be adopted.

At the moment the likelihood is of continued instability and very little of the peace and prosperity that are stated as the ultimate objectives of the Agreement, unless the impasse as between unionists and the government can be overcome. Since the failure of the Downing Street meeting of 25 February 1986, there seems little chance of this happening. Unionists insist on a removal or suspension of the Agreement. The government says that it wants talks without preconditions, but insists that the Agreement will stand whatever the outcome of such talks. This sounds to unionists like a precondition. Talks are unlikely to occur without some fudging of the operation of the Conference, and it may be that this will be offered at what is judged to be the right psychological moment. Some, however, seem to be of the opinion that the government can continue to bypass unionist opposition, or that after unionists have been 'faced down' or have gone through their trauma the Anglo-Irish process can continue. But it is unlikely that such counsels will prevail in the event of continued political deadlock and unrest. It should also be remembered that republican violence will continue. Unionists consider that the Agreement will actually incite an increase in republican violence. While republicans regard the Agreement as falling a long way short of their desires, they see it as having been produced by their action. Consequently they believe that continued action on their part will lead to even further movement towards their goal. Unionists also consider that because of a lack of will and capacity on the southern side, the security co-operation that the Agreement is supposed to produce will never reach the level where it ends the republican campaign. Experience since the Agreement has merely reinforced the unionist perception.

If it is assumed that some talks occur, the question of what this Conference will address itself to arises. The probability is that devolution will be at the top of any agenda. A problem here is that, while the Agreement puts considerable pressure on unionists, there is nothing in the Agreement to put any pressure on the SDLP to agree. In this respect the Agreement resembles the Northern Ireland Act 1982. As originally drafted it was intended to set up the sort of bargaining situation discussed above in the context of the Catherwood plan, i.e. one where no party was given a veto on the outcome of the talks, but all were encouraged to enter into talks by the prizes offered or the fear of being left behind. However, the Prior bill was amended by the insertion of a provision which meant that even if the 70 per cent level of Agreement was reached there would still be no devolution without power-sharing. As a result the SDLP knew that they could boycott the Assembly with impunity, and ignore all the proposals for progress emanating from it. The 1985 Agreement gives them the same luxury, for while the governments seem anxious that the SDLP should display a conciliatory manner, they are still insisting that there must be power-sharing. As indicated above, there is not much prospect that full blooded power-sharing will be any more acceptable to unionists than in the past. Some unionist politicians hint at a willingness to move in that direction, but it may be doubted if they can carry any significant support. Certainly they would require, at the very least, significant concessions to be offered to them with regard to the 'Irish Dimension', with genuine guarantees for the unionist position. However, there seems to be no willingness in either government or among the SDLP to make the sort of changes to the Agreement that would be necessary to give power-sharing unionists any chance of survival.

In the event of talks on devolution failing, it is unlikely that there could be a return to Direct Rule. Instead there might be moves towards what is described as integration. That is an ending of the procedure of legislating by Order and a return to the normal method of legislation. This could be accompanied by the creation of a NI Committee similar to the Scottish Grand Committee. Hints of these changes were contained in the press statement issued by Downing Street after the talks of 25 February 1986, and were renewed in a subsequent letter from the Prime Minister to the two Unionist leaders. Similar proposals have emanated from the Labour Party and the Liberal/SDP Alliance. The attraction of this to a London government is that these changes can be made without altering the agreement, and possibly without having to get Dublin's consent. Unionists could say that this fulfils the historic claim of unionism for equal citizenship and that the new procedures enable them to act as a check on the actions of the Conference. This appears to be the position of certain Ulster Unionists such as J. D. Taylor MP and R. McCartney QC, the leader of the campaign for equal citizenship, and it may also become the position of those unionists who cannot stomach the action required by more vigorous opposition to the Agreement.

The difficulty of this position is, first, that it may not be acceptable to Dublin and the SDLP. Second, if the latter are prepared to tolerate it, it becomes not just integration, but two-way integration: that is, unionists will be told that the changes will mean closer integration into the UK at the same time that nationalists are being told that the Conference will mean their integration into the Republic. One doubts if this will work.

The result is that the impetus towards some form of British disengagement will increase. In that event there seems to be only two real options, a federal Ireland or an Independent Ulster, perhaps with special relationships with its neighbours. The argument for the former was made by Dr Palley in an article in the *Guardian* on 20 January 1986. The argument is essentially the same as that put forward in 1972 by D. Boal QC (then a unionist Stormont MP), and it can appear attractive on paper, but like many interesting ideas it flies in the face of reality. The feeling among unionists against Irish republicanism is so strong that one cannot envisage a situation where a majority of unionists would say that they will enter an Irish Republic.

That leaves independence, and it seems that this is the fall-back position of most hard-line unionists and not a few of the more moderate variety. While some of the former now positively want independence, it is unlikely that unionism as a whole will present the government with a demand for self-determination in the classical manner. That demand will probably be made only in the event of a British withdrawal. In that context there is little likelihood that any real attempt will be made to obtain nationalist agreement. The position will then resemble the malign scenario sketched by O'Brien in *States of Ireland* (1972). It must be said that not all unionists are worried at that prospect.

It will be noted that the nationalist goal of a unitary Irish state is not considered likely. Militant republicans are unlikely to be able to realize the Provisional IRA's dream of compelling Protestants to assimilate into the 'Irish nation' or suffer the same fate as the French–Algerian *colons*. They may be able to secure nationalist control of some areas, but it is unlikely that the unionist heartland can be overrun without outside assistance.

The conclusion may seem to be gloomy, but a caveat should be entered. It is not inevitable that events will work out to their logical conclusion. Any one of the parties may decide to draw back from the confrontation implicit in that conclusion or may refrain from pushing matters towards it. Many times in the last decade and a half it has appeared that affairs in Northern Ireland were headed towards a precipice. Sometimes the movement in that direction has stopped and sometimes the precipice has receded. If that were to happen again, then the political impasse would continue.

6

THE NORTH AND THE REST
The Politics of the Republic of Ireland
Tom Garvin

LONG before the island of Ireland was partitioned in 1920 by an act of the British parliament, the areas that were to become the Irish Republic and Northern Ireland had shown clear signs of developing in different directions and of becoming rather different societies. This divergence occurred despite the existence of a common administrative system, good communications, and a compact geographical context which both shared. The divergence also occurred in spite of Ireland's long history as a cultural entity and even defied the existence of island-wide ecclesiastical organizations; all major churches then, as now, were organized on a thirty-two county, all-Ireland basis, as were many other organizations. Even the Grand Orange Lodge of *Ireland* sat in Dublin rather than in Belfast.

Partition, therefore, accelerated or aggravated a process of divergence that had previously existed, and did not artificially instigate it for the first time. North and South, different before 1920, came to have different, if interacting, political histories, and each have developed noticeably different identities. Within each area, the populations, simply by living together, have come to share common identities which tend to exclude those outside. Protestants and Catholics in the North tend to see themselves as having much in common which is not shared by either the inhabitants of the Republic or those of Great Britain, even if what is shared amounts often only to an acknowledgement of a common predicament (Harris 1972; Rose 1971; Hickey 1984). Similarly, the people of the Republic have come to see the people of the North as 'different', in large part because they have not shared the experience of independence, with all its rewards and penalties, since 1922. The inhabitants of the Republic have a curious liking for the British that may be partly derived from a sense of equality with them; independence has eliminated the ancient subordination. Northerners, however, are subordinated willy-nilly to a British government which is, if not exactly foreign, certainly external and psychologically remote from them. The experience of the Second World War was not shared by North and South; the welfare state developed far more slowly, and in a rather different way, in the Republic than in the North; in the North, industrialization occurred in the nineteenth century, whereas in the Republic it has occurred only in the last generation and is of a very different kind (MacGreil 1977; Rose and Garvin 1983).

Like Spain and Portugal, or West Berlin and the German Democratic Republic, the two Irelands attempted to ignore one another, while being forced by physical proximity with each other to co-operate. The Republic, which, after all, is not just the South of Ireland but the West and most of the East as well, came to pretend that it was Ireland *tout court*, while the North tried to represent the boundary between itself and the rest of the island as a wholly natural and obvious one with the physical immediacy of a range of mountains or an arm of the sea and labelled the Republic a 'foreign' country, much to the amusement of many Southerners. For good measure, the Republic denied symbolic recognition to Northern Ireland and sometimes pretended that Great Britain was as foreign and unknown a country as Outer Mongolia. In the 1960s, with the passing of the revolutionary generation of political leaders in the Republic, the will to maintain these postures became weakened, and in 1965 a series of meetings between senior leaders of both parts of the island took place at the initiative of the Republic. These meetings started a political chain-reaction that is still going on two decades later.

It could almost be said that Ireland has been united, psychologically speaking, for the first time by the shared experience of violence since the late 1960s. In August 1969, Northern Ireland forcibly entered the peaceful and parochial world of Southern politics for the first time. Two generations of unreality and make-believe on the issue of the partition of Ireland came to an abrupt end. Despite its official rhetoric of reunificationism, the Republic's governments had, naturally enough, come to legislate for the almost monolithically Catholic population of the twenty-six counties and to pay scant attention to the susceptibilities of Northern Protestants or, for that matter, Northern Catholics. After all, neither Northern community voted in the Republic's elections, and partition had been designed by the British to exclude from the North as many Catholics as possible while including as many Protestants as possible. The Republic had also developed a political liturgy emphasizing Anglophobic, pseudo-Gaelic, peasant, and Catholic themes which had reached a climax of sorts in the public celebrations of the fiftieth anniversary of the Easter Rising in 1966.

In the 1950s and early 1960s things had been changing, and the official visits of 1965 had been one of the fruits of these changes, as well as being the triggers of further change. The influence of the mass media, of relative affluence, and of Vatican II had begun to erode this liturgical edifice, which had always had a certain artificial, flimsy, and unpopular character to it. However, this official system of myths and attitudes, which I have labelled the 'liturgical edifice', was still by-and-large intact in 1969–72, when the unionist political system in Northern Ireland disintegrated; Southern politicians, paying lip-service to a wildly inappropriate nationalist ideology, found themselves suddenly having to deal with the real Northern Ireland rather than one which was a figment of the imaginations of official ideologues. In the rest of this essay I would like to discuss some of the consequences for the political culture of the Republic of this new and occasionally fearsome challenge. I would like also to speculate on the long-term consequences for the Republic of increasing demands on it from the North for changes in many of its traditional public postures.

1. THE NORTHERN CHALLENGE AND THE NATIONALIST MYTH

All political systems attempt to confer legitimacy upon themselves by reference to some superordinate set of values. Whether or not the élites themselves accept these values privately, no polity except a conquest regime attempts to rule for any considerable period without such reference. This 'political formula' may vary in intellectual coherence, in the types of values which it articulates, and in the social range within the population to which it appeals, but there is no doubt of its necessity to the system itself. This general proposition is even truer of democracies than it is of non-democracies; it is to the point to mention that one of the many circumstances that make Irish disagreements so intractable is the fact that both sides are internally democratic and leaders tend to be trapped by the public opinion of their own side. In 1965, for example, both Terence O'Neill and Seán Lemass were fearful of the reaction of their own supporters back home, and both were right.

The events of 1969–72 challenged the political formula of the Republic directly, with political consequences for the Republic itself that are not yet fully realized. The political ideology of the revolutionary élites who became the founding fathers of the Irish state was heavily influenced by a perception of English and Protestant culture as being deeply immoral and a threat to the integrity of Catholic Ireland. This ideology also asserted an Irish political identity which was thought of as being continuous from Gaelic times and which denied, both implicitly and determinedly, the permanent importance of the English-language Ireland that had emerged in the seventeenth century. After independence, this implicitly authoritarian *Weltanschauung* became a political orthodoxy and had a direct effect on state policy. Of course, this Catholic-romantic view of Irish history had its intellectual competitors; Irish literary figures, most of them either of Protestant stock or alienated from the nationalist community, were devastating in their critiques, whether solemn or satirical, of the neo-Gaelic orthodoxy. Furthermore, the neo-Gaelic, Catholic-romantic, and essentially ahistorical conception was not unchallenged within the nationalist community; after all, a liberal-nationalist and Anglophile tradition, associated with Daniel O'Connell, also existed and came to be represented in the political culture of independent Ireland. Further, the concept of a Gaelic Ireland was in competition with a very powerful tradition that regarded Ireland as being first and foremost a Catholic and non-secular nation (Farrell 1973; Prager 1986). However, the neo-Gaelic historicist ideology did become dominant in official thought and a simplified form of what Prager has termed 'Gaelic-Romantic' nationalism was taught to schoolchildren, preached by politicians and ecclesiastics, and enshrined in the laws and constitution of the new state. It was further asserted that the historical home of this half-imaginary Gaelic nation of Pearse and de Valera was the entire island of Ireland. The new constitution of 1937 reasserted this ideology in ways that forced Irish governments to pay lip-service to it. Any Irish government which openly and in law recognized fully the partition of Ireland, as distinct from accepting it tacitly for everyday administrative purposes, was in very real danger of being accused of being unfaithful to the constitution, quite apart from committing the more abstract offence of being disloyal to the nation. Issues such as divorce and contraception were also bedevilled by the legal and even constitutional provisions that were derived from the original Gaelic-Catholic ideology of Sinn Féin. Democratic party competition aggravated the situation as Fianna Fáil and Fine Gael used 'greener-than-thou' and 'holier-than-thou' slogans and postures in electoral propaganda. Two good examples of Fine Gael's determination not to be outflanked on the nationalist front by Fianna Fáil as it had been in the first two decades of independence were the declaration of the Republic in 1949 by a Fine Gael-led government and the engineering by Garret FitzGerald of the Anglo-Irish Agreement of 1985. In the latter case, the chagrin and confusion of the Fianna Fáil leaders were only too evident.

The irruption of the North into Southern affairs, therefore, threatened very directly the validity of the political formula under which the Dublin regime claimed the right to rule. Symbolic obeisance to a faraway national goal about which little concrete need be done was replaced suddenly by a frantic imperative to 'do something' (O'Brien 1972, p. 194). Irish governments were forced into a situation where they were obliged to be seen to be pursuing perhaps contradictory goals: defending the comfortable status quo in the Republic while simultaneously pursuing the goal of a united Ireland by diplomatic if not military means. Understandably, the Fianna Fáil party has ever since showed signs of internal turmoil that suggest the political analogue to a collective nervous breakdown. However, something else, essentially unconnected with the North, had been going on in the Republic's politics; by 1969 the revolutionary élite which had governed the country since independence had finally been replaced by a second and clearly post-revolutionary generation (Cohan 1972). The new leaders lacked the revolutionary charisma and value-system of their elders, were more parochial in some ways, and more concerned with bread-and-butter issues. They were the products of competitive electoral democracy in a rather parochial society rather than the products of the militant and romantic movements of the revolutionary period. These new men were more interested in economic and social development than in large, long-run, and visionary schemes for national grandeur, territorial expansion, or, for that matter, programmes for cultural and moral uplift. The relatively muted reaction of the Republic to the events in the North was closely connected with the weakening of revolutionary *élan* as the memories of the united Ireland of the pre-independence period weakened, and also with the parallel weakening of militant and fundamentalist Catholicism in the wake of Vatican II. In defiance of its own political formula, the Republic tried to minimize the spillover of violence from North to South and to restrain attempts by some politicians and others to generate spillover in the opposite direction. The Republic has, fairly consistently, attempted to negotiate with the British for either an internal settlement in the

North or for a new set of arrangements between Britain and the two Irelands. Even Fianna Fáil governments, with their long tradition of unyielding reunificationist rhetoric, have shown themselves in practice to be more concerned with the internal stability of the Republic than with traditional reunificationism. I suspect that the Anglo-Irish Agreement, which both Fianna-Fáil- and Fine Gael-led governments have been pursuing in different ways snce 1979, is intended more to hasten an internal settlement in Northern Ireland than it is to hasten the reunification of the island. But this, of course, can never be said.

It is also striking how much quiet general acceptance of this position there is in the Republic. Attempts to change the liturgy have achieved a general acceptance inconceivable before 1969. Changes in the status of the Catholic church in the constitution and changes in the law on contraception were put through against tepid opposition. The law on the status of women was revolutionized, and the old Sinn Féin version of *Kinder, Küche und Kirche* began to be demolished. In early 1974 the Fine Gael–Labour government abolished the traditional military parades which had commemorated the Easter Rising and linked together symbolically the blood-sacrifice of Pearse and the Christian sacrifice of Easter in the interests of legitimizing the state. This was a direct blow at the quasi-religious cult of the 1916 martyrs, and was supported by many clerics who had come to see it as a pagan rather than a Christian cult. What is particularly significant about this change is the deep silence with which the public accepted it. Easter Sunday as the day of militaristic commemoration of the birth of the Republic is being gradually replaced by St Patrick's Day, 17 March. Official support has been forthcoming to build up St Patrick's Day as the national day of general and apolitical self-celebration, borrowing motifs from the Irish-American tradition. The day of the patron saint of Ireland had been allowed to degenerate into a rather dreary day of prayer and morose mid-Lenten drinking, much to the bewilderment of visiting Irish-Americans, with their tradition of it as a Hibernian *mardi gras*.

Even sport began to become depoliticized, and the notorious 'ban' which prohibited players of Gaelic games from participating in 'foreign' games has been abolished. An immediate result of this was the rise of Dublin teams to prominence in Gaelic football, in part because it was possible for rugby and soccer players to participate. A parallel reduction in the authoritarianism of the Catholic church, a growing acceptance by clergy of lay involvement in running the school systems, and a far more relaxed attitude toward sexual life were results of the Vatican II changes. However, there were limits to these changes, and since the late 1970s there have been attempts, if not to put the clock back, certainly to stop it.

The general decline of strident Catholic fundamentalism dismayed traditionalists, mainly but not entirely older people, and the growing economic depression and uncertainty of the 1980s strengthened their hand. The insertion, by popular referendum, of a clause prohibiting abortion into the constitution represents a resurgence of the older tradition. Table 1 suggests that the traditionalists picked their issue rather cleverly; hostility to abortion is very general, and, although stronger in declining classes such as the smaller farmers, is as strong among the young as it is among the old. A possible reason for this is the internalization by younger people of certain Catholic attitudes promulgated through the schools. It is also significant, on the other hand, that younger people were far more likely to be hostile to the idea of inserting such a prohibition in the constitution. Table 1 suggests that, even on a valence issue such as abortion, where the population might be expected to display its traditional monolithism, differences have begun to show; it should be remembered that the population is probably almost unanimously hostile to abortion. One third of voters voted against the proposition. On issues like abortion and divorce, the party system clearly echoes differences in the support bases for the parties; Fianna Fáil voters are far more likely to adhere to traditional stances, whereas Labour voters are most likely to oppose them. Fine

TABLE 1. Attitudes toward the Insertion in the Constitution of an Anti-abortion Amendment, July 1983.

(a) By Class (%)	AB	C1	C2	DE	Large Farm	Small Farm	Totals
In Favour	45	41	48	45	33	49	44
Against	31	32	30	30	40	24	31
Don't Know	24	28	23	24	27	27	25

(b) By Age (%)	0–25	25–34	35–49	50–64	65+	Totals
In Favour	44	44	43	46	45	44
Against	34	34	31	31	20	31
Don't Know	22	22	26	23	35	25

$N = 1270$

Source: Irish Marketing Surveys, July 1986.

Gael supporters occupy an intermediate position, which would explain the divisions within the party on such issues.

Attitudes toward a divorce law are perhaps more revealing, as a prohibition on the Oireachtas (Parliament) enacting a divorce law is constitutionally entrenched and could only be removed by referendum. While opinion polls in recent years have persistently indicated that a majority favour a restrictive, 'hard cases' form of divorce, a proposal to abolish the prohibition was turned down by a two-thirds majority in June 1986.

The overall pattern of voting in 1986 was very similar to that of 1983, the rural areas being far more hostile to change than the urban areas. The anti-divorce activists, with tacit support from the Catholic clergy, nearly all of Fianna Fáil, and many Fine Gael supporters, ran an effective and clever grass-roots campaign, emphasizing traditional values, Catholic doctrines, and the anti-community effects divorce might have. There was also systematic reference to the insecurity that women would suffer if the law were changed. Emphasis was also laid on possible problems of inheritance. It is surprising, after the event, to see that one third of the voters actually voted against; the urban, better-educated, and younger elements in the population voted against the traditional official ethos. Table 2, derived from the same 1983 poll and typical of findings in recent years, shows a population which is indeed deeply divided on the issue. A striking contrast between Tables 1 and 2 is the proportion of 'Don't Knows', which is far higher in Table 1. This almost certainly reflects the cross-pressuring many people were experiencing from the impassioned campaign launched in

TABLE 2. Attitudes toward Divorce, July 1983

(a) By Class (%)	AB	C1	C2	DE	Large Farm	Small Farm	Totals
In Favour	50	60	61	45	34	29	48
Against	37	33	34	46	54	61	43
Don't Know	13	7	5	9	12	10	9

(b) By Age (%)	0–25	25–34	35–49	50–64	65+		Totals
In Favour	54	67	53	38	18		48
Against	39	27	39	52	68		43
Don't Know	7	5	8	10	14		9

$N = 1270$

Source: Irish Marketing Surveys, July 1986. On the divorce referendum see Irish Times, 28 June 1986.

that year by the Catholic church and the Society for the Protection of the Unborn Child against abortion.

I would argue that the changes in attitudes in recent years, although slow and partial, indicate that the nineteenth-century synthesis of nationalism and Catholicism is very gradually coming apart at the seams, and a huge, if shapeless, cultural revolution is occurring in the Republic. Interestingly, the nationalist components of the synthesis were jettisoned earlier and with less difficulty than are the religious components. The cultural revolution is due in part to the usual pressures for secularization that all western societies have experienced in the twentieth century, but also to the entry of the North into the South, and the all too obvious challenge it offers to the ideology of monolithic national Catholicism. The price the North pays for its communal nationalism and unionism is also obvious, and Southerners appear reluctant to share the payments, whether monetary or psychological. The psychic unification of Ireland which the media and travel have brought about has forced the South to see the North perhaps more as it is than as the Republic might wish it to be.

2. THE PARTY SYSTEM OF THE REPUBLIC

The 1969 crisis shattered both the nationalist and unionist political monoliths in the North, disintegrating the pre-existing party system, whose components had scarcely changed since Victorian times. The effects of the North on the party system of the Republic have been more indirect and subtle, but have been almost equally wide-ranging. A major difference has been that the effects have taken a long time to become visible, rather than having the sudden and spectacular impact they had in the North. The impact on Fianna Fáil was very deep, and the full consequences for that party of the Ulster crisis are not even now completely realized. Fianna Fáil saw itself as being the particular guardian of the political formula devised by de Valera: partition was not to be recognized, the neo-Gaelic ideology was to be defended, and, in general, the synthesis of anti-British nationalism and traditional Catholic values was to be adhered to, or only abandoned partially and reluctantly when popular pressure became overwhelming. Ever since the apostolic succession to de Valera had petered out with the retirement in 1966 of Seán Lemass, his successor as leader of the party, Fianna Fáil has been gripped by what amounts to a perpetual succession crisis rather, perhaps, as pre-Norman Gaelic Irish political society had been inflicted with a chronic political condition known as 'kings with opposition'. A party which had never known serious internal dissent became deeply divided, and the divisions were aggravated by the North (Garvin 1981). A long rivalry between Jack Lynch, Charles Haughey, Desmond O'Malley, and George Colley dominated the 1970s in the party, and distracted its leaders from the task of government. In 1970 Lynch fired two Cabinet ministers, Neil Blaney and Charles Haughey, for alleged complicity in smuggling arms into the Republic for use in the North. Haughey was found not guilty in court, and spent the following decade intriguing within the party to succeed Lynch (Garvin 1981). In 1979 he succeeded, but took several years to expel his rivals from positions of power; it was only in 1985 that his grip on the party became undisputed. Haughey never succeeded in gaining the general trust that previous Fianna Fáil leaders have enjoyed, and the public reaction to him, particularly among the middle class, appears to have been a major factor in the rise of Garret FitzGerald's Fine Gael in the last ten years. O'Malley's founding of the Progressive Democrats in 1985 marks the most important élite split in Fianna Fáil since its inception in 1926. The PD, liberal on moral issues and right-wing economically, is also accommodationist on the issue of Northern Ireland; in all three issue-areas it challenges Fianna Fáil orthoxoxy under Haughey, and, on morals and the North, it echoes Lynch. Haughey has clearly articulated a new ideological fundamentalism in Fianna Fáil, in defiance of the liberal trends of the 1960s and 1970s.

The effect of the Ulster crisis on Fine Gael has also been great, although of a different kind. Firstly, Fine Gael has never been as stridently anti-partitionist or anti-unionist as has Fianna Fáil, and it has little psychological commitment to the de Valera constitution of 1937, which had, after all, replaced a constitution devised by Fine Gael's founders. Fine Gael is a more middle-class party, and has tended to move from a right-wing clericalist position to a centre-left, secularist position as the middle classes have evolved politically. Fianna Fáil's troubles have benefitted the party electorally, and liberal elements in the party found themselves in a position to modernize it organizationally after a serious electoral defeat in 1977. Skilful image-building and innovative policy formation revolutionized its electoral fortunes in the early 1980s. For a while it actually began to be seen as the party of the future rather than the party of the past, and as a serious contender for Fianna Fáil's position in the system as the dominant party. It is only recently that this image has begun to fade because of a series of political embarrassments. Certainly, it is now a very different party to what it was in 1970, and it is probable that in the long run its relatively 'cool' attitude towards the North and the British will benefit it greatly.

Another consequence of the crisis was to release much of the old unconstitutional republican tradition, as represented by the IRA and its political front Sinn Féin, into the normal political arena. Sinn Féin had traditionally refused to take seats in the Oireachtas on the ground that the Republic was a puppet regime. The emergence of the Provisional IRA in 1969–70 split the movement into virulent physical-force nationalist and armed nationalist-Marxist wings ('Provisionals' versus 'Officials'). A series of politically unprofitable murders of civilians by the Officials persuaded their leadership of the hopeless-ness of violence, and they proceeded to transform their wing of Sinn Féin into a leftist-socialist party, the Workers' Party. Their presence has damaged the fortunes of the small Labour Party. In late 1986 even the Provisionals divided again into a main group who decided to try the electoral road and a smaller group who held to the older abstentionist position. Political abstentionism has been a long-distance casualty of the North's irruption into Southern politics.

The effect of the North on the party politics of the Republic has been, therefore, pervasive if not readily quantifiable. It has provoked a major crisis in Fianna Fáil and may have reversed its drift away from ideological fundamentalism, despite the weakening of such attitudes in the population in general, particularly among the middle class and the young. It has certainly accelerated trends toward internal modernization in Fine Gael and made that party's political prospects brighter. It has caused, directly or indirectly, the emergence of the Workers' Party and of the PD. It has forced the rump of the unconstitutional tradition into the Dáil and has probably damaged the Labour Party.

More generally, the North has deeply affected the public policy process in the Republic. The Irish government now spends very considerable sums on internal and border security, and the Irish Army is now a relatively serious fighting force compared to twenty years ago. A similar modernization is occurring in the Garda Síochána (police). It has been argued that the Northern violence has distracted governments in the Republic from rethinking strategies of economic development, and it is believed that the economy has been badly damaged by Northern political instability.

Perhaps the impact of the North should not be overstated; most of the internal crisis in the Republic is internally generated, and was predictable. The children of the baby boom of the late 1950s and early 1960s began to come on the labour market in the late 1970s, at a time of economic depression. Successive Irish governments have resorted to foreign borrowing, partly for productive investment, but mainly to educate the younger generation and to purchase social peace. The Republic has now by far the greatest per capita foreign public-sector debt of any OECD country, with the exception of Israel. The pressures on the party system come from an electorate that is far more worried about unemployment and the prospects for its progeny than it is about the North.

3. THE NORTH AND PUBLIC OPINION IN THE REPUBLIC

It could perhaps be argued that the Ulster crisis has had a far greater impact on élites than it has had on the general population, partly for reasons which I already have suggested. Despite all the changes in attitudes toward religious and moral issues, and despite the quiet acceptance of retreat from ultra-nationalist postures, opinion polls appear to show only moderate change in people's attitudes toward the possibility of reunification of the island. In 1968, 85 per cent of a national sample expressed a preference for Irish unity, whereas a mere six per cent positively favoured the continuing partition of the island. In June 1983, the figures were respectively 76 and 15 per cent. The small, pro-partitionist and heretical minority had grown somewhat, but the anti-partitionist majority was still overwhelming (Rose *et al.* 1978; Irish Marketing Surveys, June 1983; Davis and Sinnott 1979). On the face of it, this is a surprising finding, in view of the evidence on television screens of the intractability of the situation, and also in view of the torrent of words which have spelled out the cultural, economic, and political obstacles that lie in the way of any attempt to put together what history and Lloyd George had sundered. The popular commitment to reunification also appeared to disregard the chronic economic travail of the Republic itself and the accompanying suggestion that the Republic had its hands over-full already in trying to cope with internal problems without taking on Northern Ireland's different and even more insoluble problems. However, there has been strong support for the Irish government's recent initiatives and for the Anglo-Irish Agreement.

The presentation of figures from the years 1968 and 1983 has the effect of masking much variation over the years. In the 1970–7 period, when IRA and other violence was at its height, partitionism came to be favoured by nearly one third of the population (Irish Marketing Surveys, May 1970; Market Research Bureau of Ireland, October 1974; Irish Marketing Surveys, September 1976). In some cases, options like 'power-sharing' seem to have been resorted to by respondents as a half-way-house between orthodox anti-partitionism and a growing, sneaking preference for continued partition. Partitionism appears to grow and shrink in direct correspondence with the rise and fall in IRA violence; the more successful the IRA appears to be in its campaign, the less the Republic's population wants to have to do with the North (Irish Marketing Surveys, September 1976). I do not intend to belittle the enormous majorities anti-partitionism gets in the Republic; the lowest score it has got is 50 per cent, and it has usually been over 65 per cent.

The obvious question is, what do these figures really mean? In a recent paper Harvey Cox (1985a) has suggested that they reflect a pious and unreflective aspiration that is unrelated to everyday realities and is liable to be rapidly jettisoned as soon as its object showed any real signs of immediate realization: the Irish are not really serious about it. Cox rightly points out that the public do not expect partition to end in the immediate future; in June 1983, 64 per cent expected reunification to occur either never, within a century, or within 50 years, 39 per cent selecting the 'never' option. Only a quarter expected reunification within a quarter of a century. Cox concluded that Northern Ireland is not a practical political issue in the eyes of most people in the Republic. This analysis is convincing, but there is at least one objection to exercises of this kind: the respondents are being asked about their attitudes to, and the likelihood of, an event over which they have no personal control and over which even their government has no control. Asking the citizens of the Irish Republic their attitudes towards reunification is rather like asking them their attitudes to nuclear warfare or to the weather, which they share with Northern Ireland and Great Britain; presumably they are 'against' both. As in the case of the Ulster issue, their sentiments have no bearing on the matter, as decisions are in the hands of other, non-Irish, and more powerful agents, the great powers and Nature respectively. By contrast, Irish attitudes toward such issues as contraception or divorce have a direct impact on the policies of the Irish government, which has the capability of changing the law or initiating a referendum. In these issues, their opinions matter and influence policy. In the case of the recent divorce referendum, although a huge majority favoured divorce some weeks before the balloting, nearly 30 per cent of the voters appear to have changed their minds during the campaign; being in favour of divorce in theory was one thing, actually changing the constitution was another.

Opinion polls are therefore unreliable guides to what people really want. I would suggest that the public gives more 'realistic' and considered answers to questions framed so as to involve the respondent in making, at least in imagination, a practical political decision, in comparison to questions which seem framed to instigate an *in vacuo* response involving no real political choice with real policy consequences. A poll taken after the Forum proceedings but before the Anglo-Irish Agreement illustrates this syndrome rather well (Table 3).

Table 3 indicates that a large proportion of the Republic's people support the idea of an internal settlement in the North and are willing to soften the constitutional claim in return for a real internal settlement in the North. The constitution, it must be emphasized, can only be

TABLE 3. Attitudes to Uniting Ireland, November 1984.

(a) 'Is a United Ireland the Only Way to solve the Northern Problem?' (%)

United Ireland Only Way	31
Other Option as good, or better	57
Don't Know	12

(b) 'I would be willing to withdraw our territorial claim to the North in the Constitution entirely, if the British and Irish governments agreed on an internal Northern Ireland settlement in return for the Republic having a significant role in Northern affairs.' (%)

Yes	14
No	71
Don't Know	15

(c) 'In the event of such a settlement I would be willing to withdraw the claim and replace it with a statement expressing a desire for eventual Irish unity.' (%)

Yes	43
No	42
Don't Know	15

$$N = 1.317$$

Source: Sunday Independent, 15 November 1984.

changed by the electorate. Up to the time of the Agreement, the North's affairs were not seen as amenable to Southern control in any way, whereas the constitution was 'ours' and was not to be tinkered with without good cause. Significantly, many appear to have seen the constitutional claim as a bargaining chip which could be cashed in in return for certain concessions on the part of the agency in charge of the North, namely the British government. It may be that the Republic's population do not have a 'low-level aspiration' to Irish unity, but have a low expectation of ever achieving it, which is not the same thing. Partition in Ireland is something which resembles death and taxes, something one wants very much to be without, and something which one has little idea how to avoid. However, unlike the Angel of Death or the taxman, the British government can occasionally be bargained with, and the Irish people, being rather pragmatic and hard-headed when it comes to dealing with the British, are prepared to bargain cautiously with the few chips they have.

I would be inclined to argue further that answers to questions such as 'Is the Republic willing to make concessions in the form of legal and constitutional changes so as to accommodate northern Protestant opinion?' cannot be given, as no one is seriously offering a united Ireland. If such an offer were to be seriously and publicly made by the British government, it would turn Northern Ireland upside-down. However, it would have devastating, and possibly destabilizing effects on the Republic as well. The structure of the Dublin state is predicated on the unspoken assumption of indefinite continuance of partition, as is its party system. Furthermore, the Republic has developed a corporate identity of its own that sudden reunification would threaten; an analogy would be requiring the United States to absorb Mexico. It is not unimaginable that, in certain circumstances, the Republic's electorate would vote *against* certain kinds of reunification. The term 'reunification' is itself rather a misnomer, as Ireland has never been united as an independent, modern, democratized country; a unified democratic Ireland would be a new political system with no true historical precedent, and the past gives us no pointers to its possible shape. Despite the historicist ideology of Sinn Féin's political heirs, the electorate of the Republic appears to grasp this proposition instinctively.

7

THE CONCEPT OF CONSENT AND THE AGREEMENT*
Bernard Crick

I. TEXTS FOR A LAY SERMON

The Guarantee itself:

It is hereby declared that Northern Ireland remains part of Her Majesty's dominions and of the United Kingdom, and it is hereby affirmed that in no event will Northern Ireland or any part of it cease to be part of Her Majesty's dominions and of the United Kingdom without the consent of a majority of the people of Northern Ireland voting in a poll held for the purpose of this section and in accordance with Schedule 1 of this Act. (Northern Ireland Constitution Act 1973.)

The Guarantee guaranteed by both governments:

The two Governments (*a*) affirm that any change in the status of Northern Ireland would only come about with the consent of a majority of the people of Northern Ireland; (*b*) recognise that the present wish of a majority of the people in Northern Ireland is for no change in the status of Northern Ireland; (*c*) declare that, if in the future a majority of the people of Northern Ireland clearly wish for and formally consent to the establishment of a United Ireland, they will introduce and support in their respective Parliaments legislation to give effect to that wish. (Agreement between the Government of Ireland and the Government of the United Kingdom, November 15 1985.)

Mr Robert McCartney QC distinguishes consent from rape:

In criminal law there is a crime called rape. Rape means having sexual intercourse with a woman without her consent. Consent in this circumstance, or the absence of it, is defined in three ways. It is not consent if you have her by force, and everybody agrees that in relation to Northern Ireland force is out. It is not consent if you have her by fear . . . And it is not consent if you obtain her

* This essay was first published in Carol Harlow (ed.), *Public Law and Politics* (Sweet and Maxwell, London 1986), and is reprinted by permission of the editor and publisher.

agreement by fraud . . . because people will not accept Northern Ireland's refusal, Unionists are now worried that her consent will be obtained by fraud by a series of careful structurings . . . After a period of these closer working links she will be . . . so committed, so bound and attached that she will not be able to say no. And this, I think, breeds a lot of distrust . . . That's not the way to win her. If Northern Ireland is to be wooed, it has to be done honestly. (Interviewed in 1981 by O'Malley (1983, pp. 41–2).)

A dangerously optimistic text for seducers

And crying, 'No, no, I'll ne'er consent', consented.

(Byron, *Don Juan*.)

2. THE THEORY OF CONSENT

When is consent actually needed for government, and what kind of consent in what kind of circumstances? The Northern Ireland question is at least intellectually interesting.

When the men of Massachusetts and of Virginia affirmed in 1775 that 'all government is based on the consent of the governed', they knew perfectly well that most government was not. Most human government was based, as both St Augustine and David Hume had seen in different ways, on coercion, hopelessness, habit, and interest. Most thoughts of rebellion are stifled, Machiavelli observed, not by lack of courage but by lack of hope. The Americans plainly meant that good government is based on consent (the consent of 'citizens', at least); and they also had learnt that consent, if construed as giving power to a majority, was not a sufficient condition for good government: the majority had to act prudently, as Burke lectured a restless parliament, or better, they thought, should be bound by restraints in public law and widespread belief in individual rights. Power unchecked by constitutional law and by a belief in rights was held to be, whether in the hands of a few or of many, tyrannical and corrupting.

'The strongest', said Rousseau, 'is never strong enough unless he can turn power into right and obligation into self-interest.' He was certainly wrong on the first count, unless he meant it, as he probably did, as a moral precept rather than an empirical generalization. Only in very special circumstances do self-interest and right coincide as constitutional democracy. By 1775 in Massachusetts, Virginia, and their neighbours, white adult males with some freehold or substantial leasehold property (the laws of each colony varied) had not merely long enjoyed the franchise, but for very special and complex historical reasons had long constituted, to the frustration and annoyance of royal governors, an opinion and a power without whose compliance, co-operation, and, indeed, active consent orderly government could not be conducted. Not even taxes could be gathered if they collectively thought them to be unjust. But that was exceptional. Most people in the world, then and now, settle for peace, hope that bad government will at least be predictable and not arbitrary, and have little hope for justice based on an active consent.

Thomas Hobbes taught that for the hope of peace and to die in bed of natural causes, that is to minimize the incidence of violent death, we should surrender chimerical notions of rights in unconditional obedience to the state (which, to be fair to him, he thought had little reason to do anything else but enforce the peace and would cease to be a state if it failed in that). To most people this is common sense; even to some permanent minorities in nominally democratic regimes. And if it is not acceptable as a sufficient condition for good government, it is a minimal condition for any kind of government.

The Lockeian theory that government must rest on the consent of the governed is, fundamentally, not empirical but moral. It moralizes political theory and obligation. We should act like human beings, at best as fellow citizens, or at least, if ourselves citizens, should treat mere subjects as equal human beings. A much-used student textbook in political theory says, 'consent theory admits the legitimacy of authority . . . only when it satisfies certain moral criteria'; but it then goes on to say, of course, 'people may differ on whether any particular government satisfies them', and, indeed, on what these criteria are (Benn and Peters, 1959, p. 328). One of the difficulties of the Northern Ireland question, for instance, is whether to treat 'nationalism' as among moral criteria like 'freedom', 'individualism', 'conscience', 'tolerance', 'justice', and 'rights'; and, if so, is it an overriding principle? A large dose of nationalism seems able in the modern world to make up for a large amount of what the best minds in the eighteenth and nineteenth centuries would have seen as intolerable injustice. And, of course, to say that a government is intolerable or illegitimate is not to say that it is about to wither away. Some flagrantly unjust regimes are remarkably stable. We may accept them for the sake of peace, or as a lesser evil than the consequences of trying to change them by external pressure; but acceptance is not agreement. Indeed, to be an effective realist in politics one has to have a moral distance and to keep it.

The application of principle in the real world of policy, as well as for an individual's political actions, always involves some empirical calculation about consequences. Part of the concept of 'responsibility' is demanding that people try to think through the probable consequences of their actions. Even though we know that to be certain is impossible, we know that some degrees of risk and uncertainty are irresponsible. As Hobhouse once said, 'the ethically desirable must be the sociologically possible'. All political principles or values must claim to be workable. In fact we rarely argue directly about other people's principles, sensibly we argue about the acceptability of probable consequences. I fully accept everyone's nationalism, so long as I can question how it applies to those living in the same area who do not feel the same passionate sense of identity or read the same history books. Illegitimate governments may often be strong because people who do not identify with them nonetheless can see no practical alternative. Sometimes basically moral arguments take on a kind of 'empiricist rhetoric' in order to achieve this effect.

When Mr Charles Haughey, for instance, says that 'Northern Ireland has failed as a political entity', he really means to make, in his light, a moral statement. His view of nationalism renders Northern Ireland illegitimate and, further, the values of most people in the North affront the specific values of his party's traditional nationalism. But he puts his argument in an empirical, or at least a pseudo-empirical, vein—'has failed'. There have certainly been some instances in the modern world where organized government has broken down; but Northern Ireland, for all its terrorism, bigotry, troubles, and travails, is not one of them. There is a dangerous tendency, both in political and legal thinking, to move away from difficult but honest moral arguments into apocalyptic prophecies, masked as projections of social trends, of impending social breakdown if the prophet's case is not accepted entirely and at once. The debate about Northern Ireland is intense and deadly enough without such perpetual stage thunder.

What makes the question of consent in Northern Ireland so unusually complex is that, of course, there are two different concepts of 'the constituency' to which the consent pertains: all-Ireland or else Northern Ireland (the unionists are very wary of relating consent to the United Kingdom as a whole.) And the moralizing of consent is certainly a factor of political power. Many people do not first think in Hobbist terms before they then seek Lockian solutions; many are willing to risk (so they say, and seem to behave as if they mean it) a breakdown of government in order to gain or defend the right constituency of consent. Yet it is mildly comforting to note that over the last fifteen years opinion polls have solidly reported that a majority of people in both communities have given as their second most acceptable constitutional or institutional option the continuance of some form of Direct Rule; better at least than rule by the other side (Rose *et al.* 1978, pp. 49–51).*

Nevertheless, it is more helpful to use a moral vocabulary of consent if we can do so with our eyes open; that is to be able to recognize and admit that some illegitimate governments are remarkably stable, rather than to say with Hobbist cynicism (or minimal humanism) that stability is all one can ever mean by legitimacy. By Lockian (and American) standards the religious clauses of the Irish Constitution make it a thoroughly illegitimate regime; but nonetheless it seems in common sense, a reasonably civilized place—intolerable intolerance cannot be inferred from the letter of the law. No one's consent is total, nor can total consent be inferred by the stolid law-abidingness of the vast majority.

Locke famously attempted to deal with these questions and difficulties by distinguishing between 'explicit' and 'virtual' or 'tacit' consent. Explicit consent is to say freely (that is voluntarily and without coercion, as in a valid contract), 'I will'. When a state demands such explicit consent, it shows that there is a need for active support rather than mere passive obedience. Although republics are more difficult to manage, it was this, Machiavelli thought, that actually gave them more power in time of war than autocracies. When explicit consent is needed, whether for war or peace, it is a sign that a society has a large citizen body, and that a government, to carry through anything extraordinary, has to persuade many people politically rather than by command or coercion. 'Virtual' or 'tacit' consent is simply relative contentment, the absence of conscious and expressed disorder or disaffection; even democratic governments rely on this for nine-tenths of their administration. But there are some things that demand more positive support. Some legislation is unenforceable without a high degree of positive agreement: road safety and statutory incomes

---

* This is still the best analysis. Later polls sustain their conclusion.

policies are obvious examples, as was military and industrial conscription, or attempts to control deadly alcohol and nicotine addiction.

Constitutional change? But of what kind and where? Everyone seems to agree that fundamental constitutional change in Northern Ireland would need not merely the explicit consent of a majority but also the consent of the minority. Perhaps only tacit consent would be needed from the British and the Irish electorates. Her Majesty's Government says to 'institutional change' from Westminster, 'yes, certainly', so long as it commands 'widespread acceptance in both communities' (that is tacit consent); but no 'constitutional change' without the explicit consent of a majority. Does the 'Agreement' of 15 November 1985 between the two governments, establishing a consultative 'Intergovernmental Conference' to consider all aspects of Northern Ireland, itself constitute 'institutional' or 'constitutional' change? We must return to this question, but for the moment just note that the Irish government firmly avoids the issue, the British government firmly says 'institutional', and the unionists cry 'constitutional'. The unionist view is reasonable in light of the unprecedented extent of such an innovation, but more arguable when they say it is a 'surrender of British sovereignty' and 'the thin end of the wedge towards united Ireland'. Their feelings are so strong that they do not even trust Mrs Thatcher on sovereignty. The great issue is distorted by the Irish habit, north and south, of talking of 'the constitutional issue' as if it was only the issue of the border and a united or a divided Ireland; and everyone knows that that cannot be changed except by consent (hence the Guarantee). But what of a constitutional change for Northern Ireland that does not raise the border issue? Or possible forms of half-life between two sovereign states, extensive 'co-operation' even short of 'joint authority'? It might seem that if the 'Intergovernmental Conference' proves acceptable, does not break down, or cannot be destroyed, then what is 'constitutional' in the broad sense to us on the mainland, and 'constitutional' (and hateful) to them in the specific Ulster and Irish sense will be treated by most commentators and future writers of authority as 'institutional'. But proof of the pudding will lie less in definitions and recipies than in what happens in the eating.

Clearly consent of any kind has broken down when there is such a powerful negation of the concept as 'open rebellion' or, in the past, civil war. But where there is 'disaffection' (I find this old political and legal term less slippery than psuedo-psychological 'alienation'), it means that some have withdrawn their support from the state, and while not in open rebellion themselves, none the less tolerate and occasionally participate in obstruction, threatening demonstrations, small riots, and political strikes. Some actually tolerate violence and terrorism. Different lines are drawn. As distinct from civil war or open rebellion, some lines are drawn. The toleration of violence is most often passive, expressing itself not in participation or active support but simply in non-co-operation with the police in not informing on violent and murderous neighbours. These are measures of disaffection more deadly than the fanaticism of the relatively few active terrorists.

There is, of course, a lot of tacit consent for Direct Rule in Northern Ireland in terms of law-abiding people who are not so disaffected with the regime, but are disaffected with the choice of political parties offered them, or simply by the combative manner in which they are led. This is particularly the case in the Protestant community. Many people will only vote for a unionist party because they do not trust the others on 'the constitutional issue'; but they want no part in the membership of such a party. The phenomenon is not limited to Northern Ireland of party membership declining while voting levels remain high, so that people of extreme views find it easier to dominate the local parties and drive off the moderates. But at least they are limited in their abilities, whatever their threats, to turn their people out threateningly on the streets. (In fact, the politicians always claim that 'the people' are pushing them, but that is usually untrue; it is their party rivals who raise the stakes.) Politics does not always need agreement or high levels of participation, sometimes acceptance is enough; both for better and for worse.

Thus in Northern Ireland, to begin to come down to earth, explicit consent does not exist among a majority of the minority, and the level of tacit consent varies with political events. At times even that tacit consent, which is normally a sign that a government is (all things considered in context and by comparison with world standards) reasonably just, is wanting. Also the active consent of some of the majority can be highly selective. 'Loyalism' is, in its origins and history, a very discriminating form of consent to Acts of the United Kingdom Parliament.

3. ULSTER REALITIES

If Protestant Ulster had not threatened rebellion in 1912 and 1920 against the wishes—as nationalists always remind us—of the electorate in the last all-Ireland elections ever held, there would be no Northern Ireland today. Kevin Boyle and Tom Hadden (1984, pp. 403–4)* have put this harsh truth clearly:

> The truth in crude terms is that both the Republic of Ireland and Northern Ireland were created by a combination of military force and popular will. The idea of partition was first seriously raised when it became clear that very large numbers . . . were prepared to fight in Carson's UVF against the imposition of Home Rule by Britain on an all-Ireland basis. . . . The underlying reasons for partition were thus that the vast majority of the inhabitants in the North and in the South of Ireland had expressed incompatible loyalties and commitments and . . . had shown their willingness to fight.

At least today it has not come to that. 'The Agreement' was not seen (if judged by how unionist politicians behaved and not by what they said) as 'constitutional' (in the Irish sense), not really the ending of the Union, the great betrayal, but as a possible threat in that direction. Their 'withdrawal of consent' meant, of course, the active consent of participation in legally established institutional politics. In terms of our analysis, this is (or would be) to stop any process of change going beyond the consultative 'Agreement' towards 'joint authority' or even the weakest version of confederalism or federalism (and the very word 'process' can seem partisan). Such change would need active consent to make it workable. Coercion, on the scale needed, would not be workable and is outside the peacetime character of both the British and Irish governments. But active consent is not needed for the continuance of Direct Rule by Westminster even in the new consultative mode, only tacit or implied consent: the absence of mass civil disobedience or rebellion. People can accept as a realistic second best, out of fear of something worse, what they would never agree to formally. Such fear is not just of a new and hated regime, but the deepest and most conservative fear in us all: of a breakdown of any law and order. Revolutions more often take place because governments break down than for the reasons subsequently written into history by whatever group climbs from chaos into the saddle.

Opinion polls tell us that a majority in the Republic favour a united Ireland. But they also tell us that a majority wish this to be done only 'by consent of the North', and that the issue is itself not very high in

* This was a shortened version of a paper submitted to the New Ireland Forum and which also had a wide and influential private circulation.

the order of issues in general elections (Cox 1985*a*, 1985*b*)*. Conor Cruise O'Brien poured out a cold-bucket of commonsense when he said in 1978 (1980, p. 39):

Just as in the Republic the aspiration to acquire Northern Ireland is a low-intensity aspiration, so in Great Britain the aspiration to get rid of Northern Ireland is a low-intensity aspiration. Both have therefore low priorities in terms of practical politics.

This was written before the Forum *Report* (1984*a*) and the Intergovernmental Agreement of November 1985. The Forum did create a speculative agenda, but not an immediate political agenda. The Agreement gave a large personal boost in opinion polls to Dr FitzGerald and a small one to his party. But O'Brien's general point remains true, despite his do-nothing pessimism. Most Irish opinion is wedded to the belief that unity can come only through consent—hopefully tacit consent but realistically, as most people realize in light of actual opinion in the North, it would need active consent, positive agreement. The American 'Friends of Ireland', former President Carter, Senator Kennedy, and Congressman O'Neill et alios (now with mild Presidential support), openly favour 'the unity of Ireland with consent'. So did the Forum *Report* (the 'consent' should have been the surprising word not the 'unity'). The British Labour Party favours 'unity with consent'. But, once again, the difficulty is not just the self-deceiving unreality of such an aspiration (not deserving the name of policy) in light of present circumstances and past history, but the way the context or constituency of 'consent' keeps on shifting—within Northern Ireland, all-Ireland, or even the whole United Kingdom. All very nice and democratic; but since active consent would be needed to make such fundamental constitutional change work, to stifle armed resistance, consent in Northern Ireland itself is the necessary, though not the only, condition for this.

The dogmatic nationalist is apt to ignore consent: 'no man has a right to fix the boundary of the march of a nation', said Parnell (and some English socialists still treat anyone else's nationalism as holy). The teleology of that kind of remark is flagrant. Some people can hardly imagine how countries were ever governed before the rise of

---

* Cox concludes his summary of the opinion polls with the observation that 'it would be a conservative estimate' to say that 'certainly no more than two Irishmen to one' favour unification and that one of the two in favour of it is a 'low intensity unificationist' (p. 39).

nationalism as a distinctive and modern ideology. Elie Kedourie (1961, p. 9) in a classic work has characterized it as the belief that for every nation there must be a state, and dated it no older than the French Revolution. National sentiment can be very strong, think of Quebec, Scotland, Wales, and 'Ulster' itself; but a majority of the people in those countries wish strongly to preserve their national characteristics but not to form a separate state. They may not think it feasible or they may actually not desire it, pursuing their political aspirations through federal institutions or unusual types of regional government.

4. NATIONALISM AND SOVEREIGNTY

Nationalism assumes, moreover, a sovereign state. It is the combination of these two concepts that can cause so much harm and blind allegedly practical and pragmatic politicians to any view of possible alternatives. Lord North is not thought of as a thinking man or one, like Lord Haldane, of a metaphysical bent. Yet he asserted in response to the Franklin–Barclay unofficial peace proposal of 1776 that 'sovereignty cannot be divided'. Burke had, of course, argued in his great speeches on conciliation with America that the sovereignty of Parliament should be exercised with prudence: 'I care not if you have a right to make them miserable; have you not an interest to make them happy?' But not for a moment did he concede or believe that it could be limited in law. As is well known Blackstone regarded federalism as an impossibility, and if even Austin did not go quite so far, he did think that 'those United States' were inherently unstable. Both Mr Haughey and Mrs Thatcher seem to believe with Robespierre, for history makes strange bedfellows, that 'sovereignty is indivisible'.

The creation of a myth of parliamentary sovereignty was extremely useful to the British Government after the Act of Union with Scotland in 1707 and again in Ireland at the end of the century. What it actually meant was something as Hobbesian as this: 'if you do not surrender all power to Parliament we cannot stop you getting your throats cut by Catholic highlanders or bog-dwelling Irish peasants'. But in fact Scotland was left to govern itself to an astonishing degree, and to have the Congregational church established (an elective and popular body at every level) probably meant more to most lowlanders than the presumption to govern of a central but aristocratically dominated Parliament. The Kirk and the Law were the great national institutions. To this day textbooks both in constitutional law and in politics continue to present 'the United Kingdom' (the significance of that very formula is usually ignored) as a centralized, unitary state. This is simply old Whig English ideology. At the heart of actual political and constitutional practice in Britain there is a historically complex, but until the post-war generation, well-understood context of the management and consent of nations, not simply of classes or individuals organized in electoral constituencies. Thus to this day the special status of language in Wales and of law, education, and the machinery of government in Scotland, let alone the old quasi-federal devolution of Stormont, simply does not fit the usual English picture of central government in an homogeneous society (Crick 1982).

During the New Ireland Forum hearings Mr Haughey blundered into interesting territory when he said that the North in a United Ireland could keep its peculiar institutions as did Scotland; but he was foolish to imply that this would not need any change in the Irish constitution. Scotland's institutions arise from the Treaty of Union of 1707 and a unique national history. To create anything in Ireland remotely analogous to existing Scottish administrative devolution would plainly need a new and federal constitution.

If we believe that the sovereign national state is the best form that national sentiment can take and the almost unavoidable form of human government in the modern world, there is probably no lasting acceptable framework of government for Northern Ireland. But there are a few areas of the modern world that cannot be governed peaceably or justly within such a conceptual framework: Cyprus, Israel–Palestine, and South Africa are obvious examples where for a state to claim, in Weber's famous definition of the modern state, 'a monopoly of allegiance' is itself part of the problem, not the solution. The beginning of wisdom may be to see that Northern Ireland both historically and in the foreseeable future faces both ways. I mean not just the obvious political and confessional divisions, but the fact that there are few people active in politics whose behaviour is not a compound of both British and Irish influence (MacDonagh 1983; Lyons 1979). If Ulster Protestants do not notice it, they need telling. In English eyes they are far more different than the Scottish or Welsh; and the average Englishman finds his immigrant neighbour from the Republic less strange than an Ulsterman. This may be irrational but it is so. (Indeed, the Irish immigrant into Britain is an interesting person to consider, since he or she shows a wide spectrum of allegiance to 'Ireland' or to 'Britain', and sometimes not just differences between individuals but differences within individuals according to the situation or the company.)

To say that there are two traditions in the North, both of whom would have to consent to any constitutional change, is not to say quite the same thing as Conor Cruise O'Brien when he argues that there are two states in Ireland (and that is an end of it). Even if we accept his way of looking at things, which is a powerful and bold way, the difficulty is that one of these states is geographically contiguous but that the other, the Protestant-Orange state, is uncomfortably mixed with Irish-Green enclaves—most imperfectly partitioned for 'a state' that would reasonably (unlike Israel in the captured territories) claim a monopoly of allegiance. O'Brien is bold but he simplifies. To discredit the Sinn Féin and the IRA for their violence and lack of negotiable political policies is not to discredit the non-violent nationalism of John Hume and the SDLP.

Boyle and Hadden are closer to the ground in Northern Ireland than O'Brien. In a number of thoughtful papers and a book they have argued that the fact of two very different communities in Northern Ireland has to be faced and that they should be faced (leaving all their careful detail aside) in two ways: by legislation in the United Kingdom parliament which would virtually give equality of esteem and status to the two traditions (symbolically in flags and emblems, realistically in public employment and education); and by some joint administrative agencies between the two governments, a few bilateral projects of obvious mutual benefit that could attract a trilateral dimension (Boyle and Hadden 1984, 1985).* They argue that this can only be done from the present starting-point within the framework of British administrative law and 'the Guarantee'. They see this as a starting-point which could, in the next generation, be a finishing point too: it could go no further or could develop into—quite what is hard to predict, except that it could not be a united Ireland in any traditional sense of a centralized, sovereign state.

The Irish and British governments did not follow the Boyle and Hadden line in their negotiations. The prospects of getting agreement to practical steps towards equality between the two traditions seem poor; so they have chosen for the moment to bypass any area which needs active majority consent. But Boyle's and Hadden's ideas are likely to be influential in the future. And once the extreme sensitivity of

---

* The latter is probably the best short analysis of the problem that has been written.

the Falklands debate is over, British governments may cease to think that joint administrative agencies necessarily impugn their sovereignty (having accepting the Treaty of Rome, this view grows less and less tenable—as worries and torments the logical Mr Powell). Joint agencies may be acceptable even when they are not agreeable (indeed, some exist already, the Irish Tourist Board and the Foyle Fisheries Board, for instance; and very close degrees of co-operation also, as in railways, long-distance bus transport, and peat bog drainage).

Governments may have to proceed cautiously in such situations as Northern Ireland, but they are not mere passive reflectors of opinion or 'consent'. All governments try to build support for their policies. That most acute of American observers of British politics Samuel E. Beer once referred to one of the prime functions of parliament as being 'a device to mobilise consent'. There is nothing wrong in this. Tails should not believe that they can wag dogs. It is perfectly fair of governments to try to influence people, so long as people are free and able to answer back, have reasonable access to publicity, and are not silenced by either deliberate acts or deliberate neglect of the state (unless the state itself is in danger, which it less often is than it claims). Consent needs to be mobilized if governments would attempt rapid social change. Britain could no more be made socialist by legislation in the first hundred days of a Labour government with a majority (of whatever size) than Ireland could be united by simultaneous legislation in the Dáil and at Westminster. Consent to change involving allegiances, confessions, and deep traditions needs, as do changes involving fundamental working habits and income distribution, a great deal of preparation and persuasion. Some things can be done only by persuasion, however long it may take; and if not, then abandoned. Not only should governments not lead people into fundamental changes against their will or in ignorance by any gradual step-by-step long march of deceit, but they should realize that if people already have a tradition of free politics, they will fail.

There is a counter-argument about consent made by some Sinn Féin intellectuals and fellow-travellers. They say that 'unity by consent' means consent only to the form of unity, not to the principle of unity. They then decently offer to specify minimum criteria for unity. A unionist has reasonably called this view 'imprisonment by consent'. The very existence of such an odd argument shows the intensity of ultra-nationalist feeling. But the argument cannot explain why one should ever consent to the other fellow's nationalism in the first place (his special view of history or obsession that God created natural boundaries—'One Island, One Ireland!', or 'Ireland shall be free from sea to sea!') A nationalist who scorns political compromise has no rational argument to offer. Rival ultra-nationalists can only trade bad history and cultural insults with each other. There is no reason on earth why an Ulster Protestant, making what is to him a democratic argument, should allow the context to be pulled from under his feet into 'all Ireland'. He could be coerced into 'all Ireland'—only at a price that no one is willing to pay or live with the consequences of. But most ultra-nationalist arguments are, of course, about origins (who got there first), and so are inherently anti-democratic if population patterns subsequently change.

5. THE AGREEMENT AND 'THE GUARANTEE'

The Guarantee is thus something that cannot, in this empirical sense, be withdrawn. John Hume (1979, p. 303) used to claim that its very existence had, from the very time of partition, 'undermined any hope of political negotiation in Northern Ireland' giving 'a permanent exclusive power to one side.' Others think that if it were withdrawn organized unionism would be driven to violence. The force of it does not depend, however, on statutory declarations, still less on internationally registered agreements, but upon political recognition of historical facts. So little thought has been given, even among constitutional nationalists, to how to persuade Protestant opinion, that serious observers can sometimes wonder if they are all equally serious. John Bowman in a well-documented book found many grounds for doubting even the great chieftain's seriousness (1982). Like the British Labour Party, de Valera had aspirations to unity but no policy.* And yet the Guarantee itself recognizes a contingent, not a necessary and inalienable connection. HMG has made quite clear, both by declaration and statute, that it will legislate for unity if a majority in a referendum desired. Demography is to have the last word (not that the North would then be any more easy to govern, simply that mainland Britain would have had enough). This is perpetual gall to the Northern unionist. We view him as a Briton and a British responsibility, but not inalienably and nationalistically, only conditionally: so long as he keeps his diminishing majority. This is not a very satisfying relationship.

* Bowman summarizes de Valera's assumptions thus (p. 305): 'unity along with being inevitable, was always postponable'.

The Agreement Between the Government of Ireland and the Government of the United Kingdom, Cmnd. 9657 of 15 November 1985 has been presented by unionist politicians as a surrender of sovereignty and the primrose path towards everlasting unity. Mr Peter Robinson MP burnt Mrs Thatcher's effigy outside Belfast City Hall as 'a traitor' and Mr Enoch Powell MP in the House of Commons described the Agreement as 'treachery'. But it cannot reasonably carry that construction. Article 1 begins:

The two Governments (a) affirm that any change on the status of Northern Ireland would only come about with the consent of a majority of the people of Northern Ireland; (b) recognise that the present wish of a majority of the people of Northern Ireland is for no change . . . ; and (c) declare that, if in the future a majority . . . clearly wish for and formally consent to the establishment of a united Ireland, they will introduce and support in their respective Parliaments legislation . . .

The Guarantee could not be reiterated more clearly and the mode of formal consent is still specified in the Northern Ireland Constitution Act of 1973 (quoted at the head of this essay). And now it is a declaration of the Irish government too.

The main purpose of the new intergovernmental Conference is stated to be to 'concern itself with measures to recognise and accommodate the rights and identities of the two traditions in Northern Ireland, to protect human rights and prevent discrimination' (Article 5 (a)). As other articles make clear, anything relating both to Northern Ireland and to British–Irish relations can be raised, but in consultative not decision-making or executive mode. Article 2 clearly states: 'there is no derogation from the sovereignty of either the Irish Government or the United Kingdom Government, and each retains responsibility for the decisions and administration of government within its own jurisdiction'. The word 'decisions' is vital.

In Article 4 both governments pledge themselves to try to achieve devolution 'in respect of certain matters within the powers of the Secretary of State for Northern Ireland . . . on a basis that would secure widespread acceptance throughout the community'. Again humble 'acceptance' is specified, not stern 'consent'. Article 2 (b) makes clear that the powers of the Irish government to put forward 'views and proposals' are only 'in so far as these matters are not the responsibility of a devolved administration in Northern Ireland'. Even if the 'reserved powers' of the Secretary of State would always, in such a situation, be formidable (security, administration of justice, economic policy, administration of justice, and electoral arrangements—at least), this is a substantial exception to the Irish government's unique right of consultation and power of formal initiative. Thus in effect it said to the Irish government and agreed by them that it may advise, warn, and encourage but not in these areas, though it may discuss with us first what these areas are to be. Politically it is a carrot to the unionist politicians to return to the now perennial project of trying to find terms on which they and the SDLP can agree to work the present or some other assembly. If they can do that (as they have failed to do in recent years), they get the Conference and Irish government off their backs. However, Article 5 (*c*) states:

If it should prove impossible to achieve and sustain devolution . . . , the Conference shall be the framework in which the Irish Government may, where the interests of the minority community are significantly or especially affected, put forward views on proposals for major legislation and on major policy issues, which are within the purview of the Northern Ireland Departments and which shall remain the responsibility of the Secretary of State for Northern Ireland.

The draftsmen walked like cats on ice. Although only a consultative body, the Irish government can put forward certainly not legislation but 'views on proposals for major legislation'. Read calmly this preserves, in terms of Northern Ireland, the distinction between 'institutional' and 'constitutional' or between what merely needs 'acceptance' (as the absence of civil disobedience) and what needs, both legally and politically, formal 'agreement' (as active consent). The Agreement is not even an Act of Parliament, although it has been ratified both by Parliament and the Dáil; nor is it an international treaty either: copies of the Agreement have simply been lodged with the United Nations. But in mainland British discourse, all this is a remarkable constitutional innovation: an institution is created in which it is solemnly promised that a foreign government will be consulted before any major decisions are made about the government of a province, and has a right to raise virtually any matter or make any proposal it likes. One can see both why Ulster unionists do not like it at all—which is one of the difficulties of being a minority in a democracy like the United Kingdom; but also why they all find in it (without being, in their indigenous theories of textual exegisis, especially radical deconstructionists), a subtext of burning letters promising unity by stages.

None the less, while anyone who visits Northern Ireland at all frequently passes through a stage of being told, and passing on: 'you have got to see how it looks on the ground', yet some of us emerge to say to them 'but you have also got to see it through our eyes—the majority of the United Kingdom' (and it would not harm to lift up your eyes, if not your hearts, to look not just at modern Ireland and modern Europe but also, to avoid naming 'America', at the Atlantic Alliance). And in these wider contexts the Agreement, while unusual, appears as a reasonable mirror of hard political reality. In the United Kingdom context it is, to be quite specific, an extraordinary misreading of the British Conservative mind, and of Mrs Thatcher's especially, to think that there is a subtext of 'sell out'. It would be just as plausible and just as politically tactless to argue that the subtext from the British point of view is simply that the Agreement is a 'talking-shop' to get both Dr Fitzgerald and Mr Hume off their respective barbed hooks.

A relevant argument in construing the text is to consider its purpose. The purpose was to arrest any further decay of the SDLP vote in favour of Sinn Féin and, more generally, to achieve some diminution of Catholic disaffection in Northern Ireland so that the climate of tolerance towards terrorist operations is diminished. The SDLP boycotted the 'Prior Assembly'. This may well have been unwise on their part. Constitutional politics needs a constitutional forum, however imperfect: if the name of the game was abstention, some of the Catholic voters might prefer to vote for those with an untarnished record in that respect. But the judgement had to be that of the leaders of the SDLP. If they had taken their seats in the Assembly, they might have split and their support diminished disastrously. What is overwhelmingly clear, however, is that during the three years or more of the Assembly the unionists were not willing, despite some alleged— albeit slight—movement (Ulster Unionist Assembly Party 1984; Smith 1984), to make compromises of a kind that could have brought the SDLP in and avoided bilateral action, which had been on the cards for a long time, by London and Dublin. One might note at this point that it is often forgotten that Margaret Thatcher's impatience with the unwillingness of Unionist politicians to compromise began very early. On 12 November 1979 she gave an interview to R. W. Apple of the *New York Times* (even before addressing the House of Commons on the 'Atkins initiative') in which she was reported as saying 'that she would not permit the squabbling of political parties in Northern Ireland to block her initiative', and was directly quoted as saying that 'if they said "We don't like it and you can't do anything unless we all agree"', she would impose a decision. Otherwise, she said, 'you'll never get anywhere and we must.' (*International Herald Tribune*, 13 November 1979, p. 1). They had had their chance for compromise of the devolutionary kind, so in 1985 a compromise form of Direct Rule was imposed on them: Direct Rule by the British Government consulting publicly with an Irish government who now hold, if the analogy is apt, a watching brief on behalf of the Catholic community.

The Agreement creates neither 'joint authority' in the North nor 'power-sharing' in the North. 'Close co-operation' is the key word of the Agreement and the attached 'Joint Commmuniqué', and the reiterated objective is 'diminishing the divisions' and 'achieving lasting peace and stability'. These words if banal were well chosen. 'Co-operation' between states may be a deliberate limitation of political power, but it is no derogation of legal sovereignty. 'Diminishing divisions' is more realistic and tolerant than 'seeking for agreement' or that old weasel word 'consensus'. And 'peace and stability' will have to do until the rights of the Irish question are finally adjudicated at the 'Last Judgement', and even then there will still be some in Fermanagh and Tyrone who will not attend to the trumpet call unless they are sure what the judgement will be. We need both Hobbes and Locke. Hobbes is the precondition for any kind of political order, Locke for a just and consenting political order (when happily possible).

The Agreement is a 'step forward' when some do not want to move at all; however it is not a move towards some teleological goal of unity and enforced reconciliation but towards a plateau of wider *acceptance* of institutions of government. This is the only possible basis for future *agreement* between any possible leaders of the two communities. The next generation may rest on this plateau or move in some obvious or novel direction. Better for us to bury our dead and to leave some decisions to the future. But it is fairly clear that if a future generation did move 'forward' in a nationalist sense, it could not possibly be towards any simple form of unitary state in Ireland. Mr Haughey, Mrs Thatcher, and Mr Kinnock all need to observe that many parliamentary democracies are of a federal nature; and that it is unlikely that mankind has exhausted inventiveness in political institutions. If Northern Ireland inherently faces both ways, forms of government will have to be devised to encompass that fact. Perhaps consultation and co-operation will be enough. Perhaps not. But it cannot be anything less. Those who say they want to stay put, in reality want to put the clock back, or— among the leaders—simply to enjoy the storm.

8

THE FEASIBILITY OF SHARED SOVEREIGNTY (AND SHARED AUTHORITY)

Martin Dent

Who has made the two one and has destroyed the barrier, the dividing wall of hostility, by abolishing in His flesh the law with its commandments and regulations. His purpose was to create in Himself one man out of two, thus making peace.

(Ephesians 2: 14–15)

I speak from a full heart when I pray that my coming to Ireland today may prove to be the first step towards an end of strife amongst her people, whatever their race or creed. In that hope I appeal to all Irishmen to pause, to stretch out the hand of forebearance and conciliation, to forgive and forget, and to join in making for the land which they love, a new era of peace, contentment and goodwill. . . . The future lies in the hands of my Irish people themselves, may this historic gathering [the King's opening of the first Parliament at Stormont for Northern Ireland] be a prelude to a day in which the Irish people North and South, under one Parliament or two, as these Parliaments may themselves decide, shall work together in the common love of Ireland upon the sure foundation of mutual justice and respect.

(Part of the address by King George the Fifth at the Opening of the Parliament of Northern Ireland, 22 June 1921)

Invention is the chief of human action.

(Lord Bacon, essays)

The language of Mr Dent's pamphlet [on 'The Dispute over Falklands/Malvinas, the Road to an Honourable and Lasting Peace', in which I had put forward the concept of shared sovereignty and of administration by an outsider] is not the language of things as they are, but it is the language of things as they will be.

(Review in 'Tablet' 1982)

I must start this paper with a double apology. I have come recently to the study of the politics of Ireland from a background in African politics and as such my view is more of the general nature of the wood than of the detail of the trees. To an Africanist the intractability of the problem of Ireland and the persistence in set patterns of historical memory of past conflicts is amazing and saddening. King George's exhortation to all Irishmen to pause, to stretch out the hand of forbearance and conciliation, to forgive and forget, seems as if it were impossible to follow. Irish culture, North and South, is developed and profound, yet in the task of conflict resolution there is much to learn from situations where reconciliation follows as quickly as it did in Nigeria after the civil war and where each day is itself regarded as a new gift from God, a new age in which the quarrels of the old are no longer relevant. Politics is therefore kaleidoscopic, and the friend of today is the opponent of tomorrow and the opponent of today the ally of tomorrow, for as the Tiv proverb (in Nigeria) has it 'Ura nor man se or iyol ami'—'It has rained and we have washed our bodies in it'—all the dust of the quarrels of yester-year have been washed away by time.

Ireland has much to learn from the African experience in this respect. I write in this paper with a love of Ireland, North and South, and of all groups as well as of my own country, but if this piece is to have any value it must state uncomfortable truths to both sides with courage. The troubles of Ireland spring not only from problems of finding a means to give political expression to two different traditions, important as this is; they spring also from the need to escape from the dangerous luxury of indulgence in ancient hatreds. These hatreds exist among extremists towards Britain, and in the unionist mind, towards Ireland and Irish nationalism. To deal with these hatreds we cannot resort to the simplistic solutions of either keeping things as they are or of the opposite error of just abolishing the border and including Northern Ireland in the Republic in a homonymous state. Liam Cosgrave described the folly of assuming that the Northern Irish problem could be solved by an agreement between the majority in Britain and the majority in Ireland (*Keesing's Contemporary Archives* 1973, p. 26034, col. 2). Such an attitude he said is simplistic. 'We must see the issue in Northern Ireland in its true context. Its divisions, its bitterness, its apparently intolerable problems are not peculiar Irish manifestations, incomprehensible except in terms of national character and temperament. They are a legacy of the past of both our peoples for which each carries responsibilities. The involved and complex relations between Britain and Ireland through 800 years of involvement in each other's affairs has given to both our people the right to look forward to the resolution of the remaining issue between them.' The only solution to this last and most difficult issue between us is, I believe, that which visibly brings together the symbols of our sovereignty and the wisdom of our policy in Northern Ireland in order to undertake the task of overcoming the hatreds between the zealots of both sections of the community. For this reason I believe that far the best of the three roads forward suggested in the New Ireland Forum is that of shared authority.

Sir Winston Churchill wrote in '*World Crisis*' (chapter 8) of the 'vehemence with which [on the affairs of Northern Ireland in 1914] great masses of men yield themselves to partisanship and follow the struggle as if it were a prize fight—the glistening eyes, the swift anger and the cries of "treachery" with which every proposal of compromise is hailed'. The intensity of partisan hostility between extremists on either side remains as great as ever and might therefore seem to make the attainment of shared sovereignty very difficult. It is also true, as Professor Whyte's paper has shown, that most commentators categorize the quarrel as primarily one of 'Internal Conflict' between the two communities. It is also true, however, that the issue of sovereignty and the feeling that it is an 'all-or-nothing' choice accentuates the feeling of hostility. If there were not an issue of the border, or if the community of Northern Ireland were situated a thousand miles away from Britain and the Irish Republic, then the internal problems of unequal relationships could probably be solved in a spirit of give and take with political skill. It is the false assumption that the 'cliffs of sovereignty go sheer into the sea', and that a choice has to be made between unalloyed British rule from London or Irish rule from Dublin, which makes the Protestant community so suspicious of change and provides the republican extremists of the IRA and their supporters with an excuse for violence as part of 'a war against the British'. If we can show that there is a broad plateau of institutions in the field of shared sovereignty where an equilibrium and a peaceful solution can be found, for at least the medium term, then the internal conflicts become manageable and we can move towards a just and lasting peace.

To achieve these kinds of relations we have a long way to go. The relations established by the British government under Mr Heath and under Mrs Thatcher and the prime ministers of the Republic of

Ireland Mr Liam Cosgrave and Dr Garret FitzGerald have been admirably cordial. The statements made by both governments have emphasized the uniquely close ties that should in all reason bind our nations, yet we are still unable to achieve the most elementary of courtesies between nations—the exchange of visits by heads of states. Presidents from remote corners of the world come to Britain on state visits and their flags go up in celebration on the streets side by side with the Union Jack. Ireland also receives such visits, but ancient hatreds still festering in the minds of zealots make it impossible for the Queen to visit Dublin, and in consequence it is apparently impossible for the Irish President to visit Britain in his official capacity. African nations, who so much enjoy state visits from neighbouring heads, even though they may have been in conflict with them a year or so before, would be amazed at such refusal to reconcile.

My second apology relates to the fact that I have in this paper to present an attempt at an invention of a political category—the category of shared sovereignty. Of course I cannot claim to be the originator, since such a system has operated successfully for just over five hundred years in Andorra (as well as one sidedly in the Sudan and unsatisfactorily in the New Hebrides). But ever since the Falklands crisis of the Argentinian invasion of April 1982 forced me to think furiously of means to overcome the conflict over sovereignty and to publish in high haste a pamphlet aimed at making a contribution to the avoidance of the approaching armed conflict, I have been involved in thinking over and over again the modalities of the development of a workable system of shared sovereignty. Like all attempts at invention my paper will contain crudities and be vulnerable to criticism. The first conception of the idea lacks the perfection of the final developed models just as a Wright brothers' aeroplane is crude compared to a modern one. A new invention in political science requires a whole host of accompanying inventions and techniques in its development in order to make it work. In this sense Professor Whyte's thesis is correct, 'Simple solutions will not work'. (See Chapter 2.) In another sense, however, sheer complexity is not of itself to be seen as the answer. We have to follow the simplicity of the creative idea through the complexity of devising the means to make it operational, and this is what I am attempting in this paper.

Clearly, if it is possible to divide sovereignty, this has enormous advantages in the world, for again and again the relations between nations are poisoned by continuing and intense quarrels over sovereignty in relatively small areas. For a time the areas in conflict reach a kind of equilibrium through historical accident or the use of force or the threat of force by one side or both (as in the history of Ireland), but such solutions leave an unstable equilibrium and a burning discontent among the disadvantaged.

In this paper I shall examine the modalities of the third solution detailed in the New Ireland Forum (1984a), that of shared authority or shared sovereignty. The New Ireland Forum *Report* (para. 8. 7) puts the case for shared authority with great force—'Under Joint Authority the two traditions in Northern Ireland would find themselves on a basis of equality and both would be able to find an expression for their identity in the new institutions. There would be no diminution in the Britishness of the Unionist population. Their identity, ethos and link with Britain would be assured by the authority and presence of the British Government in the joint authority arrangements. At the same time it would resolve one basic defect of (*a*) the failed 1920–5 attempt to settle the Irish question and (*b*) the present arrangements for the government of Northern Ireland, the failure to give satisfactory political, symbolic and administrative expression to Northern Ireland nationalists.' Shared sovereignty is a concept which I first came to grips with when writing about the Falklands/Malvinas dispute at the time of the Argentine invasion. Like many others I was horrified during that Easter week to realize that we were approaching a situation of war between Britain and Argentina where very many might be killed and therefore in the white heat of concern I wrote and published a paper on the dispute over Falklands/Malvinas (1982). Necessity is the mother of invention: I was faced with the necessity of inventing a workable concept of sovereignty that could provide an acceptable solution, guaranteeing at once the Argentine sense of national pride and desire to see their flag on Malvinas (whence they believed that they had been unjustly expelled a hundred and fifty years ago), and the proper determination of Britain both to preserve the liberties of the islanders and to allow them to retain a continuing collective connection with Britain, if they wished for it. Clearly within the framework of exclusive national sovereignty no solution could be found. We were like mathematicians trying to solve a problem in three dimensional geometry on a two dimensional plane. If it could be shown to be possible to share sovereignty, then it would be of enormous advantage to do so. Such a solution would bring the two claimants together. It would provide a context for the gentle merging of cultural traditions, rather than for their sharp and destructive contrast. It would give us the situation which the peacemaker always seeks, where there are no victors and no vanquished.

I came to look at the problem of sovereignty and realized that though exclusive sovereignty is a most useful convenience for the government of about 98 per cent of the surface of the earth, it fails disastrously in the remaining 2 per cent, where there is sharp division over claims of sovereignty. Such conflicts have the capacity to cause ill will between nations out of all proportion with the size of the area in dispute. The dilemmas can be temporarily resolved by force. In the Irish case it was the force of the guerilla war that finally made explicit the determination of the British government to give self-government to Ireland, a determination which had for so long been implicit in the policy of liberal governments and yet had never actually come into being. It was the force and threatened force of the Ulster unionists that excluded Ulster from the new Irish State and brought half a million Catholics, as a minority, into the Protestant enclave of Northern Ireland. All solutions of force, however, if they involve the compulsory bringing of one group of people under the rule of a state whose legality they do not recognize or whose culture they do not share in, create a situation of unstable equilibrium.

The instability of the solution by force rests on the fact that the aggrieved party always thinks that by violence, whether in the form of sudden attack or of long guerilla warfare, it can compel a change in the map and alter the situation of sovereignty in its favour.

In many of the conflicts which arise over sovereignty and the inclusion of unwilling citizens in nations where they feel they do not belong one can find amelioration in federalism. But this amelioration is not total. We are still left with a number of situations where it is necessary to bring together two or more national traditions and connections in the government of one state.

The connection with the mother country is part of the identity which the community will not be able to surrender without loss of an important part of its identity. The juxtaposition of flags, the joint visits of heads of states and their deputies for ceremonial purposes, the singing of more than one anthem, are symbols of the bringing together of two national connections. They require also the bringing of the counsel of both nations into an advisory or perhaps a legislative body to supervise the administration of the area concerned.

Will such a system work? We have been mesmerized by the concept of sovereignty and have come to think that it must always be exclusive and that it must be interpreted in Austinian terms as a kind of mastery. This has fortunately ceased to be true even in unitary states as regards the relation of the individual citizen to the government. It is even less true in federal states, where there is a theory of division of sovereignty through a sovereign constitution allocating powers between centre and parts. It is equally untrue in practice in the external relations of states where states submit themselves to bodies set up by treaty which effectively prescribe courses of action for them in many important fields (as does the EEC for both the United Kingdom and the Republic of Ireland). Furthermore, in some small cases we have already driven a coach and horses through the concept of exclusive national sovereignty and have created happy anomolies whose very originality and lack of total constitutional symmetry is part of the attractiveness of their identity. Who is sovereign in the Isle of Man or the Channel Islands? The Pope has all the sovereignty he needs in the Vatican both for an important spiritual role and for a considerable diplomatic one in the cause of peace, yet he does not even exercise the most fundamental right of sovereignty, that of trying the Turkish gunman who shot him in St Peter's Square. The happy experience of Andorra for five hundred years under the joint sovereignty of the ruler of France and the Bishop of Ughel defies the concept of exclusive sovereignty. Why then, if sovereignty is so much less than a totally solid thing, do we continue to treat it as a 'thought stopper'—a word which we wrongly assume to put an end to all further enquiry and which creates an unreal simplicity that inhibits creative thought (I am indebted to Donald Nicholl for this concept). The actual operation of the Intergovernmental Conference set up this year shows that in the field of consultation the question of ultimate sovereignty may at times hardly arise. Each party suggests the creative idea and the best course of action he can think of and in the course of discussion all parties seek to find the best solution. In a proper consultation, rights of sovereignty might be as irrelevant as they are in a well-run seminar, where it is not the status of the speaker but the quality of the argument that counts.

There is, however, a true doctrine of political science that concentration is necessary in the management of the executive part of government. If too many manage the state, the state will be ill managed. We do not have to go to learned works on political science to prove this; it can be found in Shakespeare's explanation, at the end of

Henry the Fifth, of the reason for the decay of the kingdom under *Henry the Sixth*:

> Whose state so many had the managing,
> that they lost France and made his England bleed,
> which oft our stage hath shown.

The same doctrine can be learnt from any practical man of affairs. The import of this, however, is not that shared sovereignty is impossible, but that the co-domini must employ a manager and give him in many matters, administrative and political, a power of attorney.

This paper, which seeks to make the concept operational, will exhibit many features requiring improvement for we do not leap to new truths or to new developments in one great jump. I value, therefore, criticism in the development of the concept and of its application to Northern Ireland (and to other areas where it is appropriate). The concept is not an esoteric one devised only for the special conditions of Northern Ireland, but a more general one to apply to several areas of the world of five different sorts. All these areas are those where we can find no stable solution within the confines of an arrangement of exclusive sovereignty of one nation. The modalities of the institutions of co-sovereignty which I shall describe differ according to the case, but I shall take the analysis of Northern Irish dilemma in this respect out into the larger frame of comparison of the application of the category to a number of areas where it is needed, before returning to the final section of the paper exclusively to the working of the system in Northern Ireland. The four kinds of areas to which co-sovereignty should apply are these:

The first category is that of areas of land without inhabitants: (1) Antarctic, where we are already applying a primitive form of shared sovereignty through the meetings of the eighteen powers with consultative status and the freezing of territorial claims under the Treaty. Sooner or later we are going to have to normalize this and appoint an 'Administrator Antarctic' under the advice of the council of treaty powers (or perhaps of the UN); (2) Some similar status is going to be needed for the ocean and the ocean bed outside the two-hundred-mile limit; (3) Already we have an urgent need for Britain and Argentina to declare the two-hundred-mile limit outside the Falkland/Malvinas Islands to be subject to their joint sovereignty and to appoint a Fishing Inspector under their joint authority and give him a power of attorney to act on their behalf to conserve the fish stocks before they are all destroyed; (4) Small areas of disputed territory such as the Eastern half of the Shat El Arab and a few more or less uninhabited islands in the Persian/Arabian Gulf are in dispute between Iran and Iraq and have provided the territorial element in the most murderous ideological war between those two nations. A shared sovereignty with both flags flying and a power of attorney given to an outsider to look after the area in dispute would provide the solution to the territorial part of the Iraq Iran dispute.

The second category is that of small homogeneous groups bearing allegiance to a power separated from them by a long distance over the sea, but who are close to or contiguous with another large land-power that wishes to see its flag flying in the area as part of its national prestige. The two obvious examples of this category are Gibraltar and the Falklands/Malvinas Islands. A solution in these situations requires both flags to fly and administration to be no longer in the hands of an imperial governor but of an independent outsider as administrator appointed by both co-domini to administer, subject to the advice of a joint council of the two co-domini and the need also to reflect the consensus of the inhabitants of the area (see Dent 1988).

The third category is that of a homogeneous population in an area which has been allocated to an adjacent area's sovereignty and which has no common identity with that area but is in almost all ways akin to the state next door. The simple solution of changing the frontier is ruled out both by a general prohibition in the continent on the changing of boundaries, since if one boundary is changed all are in jeopardy. The case in point is that of the Somali-inhabited area of the Ogaden in Ethiopia. The fierce nationalism of the Ethopian ruling-group, expressed in the slogan 'Ethiopian tikdem' (Ethiopia above all), makes it impossible for them to allow any formal separation of the area from their national territory. In such a case the advantages of autonomy and of rule by a benevolent outside administrator can be combined with the retention of the formal aspects of an Ethiopian flag and presence and a similar presence from Somalia as a symbol of their reconciliation. The modalities will be difficult to devise but this is the only way to offer permanent stability.

The fourth type is that into which Northern Ireland falls. It consists of areas whose population is deeply divided by cleavages of religion and history, the larger proportion identifying with a more distant state and the smaller with a more proximate one. The other instance of this is Cyprus.

In all these cases we have to untie the bundle of functions which are put together under the general name of sovereignty and deal with each of them separately in an appropriate way. They are not attributes of a single, indivisible power. When we speak of sovereignty, we mean a number of things: centre of ceremonial glory, power to have the last word, function as grand factotum of the state, maker of laws and upholder of the constitution (having also the power to initiate procedures to alter it), source of judicial authority, and final financial authority. In a democratic society we also imply focus of representation at the most important level. In dealing with these functions under shared sovereignty we require basically four institutions.

First, the juxtaposed flags and anthems and the ceremonial visits from heads of state or representatives from both co-domini. These visits are best made together and are not for the giving of orders but for purely ceremonial purposes and hearing the views of the people. (The co-domini exercise their policy functions only through the advisory and governmental council on which they both sit.)

Flags are not like prima donnas who cannot bear to see one another on the same stage. When an intrepid mountaineer reaches the summit of a great mountain he plants the flag of his country there beside those of the countries of others who have climbed to the summit before him. When heads of state visit each other's capital we celebrate by a 'conjunction' of flags of the two countries in the streets, a temporary manifestation of what we hope will be a permanent friendship of peoples. At athletic and sporting events we fly the flags of both contestants and only uncouth soccer hooligans (the worst of whom are, alas, British!) seek to interfere with those of the other side.

In the case of Britain and Ireland there is a particular appropriateness in the flags, for that of Britain has as its central motif 'the red eternal cross', as sacred to Catholic Ireland as to Britain, while the Tricolour of the Irish Republic has been specially designed to show in equal emphasis the green of Éire and the orange/yellow of Northern Ireland separated only by the white colour of peace. (Perhaps a hopeful sign is the Public Order (Northern Ireland) Order (SI 1987/463), which came into operation on 2 April 1987. This expressly repeals the Flags and Emblems (Display) Act (Northern Ireland) 1954 and makes it legal to display the Irish Tricolour in Northern Ireland.)

The second part of the structure of co-sovereignty is the council, where the co-domini send their representatives to meet at regular intervals to give advice and guidance to the administration, to make law, to approve finance, and to appoint the administrator for a fixed term, and also the judges and heads of security services. Both sides need to be represented at levels of similar seniority, though there is probably no objection to that level varying according to the agenda. It can occasionally be at head of government level, but would normally be at that of foreign minister. It could, however, be at a lower level. This is the sole body through which the co-domini exercise their policy input into the government of the area. Involvement in the area of ministers in either of the co-domini will be by special arrangement agreed with the council, the administrator, and the representative institutions of the area under co-sovereignty.

The third and all important part of the institution consists of the 'Pure Administrator and Political Officer with Power of Attorney' from both co-domini. He is the linchpin of the mechanism, the manager who ensures that the polity does not suffer from 'too many having the managing of it'. Ideally one should seek an outsider to fulfil this role, for it is an elementary fact of performing the function of referee between parties that one does not want to be connected with either. This is as true of politics as it is in an international football match or a judicial function. The great achievements of international administrators have shown us that pure administration is indeed possible. A great administrator and political officer like, for instance, Brian Urquhart at the United Nations has achieved a status and reputation where he could act in any kind of dispute without being accused of being pro-British. The same is true of other UN administrators of calibre and of many administrators elsewhere, able to establish a position of neutrality and of empathy with all sides in situations of conflict.

The advantage of the outsider in this role of administrator and of political officer or doctor of the body politic was at times shown in colonial history, when there was not any pressure from settlers or companies to malign political control from above to interfere with it. One of the better babies that we have lost with the dirtier water of colonialism and the proper rejoicing at the ability of nations to take charge of their destinies has been the advantage of the outsider as seen in the role of the District Officer, able to win the confidence of people very different to himself and to seek reconciliation between rival sections of the community. To perform this role one needs not only political skill but a profound love of the land and people where one serves. I had the honour to fulfil this role myself for several years as District Officer in the Tiv Division in Nigeria. One must identify with the people as a whole. One must not be like Maudling, who, when he was Secretary of State for Northern Ireland, was heard, as he got back into his aeroplane to London, to murmur, 'What an awful place Northern Ireland is!'

If one can develop it, there is a role for the acceptable impartial administrator from outside the situation or conflict. Would it be possible to find a person and an authority role which would enable its holder to walk unarmed and almost unescorted up the Falls and Shankill Road and in the Bogside and be accepted by both communities as a friend? When I had written my pamphlet on peace in the Falklands Dispute, I sent copies to many distinguished people, and among several replies of support I was surprised to receive a letter from the Secretary to the Irish Prime Minister Mr Haughey, saying that he had ordered that a study be made of the concept of shared sovereignty with respect to the Falklands and also Northern Ireland. Thinking, mistakenly, that this might be a kind of Irish joke (!), I none the less replied saying that I did indeed believe the concept to have great value for Northern Ireland, but had not quoted this instance in my pamphlet since I hoped that the ideas in it might be an immediately acceptable contribution to people in the British government, as well as the Argentinian, to the avoidance of the approaching battle. I pointed out, however, how important it was to get an acceptable 'outsider' as administrator for Northern Ireland under the aegis of the two co-domini of Britain and Ireland under a co-sovereignty solution. I received no further reply.

This first role of the Pure Administrator and Political Officer with Power of Attorney (PAPOPA) from both co-domini is to treat as many issues as possible as pure administrator and to do so with no political instructions from the government of either side. The first step towards creating acceptable authority in situations of conflict is to have an authority figure who is demonstrably free from association with the political will of any larger entity which is considered hostile by either side. Furthermore, in order to reduce the political tension the PAPOPA will treat issues as 'the administration of things and not power over people'. Fisher (1964), in a study of issues at the UN, has shown how much more easily they achieve consent if they are presented as matters of administration rather than matters of politics.

The PAPOPA has also, however, a political role. It is interesting that in early colonial days the District Officers and Provincial Commissioners were referred to as 'political officers'. They were responsible for the health of the body politic as a whole and for the essential function (of which Professor Crick (1962) has written so eloquently) of encouraging 'politics as conciliation'. In his political role the PAPOPA has to be just and create consensus. Where that consensus exists he is to follow it both between the co-domini and within the representative institutions of the area concerned. His power is in this sense *kenotic* or self-emptying/limiting (a phrase of political analysis derived from the greatest concept of *kenōsis* or self-emptying as shown in the self-emptying of God himself in the incarnation). It is common for a person who is not elected and not subject to re-election to deliberately seek to fulfil a representative role. He seeks to tease out consensus where there is division of view and then obeys that consensus. If he cannot, after all his efforts, obtain consensus then he must act in his own discretion in the interests of all, seeking at least to aggregate and incorporate elements of the views of all parties in his final policy-decision.

If it is argued that this kind of role is potentially too autocratic for a democratic society, one can reply that this is very nearly the situation in which Northern Ireland finds itself today. Government is in the hands of the Secretary of State, who is representative only of the opinion of Britain, since no single candidate of a British political party won any appreciable vote in Northern Ireland and where, since the break between the Unionists and the Conservatives, all British governments are in a sense imposed upon Northern Ireland in representative terms. The Secretary of State is not in fact the servant of a Whitehall political will, since he is himself of master status and carries his office with him to Belfast, rather than having a master in a colonial office, as did a colonial governor. The evidence in Professor Crick's paper (see Chapter 7) shows that this system of government of 'pure administration by a political officer' is accepted as a good second-best type of government—far preferable in the eyes of both sections of the Northern Irish community to government by a repesentative body on which its opponent will dominate. Were the office to be filled by an outsider, appointed by both sides for a fixed term and associated with a high level of devolution in an elected power-sharing Northern Irish executive, it would cease to be regarded as alien in the way that the Secretary of State is regarded as alien by much of the nationalist community in Northern Ireland.

The role of the bearer of authority in his own person who deliberately and voluntarily subjects that authority to the consensus of the group where he presides is most common in all good administration of political bodies. A good head of department does this in a university, a wise prime minister does this over many issues in Cabinet, neither imposing his or her own pet solutions nor yet asking the Cabinet to behave like a class in gymnastics, by continually holding up their hands to vote. Rather does the prime minister take the voices, find the consensus, and then embody it in his or her authoritative statement.

In the 1973 Act the Secretary of State for Northern Ireland was expressly asked to 'initiate proceedings to find a consensus among the representatives of both sections of the community'. This is to be the perpetual role of the PAPOPA in Northern Ireland. At a smaller-scale, less sophisticated level it was the regular preoccupation of a good District Officer in a division divided by tribal or sectional conflict. His major role was that of the person who sought to use authority to effect reconciliation and produce consensus—the midwife of the idea of peace.

The fourth element in the structure of the institutions of co-sovereignty is, of course, the assembly of the elected representatives of the people in the area concerned. We are seeking to set up government which is as democratic as it can possibly be, in all co-sovereignty situations where there is a community of people in the area concerned who can express a political will. The existence of a co-sovereignty regime does not eliminate the possibility of having responsible government over many matters, with elected heads of departments accountable to an elected assembly on the Sunningdale model of 'power-sharing'. In such a situation one invokes the federal principle of division of powers. Some are given to the council of the co-domini and to the PAPOPA, others are allocated to the elected heads of department in the area concerned. Perhaps in the latter sphere one still needs a reserve power of 'tutelage' (on the French local-government model) for the PAPOPA.

In the Northern Irish case the (SDP/Liberal) Alliance Commission *Report* on the future for Northern Ireland (1985, p. 39), to which Professor Whyte (Chapter 2) refers favourably in his paper, suggests that the Secretary of State for Northern Ireland should have power to intervene to reverse decisions of a power-sharing Northern Irish executive of an elected kind if they are 'appealed against' by a specified minority of the members of the elected Northern Ireland legislature (c. 256). The grounds of this appeal would be that the piece of legislation is discriminatory or harmful to relations between communities. This is also a kind of tutelage by a non-elected executive over the decision of the elected executive. I suggest, however, that the requirement of the formal procedure of an appeal positively encourages one section to object and that a general right of tutelage to reject a provocative or discriminatory action, if used with great care and restraint by the PAPOPA, may be more flexible and better designed to lead the two sections to the harmonies of shared power.

The fifth element in the structure of institutions is the judiciary. This must have a certain independence both of the elected assembly or executive in the area and of the PAPOPA, since it acts as a check upon both by insisting upon executive action that obeys the law and legislation that is not contrary to the basic constitution setting up the condominium. Presumably the judiciary would be appointed by the council of the co-domini with security of tenure 'quam diu se bene gesserint' (during good conduct). The exact procedure for removal of misconduct could be worked out—it might involve a judicial service commission.

The three main elements of council of co-domini, PAPOPA, and elected assembly of the area allow for some variation according to need. One may well wish for the elected assembly itself to elect members to the council of co-domini. This is the model suggested by the Kilbrandon Report (1984) on Northern Ireland, which sought to set up a council representative of both communities in Northern Ireland and of the British and Irish governments, and described its role as that of a Cabinet. (I regard the role of the council of co-domini under shared sovereignty as a different one. When it achieves a consensus it can advise or instruct the chief executive for Northern Ireland and it can make laws for Northern Ireland but it is not to be an executive authority and none of its members are to have any portfolio or individual power, or responsibility. Its role is perhaps more akin to that fulfilled by a council in a University, as a kind of supreme ratifying authority and one which takes major decisions.) The Report also recommended that the elected Northern Irish Assembly elect three members to a five-member council. As the Alliance *Report* states (1985, p. 68), this could lead to a danger of a majority of three to two dominating every decision. That majority might be the British representative (Secretary of State for Northern Ireland) plus two unionists versus the 'nationalist' minority of the single Northern Ireland Catholic representative plus the Republic of Ireland representative (Foreign Minister). Alternatively, the British representative might change sides and gang up on the unionists. In either case the weakness is apparent and it springs from treating the council as an executive Cabinet taking decisions by simple majority. Executive action should be left to the PAPOPA in matters allocated to him and in tutelage matters, and to the executive of the assembly working in a power-sharing capacity in matters within their competence, provided they are able to reach consensus among themselves. The function of the council is to ratify, to advise, and to legislate by a consensus of all its members or by a substantial majority (see Chapter 7). If it numbers five, as Kilbrandon suggests for Northern Ireland, then perhaps a four to one majority would be required, thus forcing the council to seek consensus and compromise.

A further refinement might be to allow the PAPOPA himself to be a full member of the council and co-domini, thus giving an extra vote for the course he recommends. For financial legislation which has an urgency greater than that for the creation of new ordinary laws, one needs a procedure that guarantees a prompt supply and a prompt budget. In this case a procedure similar to that used in France under the Constitution of the Fifth Republic might be advisable, allowing the budget to be passed by decree of the PAPOPA if it was not passed (or rejected) within a given number of days (90 in the French case).

I have devoted a lot of space to denoting the outlines and variations in shared sovereignty in general in order that we may see it not as the 'half life between the two sovereign states', as Professor Crick describes it, but as a system in its own right with a future in the world, which we must adapt and design to suit the particular needs of Northern Ireland with the rest of the island. It is not to be seen as a peculiar one-off gimmick designed for party-political reasons in the Irish context. Nor is it to be seen as a mere stepping-stone to Irish unification under a sovereign Dublin government with sole power.

Shared sovereignty is at the least a medium-term solution for a minimum of, say, twenty years and perhaps one whose termination we do not envisage at all. The Alliance *Report* puts this well (1985, p. 66): 'The Unionists would only be able to accept it if at all, provided that it was seen as *a terminus and not as a stepping stone* to further constitutional change. The details of the leak of the Forum's consideration of joint authority (*Irish Times*, 9 May 1984) make it apparent that joint authority is seen as a transition to the objective of Irish re-unification.' Such a view would be fatal. In the long run shared sovereignty might produce a situation where Britain could quietly furl up its flag and remove its authority as it has done gladly over some fifty nations in the last eighty years, turning Empire into Commonwealth of free nations. But this can only happen if the inhabitants of those areas ask us to do this, and it will take a long period of growing together of nationalist and unionist traditions in Ireland before the unionist majority is even remotely likely to ask us to do it. I regard shared sovereignty and shared administration (the distinction between the two is, as the Alliance *Report* (1985, p. 64) puts it, 'an extremely thin one') as an equilibrium situation which is stable enough to last for many years. The far future rests with God and it is rash to assume that what one builds will last for ever. Even if the solution is regarded as provisional it is well to remember with Talleyrand that 'Ce n'est que le provisoire qui dure'.

Let us now analyse more precisely the application of the model in the Northern Ireland case. Its suitability follows with inevitable logic from the aspirations for a just and lasting peace between communities. The particular identity of the unionists is Protestant but it is also directed to the British connection. The Alliance *Report* (1985, p. 19) suggests that this is somehow 'an unconscious way of shoring up and entrenching loyalty to one's own group' in the Northern Ireland conflict situation. I doubt if this is the case. The unionists' loyalty to flag and anthem is exaggerated partly because it is threatened.

The sharpening of the conflict in Northern Ireland comes from the burning issue of the border and the assumption of a zero-sum conflict in terms of religious dominance and exclusive sovereignty. Always the unionist community suspects every move towards power-sharing and sensible contact with the rest of Ireland as being the 'thin end of the wedge'. By setting up shared sovereignty as the terminus to which the constitutional and institutional change can move, we can both demonstrate that the system is tolerable for unionists and calm their fears. We show that it is not a first step towards incorporation in a Dublin-ruled Ireland with a single (homonymous) set of laws, but is a stable 'plateau of institutions'.

The concept of shared sovereignty between Britain and Ireland is also particularly appropriate as an institutionalization of that most generous view of Irish unity which was stated in the speech of King George the Fifth with which I began this paper. It is instructive that the best speech on the spirit of Irish unity and the love of Ireland should have been made by the King himself, the *fons et origo* of the loyalist political ideology. Those who profess loyalty to the monarch only 'being Protestant' cannot be less generous in these terms than the King himself.

Under the co-sovereignty system, the input of the British and Irish governments in power terms will be solely through the council of the co-domini and through their administrator with power of attorney. Practical co-operation on specific subjects will, of course, be invaluable. But it must be in the form of specialist 'Councils for Ireland' and not a single 'Council of Ireland'. The councils will be set up by the Northern Irish authorities with the goodwill of its elected assembly, if that can be obtained, and by the Irish government. They will in no sense be the kind of bodies that could have mandatory power of a constitutional kind over the two communities. We already have a council for the Catholic Church of Ireland, and for the Anglican. We have a council for rugby and a team on an all-Irish basis, two co-operating Tourist Boards, and a Fisheries Board for Lough Foyle. Let us have more of these fields in transport, education, culture, technology, and any other useful areas. They provide a valuable Irish dimension and are also of value in themselves to all communities.

The nationalist community, however, has, as the SDLP has so often pointed out, need for a more specific Irish dimension. Power-sharing is an immense help to the attainment of such a dimension, but it also requires a specific connection with the government of the whole island of Ireland. Shared sovereignty is the means by which this can be obtained, without creating conditions which cut off the Unionist community from their 'British dimension'. Article 2 of the Irish constitution speaks of the Irish nation, whose territory is the whole island. We want Northern nationalists to share in this sense of an 'Irish Nation'. Article 3 is often misunderstood. It is one that limits the power of the Irish government rather than one which asserts it. 'Pending the reintegration' of the Island, the authority of the Irish parliament is to extend only to those areas now subject to the government of the Republic of Ireland, without prejudice to their right to govern the whole. This is *not* in my view provocative. It does, however, emphasize for us that the reflection of Irish unity in a government of co-sovereignty in which the government of the Republic partakes on equal terms with that of the government in Britain is a sufficient reflection of the Irish dimension.

While one must support the desire of the Catholic nationalist minority to establish a proper role of equality in Northern Ireland and also an 'Irish dimension' in its relation to the South, one can only deplore the use of violence to coerce the Northern Protestant unionists to join the Republic, no matter what they wish. We equally deplore the use of violence on the Protestant side. One cannot create unity by knee-capping and assassination. 'Subdue three million free people— the thing is impossible', Pitt the Elder said of the American colonists. The same is true both of the nationalist minority in the North and of the Protestant majority. Therefore, one can only seek for a solution that meets with the consent of both communities.

Professor Whyte, in his admirable letter to the Clerk Assistant to the Northern House of Assembly (quoted in Alliance 1985, p. 23), wrote of the absolute necessity of power-sharing in any divided society which has successfully overcome its internal divisions. This applies with great force to the making of any internal arrangements for representative and responsible government in Northern Ireland. But the logic of power-sharing leads to the external dimension of shared sovereignty, for in matters of identity each community must have arrangements which will ensure that the polity is not alien to them. 'In all successfully governed divided societies', Professor Whyte wrote, 'there is some set of arrangements whereby the different segments of the population share power roughly in proportion to their numerical strength, so that no segment feels permanently left out in the cold.' This is admirable as regards internal arrangement of government, but in matters of external identity one can hardly share it 'in proportion to numerical strength', one can only share it equally in a symmetrical arrangement of co-sovereignty.

We are also led to the necessity of co-sovereignty by the failure of any other arrangement to create the necessary consensus. The law of the majority is fine as a general convention of democracy, as long as the majority is a shifting one. 'It is better', as Chesterton put it, 'to count heads than to break them.' But the 1973 Act's reliance on majority decision as to national identity does not solve the problem of the alienation of the Catholic/nationalist community in Northern Ireland, and if, by some great miracle, the majority were to shift the other way, it would not solve the problem of the Protestant unionist community in a single Irish polity. The Republic would indeed need a strong stomach to digest so large a body of people who did not wish to be included in its state.

The course of leaving things as they are is no solution, even if, as I profoundly hope, we can ameliorate it by power-sharing in the government of Northern Ireland itself. The opposite extreme of rooting up the border and 'undoing the error of Lloyd George' is also no answer. Even if one can show that the 1921 settlement was a mistake at the time, that does not justify us in seeking to change it now, any more than I could go out to root up the magnificent avenue of trees below the Clock House at Keele on the grounds that they were originally planted a yard or two too near by, or too far away from, the road. History creates its reality within which we must work.

The federal solution sounds attractive at first, but it contains the fatal flaw of totally cutting off the connection of Northern Ireland from the UK government, and it also means that though some areas of law would be within the field of the Northern Irish legislature, which would have a Protestant majority, others would not. In these spheres, which would be subject to the Dublin government, the Northern Protestant majority would not only have to accept the future laws made by the united Irish Government. (Under a ruler of moderation these would, no doubt, be reasonable.) Northern Ireland would also, however, have to accept the volumes of law already made by the Dublin government since 1922. Lawyers are, by their nature, conservative and do not like wholesale change. 'The laws of England', as the Bill of Rights puts it, 'are the inheritance of the people thereof'. The same is true of the laws of Northern Ireland, and it would be a great wrench to have to accept volumes of law made in Catholic Ireland at a period when it was much less liberal than it is at the present.

Confederalism in Ireland has attraction. But again, it seems to cut the connection with Britain, though perhaps the inventiveness of Irish politicians might find a way to get round this. It also has the weakness that a confederation lacks the essential minimum of powers at the centre to prevent secession. In the United States from 1785 to 1789 it proved a weak instrument for effective government. In Nigeria the confederal proposals of the Northern 'Eight Point Plan' of the NPC were a recipe for national breakup. Fortunately, the plan was never followed. In 1967 Ojukwu's confederal stance at the Aburi Conference produced a settlement which the federal civil servants quickly had to persuade Gowon to abandon in order to preserve Nigerian unity. A confederal solution in Ireland would leave unanswered the great problem of security.

It was a difference over security powers that finally led the British government to dissolve the Stormont government and assume powers of Direct Rule in 1972. In describing the events leading up to the dissolution of the Northern Irish Legislature and the assumption of direct powers by the government of Mr Heath, Mr Faulkner, the Premier of Northern Ireland, related that when he and Senator Andrews went to see Mr Heath on 22 March 1972, the proposal was put to him by Mr Heath, that 'all statutory and executive responsibility for law and order should be vested in the UK Parliament and Government'. This included criminal law and procedure, including arrangements for appointments to courts, public order, prisons, and penal institutions, creation of new penal offences, special powers, and power over the public prosecutor and the police'. (Statement by Mr Faulkner, quoted in *Keesings Contemporary Archives* 1972, p. 25190.) If Mr Heath saw this massive level of transfer of authority as a fitting response to a situation of threat to law and order in Northern Ireland it is hardly likely that an Irish government, operating under a system of inclusion in Northern Ireland in an Irish Confederation, would be content with any lesser powers. This would be at variance with the loose arrangements suitable in the Confederal system. Furthermore, if the control of the army and the control of the police were under different governments, there would be endless room for confrontation in time of stress.

Northern Ireland needs a high degree of devolution, but this devolution has to be subject to safeguards. If it were not, the Protestant majority might well make things difficult for the Catholic minority, even in a federal Ireland. Alternatively, the power boot might shift to the other foot, in some political intervention of parties based on an all-Ireland majority. Northern Ireland needs a kind of devolution like that of a 'dog on a long leash'. There should be complete freedom to move, provided the movement is kept within the salutary bounds of justice and harmony between the communities. To achieve this the co-sovereignty situation, with its supervision through the 'Council of Co-domini', and 'Pure Administator and Political Officer with Power of Attorney' is far the most effective means.

Let us look briefly at the functions we need to fulfil in the Northern Irish context under co-sovereignty, and at the problems of introducing the system.

On 20 March 1986, almost with tears in our eyes, two thousand of us in Westminster Abbey saw the flag of Sweden taken up to the High Altar of Westminster Abbey, where the monarch is crowned, and placed there in memory of Olaf Palme, while the Court Singer of Sweden sang 'Det Ewiga' ('The Eternal'). Do we have to wait for the death of an equally beloved prime minister from Ireland before we are allowed in some way to do equal honour to the flag of Ireland as that of our dearest neighbour? The ensign of the co-sovereignty government could be the crossed flags of Britain and Ireland, like the crossed Union Jack and Nigerian flag which I have on my British Nigeria Association tie. Perhaps underneath this can also be some specific emblem of Ulster.

The 'Council of the Co-Domini' role can be fulfilled either by a 'High Council of Ulster' on the Kilbrandon model, but with the PAPOPA as a member and with a requirement for larger majorities for more important law-making functions. Alternatively, we may simply have a 'Council of Three'—one each from the Irish and British Governments plus the PAPOPA (Chief Executive of Northern Ireland).

We already have in the present Interministerial Conference created under the Agreement a first step towards a council of the co-domini of the kind I have described. We must give high credit to both governments for sticking to their guns on this matter, though at the same time they must do their utmost to explain that the arrangements are not the 'thin end of the wedge' leading to the full incorporation of Northern Ireland in the Republic and the abandonment of the British link. [During the course of the conference at which this paper was first presented, the important point was made (by Father MacDonagh) that the terms of the Anglo-Irish Agreement appear to limit the role of the representative of the Government of the Irish Republic to putting forward the case for the Catholic community. This is an asymmetrical situation which is bound to cause grievance to the Protestants, and it robbed Dr FitzGerald of an opportunity to conciliate the Protestant community and give them confidence—a task for which he was ideally qualified as the son of a Northern Protestant mother, and as a man much trusted by all. In a truly shared-sovereignty situation each member of the council of co-domini will have to pay equal attention to the interests of all sections, since they will be 'healers of the land', with governmental responsibility for Northern Ireland as a whole.]

The third element in the co-sovereignty arrangement is the crucially important one of the 'Pure Administrator and Political Officer with Power of Attorney.' Both governments together in council, after consultation with both sections of the Northern Irish community, will have to undertake a difficult task to find such a person who is possessed of the requisite skills and is not ruled out by association with either of the contending groups and identities, but rather has the background to associate with both. Possibly a pair of administrators, one Catholic and one Protestant, working as 'Chief Executive' and 'Deputy Chief Executive', in the closest possible co-operation, might meet the need. The appointment would be for four or five years, possibly renewable by Council. The best title would be 'Chief Executive for Northern Ireland.'

The Sunningdale Agreement set up a role of Chief Executive for Northern Ireland, but provided that the post should be an elected one. This seems to me a mistake. The Sunningdale power-sharing structure for Northern Ireland was based more on the local-government model than on the Cabinet-parliamentary, since it relied on government through powerful committees and on 11 political Heads of Committees appointed from all major Northern Irish parties. In the local-government pattern, the role of chief executive is a well-known non-political one, and the degree of power and discretion given to him is greater, relative to the political elected element, than it is in the case of a Cabinet Secretary or Head of Civil Service in a ministerial system.

Under the present system of Direct Rule, the Northern Ireland Office can perfectly well begin to develop the role of administrative discretion, which I have outlined, for it has the power (with the goodwill of the Irish government) to appoint a kind of *alter ego* to the Secretary of State to seek out the means to unite Northern Ireland and to work for its economic recovery. Before 1972, and later for six months under the Sunningdale Agreement, Northern Ireland enjoyed far more devolution than any other part of the United Kingdom; so that one can hardly claim that its problems came from too little autonomy. Perhaps they came from the opposite cause. British governments wanted to have rather little to do with the difficult problems of an area which, in both political and geographical terms, was peripheral to their main concerns.

Under co-sovereignty, one does not seek to impose perpetual bureaucratic or unrepresentative government on the area. Northern Ireland can break new ground in being represented by election of members of parliament in *both* the Irish and the British parliaments, though no doubt on a rather lower ratio of members to population in each parliament than the rest of either country. (Already Irish citizens in Britain and British citizens in Ireland enjoy the right, if they have a residence qualification, to vote in parliamentary elections in each other's country, as well as in their own. Already some Irish citizens resident in the North have been appointed to the Senate of the Irish Republic, and de Valera was elected for two Northern Irish constituencies. My suggestion of dual parliamentary representation for the North in the parliaments of Britain and of the Irish Republic is not as revolutionary as it sounds.) Its own elected government would also expand to take back areas of activity from the chief executive whenever, with his help, it is able to show the necessary consensus. The chief executive acts in his own discretion only in default of that consensus or in instances of countering measures which would be unjust to one section of the community or dangerous to intercommunity relations. Furthermore, the chief executive would have the role of taking positive steps to ensure greater equality of access to jobs by the Catholic community. There are already a number of bodies set up under the 1973 Act to seek to ensure equality—the Fair Employment Agency, the Standing Advisory Commission on Human Rights, and the Equal Opportunities Commission. The Stormont parliament also created in 1969 a post of Ombudsman with wider powers than those of the Ombudsman in Great Britain. His report goes to the administration and carries great weight. Access to him is direct from the citizen. The remedying of grievance will indeed be one of the important roles of the chief executive, just as it used to be for the District Officer in a colonial situation.

The precise procedure for the approval of law will require considerable study. The existing laws of Northern Ireland retain their validity. The system of shared sovereignty must be set up in a treaty between Britain and Ireland which is given the force of law as a basic constitution and 'supreme law of Northern Ireland', enforceable by judicial review through the normal judicial process of any executive action or subsequent legislation which contravenes the constitution. The constitution must expressly guarantee the constitutional status from change without the approval of a majority in a poll, as does the present Northern Ireland Constitution Act of 1973. Attached to the constitution there might well be a Northern Ireland Bill of Rights on the lines of the European Convention on Human Rights. This seems to be one of the issues on which all the major parties in Northern Ireland are agreed.

It may be that, for the sake of constitutional propriety or to keep up the idea of the responsibility of British and Irish governments for legislation in the co-dominium, new laws made by the Northern

Ireland council, after consultation with the Northern Irish elected assembly, would be duplicated by orders in council in Britain and by measures of an equivalent status in Ireland in the way that EEC regulations are incorporated into British law by a more or less automatic process. This would, however, be an endorsement of a formal kind, for the only policy input of the co-domini is to be through the council. (In Norway, Sweden, and Denmark much legislation has originated in the Nordic Council to which all three belong and occurs in identical form in the laws of all three countries. In Britain the exact text of treaty obligations entered into by the government is incorporated by Act of Parliament into domestic law. The unionist side in Northern Ireland pays great attention to the Constitution and demands a method of passing laws which involves the British parliament. Symmetry and the views of many Northern Irish nationalists requires a similar participation of the Irish parliament. We have to work out the conventions by which this can be achieved within the Institutions of Shared Sovereignty.)

The judicial function will require a judiciary appointed by the council and with its own independence of tenure and status. At the apex of the judicial pyramid one could perhaps have a court consisting of a judge from the Irish Republic, a judge from Britain, and a judge from Northern Ireland as a final court of appeal.

The administrative and financial aspects of government are all important. They come under the general supervision of the chief executive, in interplay with the elected Northern Irish political heads on a power-sharing basis, when these are available. The essence of the settlement is one of devolution wherever possible. Therefore in matters of finance Northern Ireland would become a financial unit on its own. Contributions would be made to the budget of the co-domini for defence and foreign affairs and existing involvement in social security schemes of the UK will be maintained. The result of this exercise will, of course, be a colossal Northern Irish deficit. Government expenditure per head of population in Northern Ireland is easily the highest in the United Kingdom—°452 in 1973. The United Kingdom nett subsidy to Northern Ireland was reckoned by the 1973 Green Paper on the Northern Irish economy at °313 million out of a total Northern Irish Government expenditure of °841 million. It is now estimated at °1,500 million. It is altogether fitting and proper that this help should continue, but it is also appropriate that it should be openly seen as a subsidy to be approved on a yearly basis by the UK government. It is not unreasonable to expect that the existence of such a discretionary subvention will make it clear to the more rebellious elements in Northern Ireland that a British Government which pays so great a yearly amount to the piper has some right to demand moderation to the tune.

The main problem of Northern Ireland is at least as much economic as constitutional. It is in this sphere that the combined efforts of Britain and of Ireland, and of the EEC and of any outside well-wishers, such as the United States has just shown itself to be by its £300 million contribution to all Ireland, must be brought to bear to help. The chief executive will have as his perpetual and burning concern the improvement of the economy and the provision of jobs for the very high proportion now unemployed.

The problem of the difference between British and Irish currency will no longer be a problem if Britain joins the exchange rate mechanism of the European monetary system.

A study of the economic deprivation of Northern Ireland would require a long paper to itself. It is sufficient here to show that this is a problem of the greatest urgency requiring the *combined* energies of Britain, of Ireland, of the council proposed in this paper, of the chief executive, and of Northern Ireland's own elected assembly. Much of the economic decline has sprung from the *security* problem and it is to this that we must devote urgent attention. Without an improvement in the maintenance of peace and of the rule of law, nothing else can be achieved. Already we have as part of the Agreement provision for co-operation of security services, north and south of the border. It is strange that the unionist community should object to this, since they themselves have asked for it so often in the past. Under a full system of co-sovereignty we shall be able to deploy the combined forces of Britain and Ireland in the North, and this will give us a great additional strength in dealing with republican and loyalist paramilitaries. We shall also be able to deny to terrorists the 'safe haven' of the border. Soldiers are professionals and know how to co-operate beyond the barriers of nationality, as we have already seen in NATO and in UN multi-national forces in the Congo, in Cyprus, and on the Israel/Syrian border (where there is an Irish contingent). The establishment for the principle of a joint British–Irish military presence will be difficult, but once it is achieved we have a very powerful weapon for peace. Extremists using violence are better controlled by sensible people of their own community than by outsiders associated with a rival one.

The failure of the IRA and its associates to make any headway in the Irish Republic demonstrates this. A joint patrol of British and Irish soldiers, particularly if they wear a very similar sort of battle-dress, would be less likely to be fired upon by the IRA than would a British unit. Similarly, Protestant men of violence who would fight a purely Irish army to the death would be less inclined to do so if it were mixed up in a joint Anglo-Irish force. In fact, the New Ireland Forum *Report* (1984*a*, para. 8. 7) places great emphasis on the security benefits of shared sovereignty, which will be greater than those achievable under the present Anglo-Irish Agreement.

The chief executive, though not himself the head of the police, must have a strong advisory role in its constitution and operation. A delicate interplay between police and general administrative authority is required.

The representation of Northern Ireland in the parliaments of the co-domini requires a provision without precedent. There must surely be provision for the representation of Northern Irish people in the two sovereign parliaments at once. Whether this should be by direct election or by delegation from a Northern Irish parliament is not clear. One would have to guard against the danger of a unionist candidate winning the election to the Irish parliament merely in order to sabotage the arrangement by refusing to attend once elected.

The problem of foreign policy presents difficulties. Unionists would not wish the change of status to involve separation from the Commonwealth or NATO. Fortunately, however, the foreign policy relations of Northern Ireland itself with outside countries other than Britain and Ireland are not very intimate or important, and some way can be found to deal with the dilemma.

The final element is the most important. The object of all our constitutional and political procedures is, in the end, to produce harmony and unity. 'They be two things, unity and uniformity', as Bacon says in his Essays. None the less, we do have to create a new sense of Northern Irish identity transcending religious attachment.

In the religious sense, theologians are already going ahead and undermining the 'middle wall of partition' between the viewpoints of the two communities. More and more recent scholarship and religious thought has shown that the division in the church springing from the Reformation was a tragedy upon both sides. Reformation is now generally agreed to have been urgently required in the sixteenth century, but at the same time we see that given a more perfect

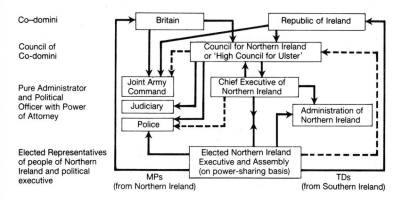

Participation in Specialized All-Ireland Councils

Interrelation of Shared Sovereignty and Power-Sharing

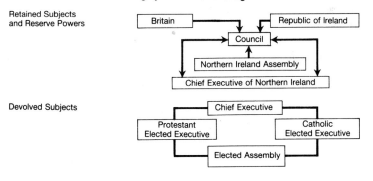

FIG: Possible Institutional Structure for Shared Sovereignty
in Northern Ireland

dedication on both sides it could have come without schism. The great emphases of the reformers—the equality of Word and Sacrament, the doctrine of the priesthood of all believers, the proper balance of faith and works, the translation of Bible and liturgy into a 'language that can be understanded of the people', the autonomy—within certain limits—of the congregation and the bishop and the collegiate, as well as the personal nature of church authority, have all been accepted in large part by the Catholic church. Inter-communion is a long way away. But, as the theological dividing walls in the one Christian community are seen to be less important, the theological reason for continued hatred in Northern Ireland will decrease and, without that element of justification for hostility, even the zealots may find it hard to polarize the ordinary people into rival camps.

This, however, is for the theologians and the long term; our work as political scientists is with the political and the reasonably short term. The equal balance of the institutions we can set up under shared sovereignty or shared administration provides the basis for a Northern Irish political identity. The provision for peace among people is more important than is that for symmetry for the tidy minds of lawyers. Provided that our political institutions are workable, they can create unity. If they are, in Hopkins's words, part of 'all things original, spare, strange', that is something for which we can be grateful. The warmth and attractiveness of Northern Irish friendship in both sections of the community is a basis for our endeavour.

In his book *Towards a New Ireland* (1972, p. 159), Dr FitzGerald asked for the use of categories for which there is as yet no precedent. I suggest this model of shared sovereignty as one of them. I present these proposals in a spirit of deep respect for both traditions in Northern Ireland.

9

CONFLICT AND CONCILIATION
A Comparative Approach Related to Three Case Studies—Belgium, Northern Ireland, and Nigeria
James O'Connell

INTRODUCTION

This paper falls into four sections. The first section deals with general factors that appear to be found in most situations of group conflict within societies. The second looks comparatively at three case studies—Belgium, Northern Ireland, and Nigeria—that present in differing ways situations of conflict. The third section, drawing on the case studies, makes more detailed and empirical analyses of the factors underlying the main points of the first section. The final section deals with the possible shapes of conciliation in such intergroup conflicts. One of the crucial points to be made is that while conflict arises in measure out of misunderstandings between groups, these misunderstandings themselves usually arise out of conflicts of interest. For that and other reasons it is unlikely that approaches can be made to resolving or reducing conflict without facing up to conflicts of interest.

I. GENERAL FACTORS UNDERLYING CONFLICT

1. In certain conflict situations—and these are the kind we are concerned with here—there is present in a group or groups a socially strong and distinctive mark or characteristic that is in some way problematic. By a socially strong distinctive mark some feature is meant such as race, ethnicity, religion, or language that separates groups from one another. By problematic is meant initially a form of contrast between groups that is unacceptable in some way to one or more of these groups. What this socially strong and problematic mark does is to delineate the boundary between groups. It also tends to have the role of creating or facilitating linkages within groups. Language, for example, with its oral and literary traditions is an obvious

foundation and vehicle of linkages within a group. Moreover, it can be a powerful distancing factor between groups.

Contrast in itself does not create conflict. There are countries in which language groups live with one another in such fashion that friction based on language differences is kept to a minimum. Similarly there are many countries where religious differences do not make for social or other conflict. Switzerland is a good example of a country where language differences are not socially divisive. In the United States, though religion can enter as a factor into politics, religion by and large is not used to underpin political and social differences.

2. Where strong and socially distinctive marks become problematic there is usually a historical inheritance in which, for various reasons, these marks have been used to structure competition or opposition. One of the common results of history is to leave persons and groups unequal in the possession of political power, in the access to economic benefits, and in the enjoyment of social prestige. It is equally true that competition for power, money, and status tends to be structured in societies around inherited allegiances—ethnicity, class, religious allegiance, etc. One (or more) of the socially salient factors can become politically crucial where it provides an organizing focus—and in consequence a boundary—for preserving inequality or, conversely, for providing a rallying point for an assault on inequality. In this sense race (in a particular definition of it) has been used in South Africa, colour in the United States, ethnicity in Malaya and Sri Lanka, and religion in terminally colonial India to allocate—or more correctly to organize the allocation of—socially desirable goods.

Even where socially distinctive factors are used to sort out access to social goods, and where they are, in consequence, in measure problematic, groups marked off by these salient factors can spend long periods in which they remain on tranquil terms with one another. At one extreme such tranquillity may emanate from apathy or a sense of powerlessness, as was the case of black South Africans during the period 1930–50, from a gradual lessening of distance, as was the case of Catholics and Protestants in Northern Ireland during the early 1960s, or from non-activation of distinctiveness or lack of consciousness-raising, as was the case with the Belgian Flemish during the years between 1870 and 1919. Where certain forms of social change intervene, especially where rapid social change does not give enough time for adjustments between groups, social differences can become acute as competition intensifies and opposition sharpens. Among such factors of change are demographic patterns, especially where an under-group grows faster in numbers than a socially dominant group (Muslims in Lebanon or Catholics in Northern Ireland); new patterns of education through which an under-group either becomes more conscious of its rights or more skilled in competing for jobs (Ibo in Nigeria, Flemish in Belgium, Catholics in Northern Ireland); mineral discoveries or altered patterns of economic growth (Baluba and others in Zaire); outside intervention or intervention in colonization or decolonization (many African countries); missionary interventions (again many African states); and the impact of ideas from fellow ethnics or co-religionists elsewhere (Shia Muslims in various Middle Eastern countries influenced by Iran, and in pre-1939 Europe German communities in various central and eastern European countries). It is seldom, however, that these influences do not operate directly in an economic context; it is seldom also that more than one factor is not at work; and it is seldom, finally, that the awakened social perceptions do not lead to more competitive or oppositional behaviour when the economic situation of groups deteriorates or where groups are not making the economic progress that they have come to expect. It is in this context that a sense of relative deprivation can deepen.

3. Crucial though social distinctiveness and contrast are, and important though political and/or economic competition is, conflict in a society seldom if ever takes place unless there is organization that sets out to consolidate boundaries and to mobilize political and social grids to carry out opposition/competition. Such organization readily takes the form of political parties but it may also take the form of communal social organization. Formal organization/discrimination can be built into legal, economic, and educational structures. South Africa, Sri Lanka, Spain, and Canada provide examples of different forms and varying degrees of political, economic, and social organization that maintains ethnic, religious, or linguistic differences and that regulates relations between groups for the benefit or partial benefit of one or more groups in their dealings with others. The trouble with organization is that it hardens boundaries, distances groups from one another, creates vested interests for leadership élites, and makes competition/opposition more visible and articulate and more open to reprobation and stereotyping by other groups. Yet often there is no alternative to organization to protect or secure group interests.

2. THREE CASE STUDIES

What this section of the paper does is to take the broad theory of the previous section and suggest how such theory is useful in describing the situations in Belgium, Northern Ireland, and Nigeria, and in distinguishing the factors of conflict in each specific situation.

Belgium: language, power, and money

Belgium as a country was accepted by great states to provide a neutral zone in north-west Europe. Internally it held Dutch and French-speaking groups who gradually consolidated a will to belong to neither Holland nor France. More so than its European neighbours it was a state (a political entity) rather than a nation (a community of common history and culture). For long years after its foundation it was ruled by a French-speaking aristocracy and haute-bourgeoisie who also controlled its main industries, mines, and commerce, as well as filling the upper ranks of the public service and the clergy. Such rule continued down to the end of World War II. Even as late as 1954 it was typical of the ruling groups in Belgium that the vast majority of Belgian ambassadors were Walloon. Changes were, however, taking place. First, the Flemish birth rate was higher than the Walloon, and by 1945 the Flemish clearly constituted more than half the population. Simultaneously, Flemish advances in education brought a middle and lower bourgeoisie into the urban and public job markets that had traditionally been the preserve of the Walloons. The new Flemish bourgeoisie drew on a sentiment of ethnic solidarity that owed much to a Flemish literary revival. These changes occurred at a time when new coal mines were being opened up in Flanders and new industries were shifting to that region, while the older Walloon mines were being exhausted and the heavy industries located near them were in the process of being run down. In short, demography, literature, education, and economics combined to give the Flemish a more defined sense of identity, greater skills, and new urban and occupational patterns. At the same time they encountered the resistance of the Walloons, who controlled the public services, owned most of the country's capital, and resented the demands of a group whose language and culture they despised and whose numbers and energy they feared. The stage was set for confrontation.

The new Flemish bourgeoisie (the traditional Flemish bourgeoisie had been French-speaking) sought a way into sectors of public and economic life that were blocked off against them by families and classes already in possession. They had a ready weapon to hand in the language issue. At one and the same time it symbolized their social unity, facilitated in-group communication, and permitted them to claim that discrimination against the Flemish language was discrimination against Flemish citizens. In arguing for and in prevailing in a demand that public officials be able to use both languages, the new Flemish lower bourgeoisie gained an immediate advantage over Walloons, who were mostly mono-lingual and who only slowly accepted that their children should learn Flemish. Beyond this demand for bilingualism which gave the Flemish an advantage over Walloons at entry into public posts the Flemish also used their power within the two main political parties, the Christian Democratic Party and the Socialist Party, to insist that existing imbalances between the two linguistic groups in the public service be remedied faster than existing seniority and experience would have permitted.

Walloon reactions to Flemish insurgence included political and administrative resistance, cultural revulsion and rejection, concessions made under political pressure, and straightforward conciliation in the face of recognized injustices and the need for both peoples to live together within one state. Once the official parity of the two languages had been conceded and the linkage between schooling and language acknowledged, Walloons accepted with reluctance but with a sense of inevitability that a linguistic frontier should be drawn in the country. Though there were linguistically uncertain areas which were bitterly disputed, the broad geographically separated locations of both language groups enabled a line to be drawn on each side of which one of the languages held chief status in public life and education. The complicating factor, however, was Brussels, the capital city, which grew rapidly during the quarter of a century after 1945. Brussels was officially bilingual but in pratice most Flemish families who settled there tended to become French-speaking over one or two generations. In consequence, Brussels offered considerable reinforcement to the French-speaking groups. Yet the success of Flemish speakers in making inroads into public service employment provided an influential group whose interests lay in both supporting the Flemish cause and in protecting the interests of the capital city.

In a crucial sense the blurring of the lines of linguistic confrontation in Brussels, which continued to remain bilingual in schooling and public life (and in strong minority linguistic practice in economic and private life as well), characterized much of Belgian living. The language question never fully polarized Belgian politics for any long period, although every now and then the country seemed about to tear itself apart on that issue in irreconcilable division. It enabled the newly educated and newly arrived Flemish middle classes to press their case for posts and promotions and to build up an educational system in Flemish that consolidated their sense of ethnic identity and cultural expression and that pushed back the earlier Frenchification of the Belgian middle classes. The expanding economy absorbed the newcomers without excessive cost to those who were already in position. And while Flemish speakers used their numbers and language skills to lay claim to public service posts, French speakers held on to a disproportionate share of posts in the private sector of the economy.

Though on certain issues the linguistic groups had divided politically—the most bitter of these was the royal question immediately after World War II, in which the Flemish dominantly supported King Leopold, who was obliged to abdicate eventually as widespread opposition prevented the monarchy in his person from being a sign of the unity of the state—there were many other issues that cut across the linguistic groups. Most Flemish supported church-related education; Walloon Catholics welcomed such support against majority opinion in their own community. Similarly, Walloon churchmen preferred to conciliate Flemish opinion than run the risk of a heavily anti-clerical Walloon state. French-speaking industrialists and the commercial middle classes, whose financial interests lay with Belgian unity, preferred to join in the Christian Democratic Party with Flemish workers who wanted moderate social reform and improved working conditions but not the transformation of social structures which was favoured by the Walloon workers and the Socialist Party. The Flemish movement within Flanders had originally a strong class base and was immediately directed against the Frenchified haute-bourgeoisie. Walloon socialist workers, who were more ideologically sensitized than their Flemish counterparts, saw their interests as workers allied with Flemish workers against a capitalist class and had no wish to break the unity of the working class. Flemish socialist leaders, who had difficulty in winning more than a third of the votes in Flanders, recoiled from any break in the country that would have left them out of power indefinitely and at the mercy of conservative clericalism. In this kind of situation successful language parties have not been able to grow. The two main parties have divided on ideology and economic strategy, but in spite of recurring bouts of tension have kept both language groups within their ranks. Even the smaller Liberal Party has tried to reconcile appealing to the interests of the commercial middle classes by opposing tax rises and worker agitation among both Flemish and Walloons while concomitantly appearing as a French language defender in Brussels and Wallonie. Typical of these converging and over-lapping tends has been the informal understanding among the political parties to have equal numbers of Flemish and Walloon members in Belgian Cabinets.

In short, though there have been many groups that have sought to polarize both communities on the language issue, they have not been able to undo the criss-crossing interests of different sections of the population. In this sense a crucial overall organization or mobilization along the language divide has not occurred for any length of time in Belgium. Interwoven interests have fostered conciliation, not least among the inhabitants of the capital, who have decided that they can live with official bilingualism and who know that their interests depend on representing a united country. Brussels itself, with its immense investment and its leanings towards French, is too precious a prize for most Flemish nationalists to abandon, apart from the problems of political and economic viability for an autonomous Flemish state. The accommodations and concessions that are made in this kind of situation are all the more powerful because no matter how reluctantly made by the representatives of both sides they are rooted in the self-interest of nearly all Belgian groups.

Northern Ireland: history, distinctiveness, and fear

The broad context of the Irish question is the location of the smaller island of Ireland alongside the island of Britain. British rulers, through a defensive wish to protect their flank as well as historical expansionist inclinations, took over control of the smaller island. When a long period of British political rule came to an end with Irish independence in 1921–2, complications of history, not least those that had seen Britain become Protestant and Ireland remain Catholic, led to the six north-eastern counties of Ireland still remaining attached to Britain and forming part of the United Kingdom, albeit with a form of devolved government.

After the collapse of the last traditionally Gaelic resistance in Ulster, Britain introduced Protestant settlers, mainly but not exclusively Scottish, during the seventeenth century. These settlers dispossessed native landholders (some of whom also changed religion and joined them) and took over the best agricultural land. It must be said as well that they developed enormously land that they took over. They eventually constituted the majority of the population in the north-eastern counties. When the Industrial Revolution reached Ireland, it made its greatest impact on Ulster, particularly with the growth of Belfast. The more numerous and more prosperous Protestant community in those counties showed outstanding entrepreneurial flair, benefited most from industrialization, and extended their previous dominance into the new urban sectors of the economy. Moreover, in Belfast and other centres, particularly in working-class areas, much housing developed along segregated lines as new immigrants from the countryside set up house alongside their co-religionists, much as ethnic groups were doing in the industrializing United States or as they have done in contemporary African cities. As Irish Home Rule agitation grew during the nineteenth century, Protestant rural and urban reaction converged to resist a solution which would have left them a minority in a self-ruling and Catholic-dominated Ireland. The Protestant rural communities, proud though they were of having developed land that they had taken over, retained a settler mentality (they knew that many Irish still regarded them as interlopers); and in the context of a long oral tradition linked to land attachment they felt their own tenure to be insecure. Protestant urban capital in its turn believed its interests to be linked with the British economy and desperately wanted to avoid being carried into a dominantly agricultural country and risking loss of access to British markets. The 1921–3 compromise that gave independence to 26 Irish counties and left 6 still part of the United Kingdom owed much to the threat of Protestant violence. It also owed something to a British reluctance to let Ireland go completely, as well as to the realization in Dublin that the North could not be fully integrated at that moment in history.

The spread and size of the Northern Irish state (sub-state of the United Kingdom) was designed as a compromise between an area large enough to be viable demographically and economically and small enough to provide a sure Protestant majority. It eventually contained six of the traditional nine counties of Ulster and two Protestant inhabitants for every one Catholic. Those of the Gaelic and nationalist minority, nearly all Catholics, refused initially as much as they could to recognize the legitimacy of the institutions of the new state and refused to co-operate with them. This reluctance, in line with a long nationalist tradition, confirmed Protestant and unionist beliefs that the Catholic minority was subversive. Anti-partition propaganda from the South and the special position allocated to the Catholic Church in the 1937 Constitution served to make the Northern government more defensive. The unionist distrust of the Catholic opposition deepened as birth-rate statistics suggested that Catholics were increasing in number faster than Protestants. The fear underlying the distrust had roots in the history of the land plantation, differing ethnic origins, theologically hostile religions, and relative social separation/demarcation by living-place, school, and even workplace. The trouble was that in the face of the Catholic hostility and threat the Protestant government supported by its Protestant people (one Northern Ireland premier declared that his was a 'Protestant parliament for a Protestant people') discriminated in some measure, especially in the first two decades of the state's existence, against Catholics in jobs, voting arrangements, and housing allocation. In the process the balance of prosperity was tilted more acutely against a minority population that was already weaker numerically and economically. Catholic alienation inevitably deepened. Yet, especially in the years after World War II as their co-religionists in the South (after 1948 officially called Éire or Ireland) struggled against economic diversity, Northern Catholics were conciliated by the benefits of the British welfare state and growing employment prospects. If they resented the deprivation and injustice of their position in Northern Ireland, they also felt relatively—and in fact were—more well-to-do than the Southern Irish. During the period between 1945 and 1965 most Catholics became unionist in all but open admission of the fact. It was a reluctant unionism, based mainly on economic calculation, and it was all the time threatened by perception of Protestant discrimination and a residual nationalist tradition. Discrimination was almost certainly less than it was perceived and the nationalist tradition was weak. But both factors lay in wait for changed conditions.

The crucial change that took place in the Catholic population in the post-war period was that Catholics profited from the extension of the Butler education reforms from Britain to secure secondary schooling in greater proportion and numbers than ever before. By the mid-1960s

Catholics made up a third of the students at Queen's University, Belfast—roughly proportionate to the numbers in the general population. The expansionist economic policy around this period also drew many new companies, mainly multinationals, to the province. Their managements ignored received hiring practices and employed Catholics and Protestants without excessive distinction. Through these factories and other developments Catholics were able to share in the growing prosperity of Northern Ireland.

In this period as well liberal developments began to take place in the Unionist Party. Terence O'Neill, who had succeeded the traditionalist Lord Brookeborough as premier, held discussions and meetings with the Southern government and made various conciliatory gestures towards Catholics. In doing this he raised Catholic hopes but alarmed hardline Protestant fears. Unfortunately, he had little success in liberalizing internal politics. A crucial turning-point came with the decision on the siting of a new university. Regional balance, employment needs, and an existing embryonic academic institution pointed to Londonderry as the most suitable site. The Unionist Cabinet preferred the Protestant town of Coleraine to Catholic Derry. With this decision the new Catholic middle classes concluded that since they could not secure such obvious justice they were going to remain deprived of rights.* Out of this disappointment and other perceived anti-Catholic stances came the civil rights movement, which started from a protest against a case of injustice in housing. It carried the resonance, terminology, and methods of the struggle of black Americans. There was also more than an echo of Irish nationalism in the civil rights movement, but it was not the dominant note. However, the Northern government failed to play this new type of opposition coolly. Cabinet members saw it as part of endemic Catholic subversion and dealt roughly with civil rights marchers. The police showed in crucial episodes that they were sectarian in allegiance rather than responsive to the whole community. The situation became more

* Two correspondents whose views I respect suggest that I have over-emphasized the importance of the decision on the location of the university. One writes that the references above 'illustrate Catholic perceptions rather than reality'. Be that as it may, the situation of Northern Irish society by the late 1960s was awaiting a spark that would ignite it—educational and economic changes within and external influences, coming not least from liberalizing influences in western countries and the new media explosion— had begun to affect a society that had remained too rigidly set in traditional moulds. For a good discussion of the university issue see R. D. Osborne, 'The Lockwood Report and the Location of a Second University in Northern Ireland' in Boal and Douglas (1982, pp. 167–78).

complicated as Protestant hardliners—who had a gifted spokesman in the person of the Revd Ian Paisley, a Poujadiste-type leader—organized mob attacks on Catholic districts. As violence got out of hand integrated working-class areas were torn apart and thousands of families from both communities were forced from their homes and into areas populated by their co-religionists. Out of this confused and bitter mob violence, in which the minority community was most at risk, the almost defunct Irish Republican Army emerged, phoenix-like to claim to defend the Catholic community. Within a few years its organizers and gunmen had created a formidable guerilla force that 15,000 British troops, 4,000 part-time locally recruited soldiers, and a vastly expanded police force were able to contain but not defeat.

In reaction to the beginnings of the IRA campaign the Northern Ireland government persuaded the British government to go along with a one-sided internment operation in which Catholics were indiscriminately imprisoned and Protestant extremists left virtually untouched. The result was greater Catholic sympathy for the IRA and increased guerilla recruitment and activity. With further deterioration in the law and order situation, especially after the army violence of Bloody Sunday in 1972, the British government assumed full powers in the province and suspended the Stormont government. Apart from one interlude in 1973–4, during which Protestant and Catholic politicians came together in a British government backed power-sharing arrangement which was ended by a loyalist general strike, the province has been ruled directly from Westminster.

There is a crucial contrast between the Northern Irish and Belgian situations at parallel moments of development. The Belgian economy was expanding fast enough to allow Walloons to accept that the Flemish thrust for jobs be met as education and aspirations combined to underline the Flemish demands. Whatever the objective situation might have been, Protestants in Northern Ireland did not believe that the new Catholic economic thrust could be met—without excessive strain on scarce resources. Moreover, Protestant fears were political as well as economic: they were afraid for the foundations of the state that they controlled. They were defending a state that they regarded as under siege by nationalists/Catholics from North and South—not for nothing did the 1690 siege of Derry as a symbol and its 'No Surrender!' slogan lie at the heart of their imagery. They wanted nothing that would cross or confuse lines. In consequence, the only place for Catholics who were by definition nationalist and subversive was outside. The trouble was that, though they were relatively marginal in terms of power and patronage, they were inside and utterly part of the province and were able to claim the legitimacy that history gave them among communities more than normally sensitive to the weight of history. From 1970 on an active minority of Catholics less and less accepted the legitimacy of the Northern Irish political community, especially when British politicians were drawn directly into the conflict as they tried to maintain the basic status quo of the Union. The nationalist struggle also turned more directly beyond the unionists on to the British army, the British government, and the British connection. At least up to 1981—the hunger strikes and the Fermanagh election may prove to have been a watershed—there was probably a Catholic majority for the union, at least in the negative sense that it was an easier and less unpredictable political and economic solution than a united Ireland. But there was too much nationalist nostalgia and too much resentment of military brutality in the Catholic community to dry up the supply of IRA recruits. Moreover, too many Catholics were afraid that if the violence stopped the Protestant politicians would, Bourbon-like, seek to restore Stormont and all that it had stood for and done. For that reason the Catholic community offered enough connivance to gunmen to make possible the milieu which guerillas needed for their operations. In short, two fears confronted one another: Protestants feared for the foundations of their community and power; and Catholics feared the injustice and bias of the distribution of power in the state in which they lived. In that sense the most embracing theory for explaining the Northern Irish conflict is that of the double minority—the Protestants are afraid because they are a minority in Ireland, while the Catholics are afraid because they are a minority within the existing Northern boundaries. It is such fears that in good measure generate hatred.

If the two main communities in Northern Ireland were socially distinctive in respect of one another and if they were in political and economic competition, it is also true that they were organized against one another. The main political arm of the Protestant community was the Unionist Party. Catholics were not welcomed in the party, even if they were unionists, and no Catholic ever held office under the Party. The Unionist Party itself was flanked, penetrated and supported by the Orange Order. This latter organization banded together a great proportion of the urban working class, farmer and farm labourer, and a significant minority of middle-class Protestants. It was ostentatiously anti-Catholic and mounted massive celebrations each year on the twelfth of July (and other dates as well) to commemorate the victory of the Protestant King William of Orange over the Catholic King James II at the battle of the Boyne in 1690. Nearly all Unionist MPs were members of the order in which working-class people could speak on a basis of equality with their social superiors. Many Protestant middle-class persons sought, however, to foster their economic interests through belonging to the Free Masons. Political and economic control wielded by government and the main Protestant organizations and informal networks ensured in a small-scale society that power and patronage remained in Protestant hands. Eloquent employment statistics were available to make this clear. Some Protestants saw value in discrimination or favour for Protestant job applicants as a way of forcing Catholic emigration, and many Catholics saw the policy in this light. It is the case that while Catholic births nearly matched Protestant births in absolute numbers, the population proportions in the province changed little over 50 years—though it should be noted that Catholic emigration, stemming from a weaker economic position, would have been higher than Protestant emigration even without discrimination.

Excluding themselves initially from the structure of the state Catholics not only confirmed Protestant fears of subversion but ensured that key groups like the police (the Royal Ulster Constabulary) would have few Catholic members. Moreover, once recruitment patterns were established they were inevitably resistant to change. Though Catholics gave up their parliamentary boycott with time and transformed an old fashioned nationalist party into the Social Democratic and Labour Party, which had a moderate socialist orientation and which tried to put the partition issue into parenthesis, Protestant fears were not assuaged. Finally, though there was no Catholic organization equivalent to the Orange Order, many smaller organizations, church linkages and education, and ghetto-dwelling maintained a relative unity in political attitudes among Catholics.

In short, Protestants feared political control and economic loss in an all-Ireland state; and they feared cultural and religious suffocation in a state where they believed that the Catholic church would exercise a dominant and oppressive influence. Catholics in their turn reacted against the loss of the nationalist birthright as fellow Irishmen gained freedom; and they resented discrimination and the stigma of second-class citizenship. Christian divisions brought inherited dislikes to bear on the problem, but the problem was not primarily religious.

Religion—as language in Belgium—only served to provide boundaries for a share-out that was inadequate for the members of the society. It also helped to sharpen antagonisms, but it took on political meaning only through secular competition and organization. Unlike the criss-crossing of interests of Belgian groups, there were, however, few such linkages in Ireland. Protestant and Catholic working classes were violently polarized in sentiment and even (this is true at least in the short run) in job interests. The Protestant industrial and commercial groups believed also that their economic interests lay entirely in union with Britain. To a lesser extent the Catholic middle classes believed this too, but for them it was in measure offset by unionist rejection as well as by elements of discrimination. The British social welfare state conciliated in a certain measure working class and unemployed Catholics. Catholic sentiments, however, remained unconciliated. It may not have been possible for the majority community to meet nationalist political demands, but its members made little effort to proffer economic or cultural conciliation. In consequence, Northern Irish society had a rift running down its middle. It could hold together during the social apathy of the slump in the 1930s and during the enthusiasm of economic growth in the early 1960s. It could not readily bear the faltering economy and bruised hopes of the late 1960s and the 1970s.

Nigeria: ethnicity, social change, and competition

Much of the Nigerian political development after 1950 cannot be understood without taking into account the growth of ethnic sentiment. The basic units of social identity in Nigeria are the traditional communities—villages, groupings of lineages, towns, district, emirates —which vary in size and shape with the social structures of the individual peoples. Within these communities an individual inherits his traditions, shares most deeply his fellowship, and seeks the esteem of his peers. The élite members of the communities were their opinion leaders, who guided their political decisions. These men—civil servants, local government officials, teachers, clerks, produce buyers, traders, building contractors, small industrialists, traditional title-holders—formed the bulk of the participants in and the audience for politics. Since these élite members functioned mostly in the modernizing sectors of society, where they had to cope with members of other ethnic groups and where community differentiation and representation was less important—if only for the reason that the number of educated persons from any single community tended to be small—they combined, once representative politics began, most easily amongst themselves along ethnic lines to protect and advance their interests. Hence, both the struggle for political power and the competition for jobs and contracts evoked ethnic alignments. The resulting inter-ethnic hostility tends to be called 'tribalism' in Nigeria.

Tribalism is the competitive struggle of the élite members of ethnic groups for the rewards of the modernizing sectors of society. All the strains of social change—and they are considerable—have served to embitter this competitive ethnic modernization. Only within their own ethnic groups did individuals reckon that they could safely predict the actions of others and find the co-operation with which to protect and promote their interests in an environment to some extent alien. One of the worst features of tribalism was that it led members of competing groups to see one another through unfavourable stereotypes, and so to dislike and distrust one another. Hardline tribalists constantly urged that decent conduct towards members of other groups was a form of weakness because the others, who acted badly as a matter of course, only took advantage of fair behaviour. Under these conditions a two-fold social morality developed: law/morality held only for relations within the group; outside the group only power relations existed. Inevitably ethnic lines hardened and lack of communication intensified ethnocentricity and deepened distrust.

The main tribalist conflict was carried on initially between the two large and rapidly modernizing Southern peoples, the Yoruba and the Ibo. The Yoruba had early taken to Western-style education, and had for long in the colonial era held most of the administrative and commercial posts open to Nigerians. The most developed of the Nigerian towns and the administrative and commercial capital, Lagos, was in Yoruba territory. The Ibo challenged the Yoruba quasimonopoly of posts from 1940 onwards. They displayed considerable energy; they gave every proof of understanding the role of formal education; and they adapted their traditions quickly and subtly to the requirements of a money economy. The Yoruba disliked the arrival of their Ibo competitors, resented their presence in a capital on Yoruba soil, and condemned them as alien and backward. The Ibo remained sensitive to this hostility of the people of the land. Attached to land even more than the Yoruba, they remained uneasily present on what, for all their nationalist logic, they kept on considering to be alien soil. And they could only hope to compensate for this hatred of the people of the land by making their gains in status and wealth.

The two worst periods of tribalist conflict between Ibo and Yoruba were the years between 1948 and 1952 and the years after 1964. In the first period, with the advent of elections, the political activists in the nationalist cause split largely along ethnic lines. The Action Group party, based dominantly in the Western Region, explicitly sought Yoruba backing and campaigned on an anti-Ibo platform. At the same time, with the effective opening up of the senior ranks of the public service to Nigerians, the educated élites battled to get in on the ground floor of an expanding public service that expatriates were beginning to leave. After this unpleasant encounter there was a lull. In politics the country's parties set about consolidating their hold on the federal regions they had taken over after the 1951 elections. Moreover, the emergence of the Northern People's Congress, whose leaders were allied to the emirs and who were committed to the protection of Hausa-Fulani and Kanuri traditional social structures, led the southern party leaders to realize belatedly that Northern traditionalists might benefit most from the gains of the nationalist movement. But wounds left by the 1950s clashes between the Yoruba and Ibo leaders kept on festering and were a decisive factor in preventing a Southern alliance from forming a federal Cabinet after the 1959 federal election. Instead, the Ibo-led NCNC joined with the NPC to form a federal coalition government. The two parties co-operated to dislodge the Action Group-controlled Western Region government in 1962. And during the suspension of the Western government they pushed through constitutional measures to enable the non-Yoruba minorities of the West to set up their own Mid Western Region.

The second tribalist flare-up began in 1964, once the Southern élite groups had divined that opportunities were closing up in the federal administration and public corporations and a scramble began for the last top posts. The same phenomenon occurred in the federal universities. Antagonism broke out openly to the point of student riots and staff manifestoes and counter-manifestoes when in 1965 a Lagos University board of trustees with a Yoruba majority arbitrarily replaced an Ibo Vice-Chancellor with a Yoruba. The conflict over this post was particularly intense because more than other posts the few university Vice-Chancellorships revealed how quickly top posts were being taken up and were about to be filled for a long time by comparatively young men. The general struggle between Yoruba and Ibo élite groups, whose numbers were increasing rapidly due to the growth of schools and universities, was exacerbated by the arrival on the scene of Northern contenders, whose entry to the public service and promotion were being facilitated by the Northern control of the federal government. Moreover, the NPC politicians had few scruples in advancing élite members of Northern minority peoples, who were proportionately and in absolute numbers more advanced in education than the Muslim peoples of the emirates. In this way a certain solidarity was created among the Northern élite, in spite of political hostility between the Hausa-Fulani and Kanuri-controlled regional government and most of the Middle Belt minority peoples.

The significance of these tribalist struggles was that they extended conflict far beyond the political realm and into spheres which made the inter-ethnic struggles tangible to the different élites in the loss and gain of status, roles, and money. In that sense the general Nigerian belief that tribalism was a phenomenon generated by politicians was a misleading simplification. The first military regime which succeeded the civilian politicians in January 1966 tended to accept this simplification and paid dearly for it. Political tribalism was only—the climatically inappropriate metaphor will be forgiven—the tip of the tribalist iceberg. These struggles, too, were taking a psychological toll on their participants. Individuals were growing weary of forms of competition whose rewards were considerable but whose cost in insecurity and bitterness was high. Yet the various élite groups might have gone on paying the price asked for their achievements but for the hazards of political change which caused the strains imposed on the Ibo élites to pass beyond what they reckoned to be the bounds of physical security and psychological endurance after the 1966 pogroms in the Northern Region, which were carried out mainly by the Hausa-Fulani. When this happened after the second military coup in July 1966, it became perfectly clear that Ibo bureaucrats who were lobbying for secession were at least as much socially marked by their conflict with the Yoruba as they were politically influenced by their hostility to the Hausa-Fulani. In a sense they were more deeply alienated from Lagos, though they stated more openly their aversion to Kaduna.

Were one to try and sum up the situation existing between the ethnic groups—and to some extent the communities—in Nigeria by the early 1960s, one might say that it came close to being a state of international relations between them. But the various groups were without the safeguards of genuine international relations because they lived within one state.

The British had forcibly united different nations and communities within the colonial boundaries. These groups were thus drawn together by a common administration, a shared set of laws, and a single currency; they expanded their economic relations with one another; and in the later stages of colonial rule they built up a certain unity as they collaborated against the colonial administrators to hasten the advent of independence. But they did not have time enough nor were communications between them good enough for the different groups to become integrated into a political system of strong common identity and trust. While the British stayed, there was an arbiter who, partial though he might be on occasion, was accepted as ready to prevent extreme exploitation of any people or community. After independence the communities had to live together alone and accept a federal logic in which the central and regional government could to some extent act on each community in determining roles, deciding facilities, and allocating rewards. The federal system was designed to offer political safeguards to the three largest peoples. But developments subsequent to independence, in particular the suppression of the Western Region government, led all groups to doubt the efficacy of those safeguards. And the federal system left unconciliated minority peoples in each region who considered themselves discriminated against by the regional governments and who were substantial enough in numbers not to have their claims to regional self-determination entirely disregarded.

Since considerable tensions existed between the communities, it is in some ways surprising that the unity of Nigeria went unchallenged— or relatively unchallenged—as long as it did. Various reasons explain this lack of challenge: the remnant of nationalist ideology left over from the independence movement; the ruling groups were willing to employ the coercive power of the state against any single group that sought to break away from the political community; and no substantial set of élite groups had yet concluded that it had become impossible for them to achieve their particular interests within the Nigerian state. Understandably in those circumstances the first violent challenge to the political system was made to political authority in the first 1966 coup that overthrew the civilian government and not to political community. But once the first break took place, Pandora's box was open. Before long worsening relations between the peoples led to political community being challenged as well as authority. The violent break in constitutional development, the fear of an international system without safeguards, and the socio-psychological traumas of modernizing change combined to worsen relations between different peoples and to shake the unity of the country.

In other words, if the central government (and to a lesser extent the regional governments) could maintain stability and unity by conciliating élites and communities through its allocation of roles and rewards and preserve order under certain circumstances through its control of coercive power, it could also provoke dissent among those groups who considered that they had not been conciliated. In post-independence Nigeria each group that was dissatisfied with its access to central and/ or regional power felt alienated. Also, there was no group that did not think it was being dominated at one time or another by another group and did not seethe with consequent resentment. In the alienation there were sentiments of hurt pride, concern for the integrity of local traditions, fear of utilitarian interests being harmed, and resentment of real or imagined injustice. But more corrosive than anything else was the distrust of the intentions of other groups. The post-coup developments brought out with great clarity the correlation of dissent and distrust.

By 1965 the Nigerian political system had reached an impasse. Formal political opposition continued from the rump of the Yoruba Action Group. But nearly all Southerners were dissatisfied with Northern domination, and there was talk of Southern secession. When trouble came, it was sparked off in late 1965 by a rigged election in the Western Region, when the federal government connived with the Yoruba NNDP (an anti-Action Group Yoruba party) to keep the latter in power. Populist disorders broke out in the West: law and order broke down in the face of riots, robberies, and murders. In January 1966 an army revolt overthrew the federal and regional governments. An army regime then set about creating a unitary political system to avoid the regionalist mistakes of the past. This move alienated the North, including the Middle Belt peoples who made up the rank and file of the army. An army split in July 1966 overthrew the Ibo-led army command. The Ibo officers who formed two-thirds of the officer corps were either killed or obliged to flee. A Northern officer from the Middle Belt, Yakubu Gowon, took over control of the army. Those Ibo officers and men who had fled formed an Eastern army under the Eastern military governor, Colonel Ojukwu. He, moreover, used his control of the regional administration to put his region into a state of virtual secession. There had been a massacre of Ibo in May 1966. This May massacre, the army killings, and a second massacre of Ibo in September 1966 united Ibo intelligentsia and common people alike in a desire to secede from Nigeria. By this time also Ibo leaders had concluded that the secession of the Eastern Region would enable them to control the lion's share of the growing oil revenues of the country. Secession, in consequence, seemed to provide a route to both security and prosperity. However, it was unfortunately the case that the Eastern Region contained minority peoples who made up almost two-fifths of the population and who were violently opposed to a secession that removed federal protection from them in their struggle against Ibo control. Moreover, nearly all the oil was to be found on minority territory or off their shores.

A constitutional conference in September 1966 revealed that the Far Northern Hausa-Fulani, Kanuri, and Fulani groups wanted to break up the Nigerian federation. So did a large part of the Yoruba political leadership. The Ibo leadership obviously did. The minority peoples who saw that break up would leave them under the heel of a single dominant people in each region were opposed to the break. They were supported by most members of the central bureaucracy. They also got support from the Edo groups who made up most of the Mid-Western Region—the latter feared a takeover bid from stronger neighbours in the event of a fragile independence. The minorities' crucial strength was that they controlled the federal army. They argued at the constitutional conference for a renewed federation with an enlarged number of state units. Once they saw that the federation was not going to break up easily, the Ibo leadership declared a unilateral independence and set up the Republic of Biafra in May 1967. Civil war broke out and lasted until 1970. It ended in Ibo defeat after great losses of life in the fighting and the hardships of blockade.

Gowon, the federal leader, ensured that the aftermath of the war saw few recriminations or reprisals. He also put into full effect the decision to break the Northern Region into six regions or states. The increasing oil revenues which were augmented greatly after the OPEC price rises of the 1970s enabled generally rising standards of living and the increased administrative costs of the new states to be funded. Constitutional changes also gave resources to the federal centre as against the states. At the same time the greater number of states facilitated the federal centre's growth in power. Overheating of the economy by 1975, however, created galloping inflation as well as provoking labour and student troubles. Gowon was overthrown in a palace coup. The successor regime was sensitive to the unpopularity of army rule and promised a return to civilian government. After a new constitution had been worked out and more states created (19 in all) a civilian regime took over in 1979. Ethnicity provided the organizational principle in Nigerian politics as it did in Belgium—though the use of a neutral language, English, prevented the indigenous languages from being an issue. The independence version of the Nigerian federation had enabled the three large peoples to take control of the three regions, reduce the other peoples of the regions to a position of political subjection, and left the centre little more than a collection of regional representatives. At one stage it looked as if organizational forms, in particular the regionally based parties and administrations, would lead to the break up of the country. There were, however, factors that balanced the fission-tendencies of the large peoples. First, the minority peoples held on to the federation as their sole protection. Second, the federal bureaucrats, as well as the Lagos-based and Western region intelligentsia, judged that their interests lay with the federation. Third, the army was mostly made up of minorities. In the event the minority groups, allied with those groups with federal interests, used the organizational apparatus and resources of the federal state to hold it together. The constitutional outcome of the debate and the negotiations preceding civilian rule set out to create a strong centre, more numerous small states that both catered for various ethnic groups and were too weak to be able to challenge the centre, and political parties that could seek central power only by allying many ethnic groups together. Finally, when the new civilian regime, set up in 1979, floundered into incompetence and corruption, suffered a drop in government revenues from falling oil prices, and was overthrown in the mid-1980s by another army coup, the challenge was to authority rather than community. It seems now that it is the shadow of pretorianism rather than secession or breakup that hangs over Nigeria.

3. FACTORS BUILT INTO CONFRONTATION

The previous section set out to provide three case studies. In each case the description was broadly—and hopefully not over-rigidly—structured around a problematic social contrast, competition/opposition in the context of social change, and the relative presence or absence of organization around the contrasting social saliencies during that change. What this section sets out to do in its first part is to take five features which serve to specify and/or condition the nature of social competition in such cases. In other words, while this paper tries to explain further the three countries described, it also seeks in this section, as in the first section (all in drawing on the second section), to suggest comparative factors that may be looked for and considered in order to see their impact on the present three situations and other similar situations.

(a) *Structural factors*

1. *Relative population size and rates of demographic increase*: The Flemish determination to challenge Walloon social and economic dominance drew great strength from the realization that they outnumbered Walloons in the Belgian state and that their higher birth rate was strengthening their numerical superiority. At the same time they knew that through linguistic seepage many more Flemish became French-speaking than did Walloons become Flemish-speaking—the latter number was negligible. For that reason the Flemish-speaking leaders consistently opposed the publication of linguistic censuses. This refusal helped them to consolidate the accepted linguistic frontier but weakened their case for overall control of the Belgian state. In the event both communities accepted a social rather than a mathematically demographic equality between them. As the Flemish grew more satisfied with administrative and economic gains they drew back from stressing their numerical superiority, at least in public. The outcome left the state awkwardly and evenly divided. Yet the state had a built-in conciliation process on a crucial issue.

In the original Nigerian federation large ethnic groups dominated in each region—the Hausa-Fulani in the North, the Yoruba in the West, and the Ibo in the East. When the fourth region, the Mid West, was created in 1964 it was mostly Edo and in good measure avoided ethnic, though not communal (in the sense of local communities) politics. Initially, numbers played a crucial role in Nigerian politics. The Northern Region was reckoned by the 1952 census to have had more inhabitants than the other regions added together. As party politics and voting got under way the Hausa-Fulani, and allied groups like the Kanuri, used the regional administration of federal elections, the control of patronage, and the manipulation of the courts to beat down opponents and to establish a majority control over the lower and more powerful parliamentary Chamber. The other regions hoped that the 1962 census would eliminate, or at the very least reduce, the Northern population estimates. That census, and a subsequent census a year later (and a much later census again in 1973), was falsified because each part of the country inflated its numbers. Northern dominance seemed to be established indefinitely and could not be challenged through the ballot-box. The frustration ensuing on the census debacles and controversies of the 1960s was no small factor in leading to the 1966 coup.

One other feature of the Nigerian population proportions needs mentioning. The two largest Southern élite groups, the Ibo and the Yoruba, who were rapidly modernizing through formal education, fought bitterly with one another for posts and patronage and detested one another. They also looked over their shoulder at the Hausa-Fulani, who had come to education late but who were beginning to insist on their right to posts and promotions. Yet all three groups in good measure ignored small groups like the Idoma and the Itsekiri, who had done well in jobs and who were disproportionately well entrenched in the public services and business. Because the absolute numbers of these groups were small they could be discounted. Yet the evolution of Nigerian politics was not only to break up the Northern political monolith so as to get rid of the imbalance of a federation in which one unit was larger than the rest added together, but also to break up the three large groups themselves among different federal units or states and to let nearly all the larger minority groups have their own states. In the process the whole balance of the Nigerian state was changed: the fear of dominating groups was greatly reduced; and power was much more widely spread.

In the Northern Ireland case study the fears of the Protestant community over the higher Catholic birth rate were mentioned. Protestants saw the higher rate as linked to Catholic anti-contraception stands. In real truth there was—and is—probably a greater connection with lower Catholic incomes than with doctrinal convictions. One fearful possibility in the event of conciliation continuing to fail is that following on from a seemingly precarious demographic majority Protestants may agree to a repartition of Northern Ireland in which mainly Catholic areas move to the Republic of Ireland. Protestants could then consolidate the smaller enclave in which they would have a proportionately larger majority and would be able to hope for its eventual full integration into the United Kingdom. Catholics who see time on their side tend to be more opposed to repartition. It would in any case be a solution that ran the risk of population shifts and much human suffering.

Overall the conclusion seems to be that demography may add crucially to a conflict situation where groups are polarized and are equal or potentially equal in numbers. The existence of more than two groups seems to help in creating a more peaceful equilibrium—provided that alliances are not so formed as to create a new polarization. Yet in situations where there is no endemic conflict such numbers may play no significant role—Switzerland is an example here.

2. *Values of tolerance*: Some societies do seem to have a greater level of political and other forms of tolerance than others. The Western democracies have been better than most countries in tolerating political dissent—though the latter has in recent times mostly not threatened the existing political systems. There seems to be some evidence of a reasonable level of tolerance in Belgium. The Nigerian evidence is more ambivalent. Once the Nigerian system became more ethnically pluralist there seems, however, to have been a growth in tolerance, that is, in the capacity to accept political differences or rivalry. The Northern Ireland majority community has a poor record of tolerance—the minority community has had few opportunities of showing its real face on the matter. What history suggests is that tolerance is very much the social outcome of periods of basic agreement in societies rather than the reverse. But it is also on occasion the outcome of a situation where groups know they will continue to live with or alongside one another and where they have realistically accepted that dominance is not a sensible objective in the wake of inconclusive conflict.

3. *Distribution of political power*: This factor is closely linked with the former. It has explicitly or implicitly been discussed at some length in the case studies. Where there is trust or confidence in a state, power distribution is not critical—Catholics in Britain are under-represented in British Cabinets but make nothing of the fact. The opposite is the case in Northern Ireland. In Belgium activists resolved a problem of a relative lack of confidence by having equal numbers in a Cabinet as well as allied arrangements. The Nigerian system did not reach relative stability until the domination of large groups or close alliances of groups were eliminated. In fact, the civilian Nigerian Cabinet had to

have a representative from each state; and the military governments have followed the same pattern. Perhaps the most important remark that might be made in this connection is that in a period of rapid social change people seem to prefer to have governments that distribute goods fairly rather than governments that claim to foster rapid economic growth; and representation in government is seen as basic to access to power and patronage.

4. *Access to the economic rewards of society*: In countries where a disproportionate amount of goods comes through the state (or in a developing country where a disproportionate amount of the goods of the modernizing sector comes through the state), competition for political power can easily become envenomed. In other cases where a group without political control but which makes economic gains that are greater (or look disproportionately greater) than those of others with more political power there can be grave dangers to peace. The Ibo in Nigeria, the Chinese in Indonesia, and the Bengali in Burma are among those who have suffered bitter persecution in such situations. In Northern Ireland the economic weakness of the minority, together with a sense of resentment against discrimination, served to produce alienation and to underpin conflict. Without going as far as conflict Oriental Jews in Israel, who now make up most of the population, carry a similar sense of deprivation. The most horrific examples of economic discrimination against majorities, however, occur in Latin America and in South Africa. Finally, it should be said that economic discrimination —whether along social class or any other lines—does not feed into political conflict until deprived groups are sensitized or have their consciousness raised by other developments, notably but not exclusively by the spread of education.

5. *Pace and patterns of social change*: Social change tends to create insecurity for individuals and groups because it upsets established patterns in society. Predictability, and in consequence, trust suffers. So does communication. All this is sharpened if change brings new forms of group competition or alters the status of some groups for the worse. In each case study we saw the pace and patterns of social change become a factor in creating a worsening conflict. In fact, a model of change in plural communities may well embrace the following scenario: competition organized around ethnicity/language/religion/ colour/caste changes received relations and creates unpredictability; in the process communication breaks down between groups and stereo- typing becomes easily possible; and confidence is harmed, dragging in

fear and creating dislikes that can turn into hatred. Finally, a point that needs to be made is that the factors that we have been considering—demographic, political, economic, and social change—most often go together. When they do, they tend to reinforce divisive effects. The worst situations are those in which siege societies—Lebanese Maronites, Sinhalese, Sri Lankans, South African whites, and Northern Irish unionists—develop.

(b) *Immediate factors in a conflict situation*

Where this section differs from the previous section is that it deals less with objective factors than with epistemological and psychological factors that condition relations between groups where the objective factors already dealt with—and others—operate. This latter set of factors, conditioning ways of knowing and reaching deep into emotions, grows out of structural relations. These factors also prolong confrontation built into structural situations, often in a vicious spiral of accumulating bitterness.

1: *Inter-group relations*

(*i*) *threat to possessions* Economic threats to possessions or prospects may be real but often they are more perceived than real. Moreover, in situations like the Northern Irish or the Nigerian, a sense of deprivation that sees justice affronted or the 'rules of the game' broken impedes forms of economic growth that would benefit all groups in the longer run. In particular, where gains are being newly made by groups—like the Flemish, Northern Irish Catholics, or all the Nigerian groups—such groups hold their gains with psychological fragility and react oversensitively to any challenge, no matter how legitimate. In these situations it is crucial that justice not only be done but be obviously seen to be done, and even that almost always will not be enough. Having said that, Belgium offers a good example of a country where economic growth has served to offset a considerable degree of economic competition and cultural bitterness.

Often the crucial psychological factor in political threats is that groups regard those who rule over them as doing so illegitimately. Legitimacy is a complex notion. For practical purposes, however, it can be said to be made up of two components: acceptance that the right persons are ruling and that they are ruling rightly (efficiently and justly). Terminal colonial rule was especially challenged on the issue of the 'right persons'. Here lies the roots of the desire for freedom and independence. Where both elements of legitimacy are missing, a festering resentment and eventual challenge to either political authority or political community or to both are almost certain to emerge. Northern Ireland and Nigeria have experienced such challenges to the full.

The precise meaning of what constitutes a cultural threat in this context is often relatively vague in its broad definition. It may, however, be extremely precise in the minds of those concerned. Outsiders may perceive little religious difference between Northern Irish Christians. Yet Northern Protestants fear incorporation into a united Ireland in which in their view Catholic clerics and Catholic values would exercise undue influence: incorporation would bring mental and moral damage. The present-day easy acceptance of Irish nationhood by Southern Protestants makes no impression on Northerners. In Belgium, while the Flemish reject linguistic Frenchification for their children as an approach that demeans their cultural dignity, Walloons who perceive Flemish as a language of a coarse petite-bourgeoisie and peasantry reject Flemish mono-lingualism for their children (or more likely their grandchildren) as a form of cultural stultification. Such stultification is considered to involve cruder linguistic conceptualization, restricted literary heritage, and inhibited access to an outside world. Walloons for long largely ignored the cultural wealth of the Dutch nation, which they respected as much next door in Holland as in Belgium they condemned the Flemish who shared the same language as the Dutch. This situation has, however, changed as membership of the European Community has softened ethnic ethos and as requirements for public service positions have led Walloon parents to motivate their children in the learning of Flemish/Dutch. In Northern Nigeria, Muslims claim to perceive threats to their religion in a secular Nigeria and take little notice of how easily and freely Western Nigerian Muslims have lived under the same conditions. These reactions should never be underestimated since they often outweigh more rational calculations of interest.

(*ii*) *communication* The breakdown of communication in the stress of competition and social change has already been referred to. This lack of communication is, however, not merely negative but is often compounded by reactions such as aesthetic revulsion, clashing ideologies, differing languages, and double-talk. Walloons constantly cite Voltaire's remark: 'Flemish is not a tongue, it is only a sore throat'. Differing languages create real obstacles to the inter-personal present-ation of a common humanity. Language is so much the person that where normal linguistic intercourse is not possible not only is communication hampered but humanity is perceived in a partial, and hence often diminished, way. Above all, what is most pernicious in a competitive/conflict situation is that the groups use double-talk: one form of language and even set of words for in-group communication and another (more antiseptic and anodynely inoffensive) for the out-group. In consequence, it is difficult, whether in Northern Ireland, Nigeria, or Belgium, to hold upright private conversations in mixed gatherings, difficult to discuss honest differences, and difficult to believe that others are straightforward in communication (not least because each group is conscious of the limited integrity of the face it itself presents). It takes gifted language or gestures, high integrity, and a relatively favourable conjecture of circumstances to overcome these problems.

(*iii*) *confidence* In reflecting on the difficulty of communication, the breakdown or trust of confidence has already entered as a factor. The trouble is that good communication and existing confidence enable confidence to be deepened, whereas their lack impedes its develop-ment. Moreover, those members of a group who seek to build confidence by offering accommodation find often that opponents see such efforts as weakness rather than conciliation, while supporters see the same efforts as betrayal rather than statesmanship. O'Neill and Faulkner both suffered this fate in Northern ireland and the SDLP party is constantly hampered by such perceptions. Dealing with this problem takes all the gifts and circumstances that creative communi-cation, which is closely linked to it as a problem, requires. Not for nothing have peace theorists in issues ranging from community relations with the police to relations between the super powers discussed the necessity for confidence-building measures.

2: *Community and wholeness*

(*i*) *impurity reaction* Where groups recognize boundaries and are forced to accept that persons of other groups exist within those boundaries there is a temptation, especially where a group is in a majority and believes that a region properly or rightly belongs to them—in the sense of land cultivation or urban construction—to reject an opposition group as sullying the community. Inevitably the image of the community that is sullied is an idealized one; and it is usually also built into highly interpretative historical accounts. The Orange symbol of unviolated or unsurrendered Londonderry as the 'maiden city' is typical of the symbolism of such communal views. Conversely, Irish nationalism with its concept of sacred territory ('holy Ireland') sees Protestants as interlopers. One of the consequences of such views is that the majority (Protestants in Northern Ireland and Gaelic nationalists in the whole island) refuse to negotiate with those perceived as 'outsiders'. It is difficult for persons to treat fully or properly with those who appear to break the symmetry or wholeness of community. Yet such persons (Northern Ireland or the island of Ireland are no exceptions) are not likely to go away—unless they are driven terribly away as Ibo were in Northern Nigeria. The lack of sentiment around the artificially created Belgian state has avoided the worst of this problem in Belgium.

(*ii*) *stereotyping* Where impurity reactions exist, where competition is excessive, and where communication breaks down stereotyping creeps in. Thus: 'Catholics are dirty', 'Ibo are greedy', 'Flemish are crude', 'Walloons are superficial and unreliable'. Research on the stereotypes of black Americans among Southern Whites joins with an historical record that reaches back into the European Middle Ages (not least describing 'demons') and is flanked by similar reactions throughout the world. The problem with stereotyping is that it cramps the ability of persons to receive accurate perceptions of other persons and groups by concentrating on undesirable characteristics. In the process the humanity of others is reduced. It is then easier to deny justice to those of diminished humanity than to those whose humanity and, in consequence, deprivation would have to be fully recognized. At worst such persons are regarded as pariah, dangerous and privileged pariah, and legitimate objects of killing as has happened to Ibo in Nigeria, Jews in Europe, and Chinese in Indonesia. It takes the greatness of a Gandhi to cope with stereotyping and to turn 'untouchables' into 'harrijans'; and even Gandhi had limited success.

(*iii*) *organization on competitive lines* This section does not need to add to the opening section that dealt with organization. It is enough here to remark on the divisiveness that exists where impurity reactions, stereotypes, and confrontation organization reinforce one another in conflict relations within one political or social entity.

4. BROKERAGE AND PROCESS

(a) *Brokerage*

The crucial concept in this last section of the paper is brokerage. Brokerage includes components of mediation, suggestions of conciliation, capacities to move with more than one side and, above all, an ability to identify the interests of different groups and common interests. Not the least part of brokerage is to seek to work within an existing situation rather than to try to change a situation too directly or too quickly or to postpone a search for accord until conditions have become entirely favourable.

1: *Normality and fear*

In divided societies, individuals and groups are usually afraid, especially in those areas of life that are part of the conflict. It is important to acknowledge this fear and the distortion of perception that it brings. But it is even more important to retain the conviction of common or normal humanity. Political murders mar the Northern Ireland scene. But before the present flareup there were fewer murders or any kind of violent crime in that province than elsewhere in the United Kingdom. Nigerian Hausaland where Ibo were slaughtered is one of the least policed and most peaceful parts of the world. It is important to know what fear does to ordinary human beings and at the same time to retain the conviction of the presence and worth of common humanity.

(*i*) *translation* To overcome a lack of knowledge of other groups is always a contribution. Moreover, it is essential to the elimination or reduction of stereotyping. Nigeria lost much in not using its radio services to build a knowledge of groups across ethnic boundaries. Similarly, Northern Ireland's Protestants have lost much in not having better used their schooling and broadcasting systems to provide access to Irish history, including their own history. Belgians are greatly divided by the differing languages of their media. Simplistic if well-intentioned public descriptions of other groups—which sometimes verge on the double-talk of a conflict situation—may do more harm than good. But there is no alternative to good explanation and to accurate description and honest discussion. It is much better that differences be acknowledged than suppressed or avoided. It is better that differences remain after discussion, even after good information has highlighted them, than to have a gentleman's agreement to ignore differences or conflicts of interest.

(*ii*) *leadership and confidence* If group hostilities are to be transcended leaders will at some stage have to emerge who are less wounded than others by fear, who are better able to take the stresses of change, and who are more open to human meeting and common concerns. In other words, such leaders need to be persons of confidence, courage, and vision. In actual reality people will not exist who conform to this pure model. Rather is it that societies require persons who more or less adequately possess those qualities. Such persons have to be able to reassure their own groups as they lead them towards change; and they have in some measure to be able to reach out to opposing groups. There will be times when circumstances prove too adverse for even the best leaders. Yet without persons of calibre, historically or economically adverse circumstances will pull groups away from one another. In multi-ethnic situations such persons often emerge from minority groups—Gowon in Nigeria or Nyerere in Tanzania. Such persons emerge with greater difficulty in a confrontation situation between two groups only.

Perhaps in a polarized duality the best hope is a lot of middling and muddling leaders with earthy canniness and no excessive commitment to ideological positions. The Belgians have consistently produced such leaders. The weakness of the Northern Irish situation has been the absence of such leaders on both sides, perhaps particularly on the Protestant side, where there appears more to lose and where a frightened siege outlook has been ever ready to reject those, like O'Neill and Faulkner, who might cross or blur lines.

(*iii*) *convergence of interests* Where conflict is total, politics or social competition is seen as a zero-sum game: one in which a gain is necessarily a loss to, and at the expense of, another or others. Unfortunately, underlying Protestant attitudes in Northern Ireland is a fear that a redistribution of goods in society to meet Catholic demands can be made only at Protestant expense. At several phases of Nigerian development such attitudes also prevailed. In the last resort this problem may well be rooted in the constitutional structures of society or in its social and economic arrangements. There are several ways of facing up to it as a problem. First, it may be possible for groups whose interests cross divisions to press such interests. Bureaucrats did this in Nigeria. Political, economic, and administrative groups, especially but not exclusively those linked to Brussels, have performed the same function in Belgium. Few Catholics have appeared among equivalent groups in Northern Ireland. Second, groups may find that their interests criss-cross to prevent polarization: Belgium again offers an excellent example. In Northern Ireland Catholic middle-class groups were beginning to share such interests with the Protestant middle classes in the 1960s. But disruption occurred before sharing had been consolidated and common interests thoroughly recognized. Third, groups may find that their own interests converge. This happened in Nigeria when the minority groups discovered on the eve of the country's dissolution that they could best protect their interests only within the federation. Almost all the Nigerian groups except the Ibo came round to this view. What is needed in most countries where hostile attitudes are organized around particular social saliencies is to work out constitutional and other devices that lead groups to accept that their interests can be adequately, if relatively, secured; that their fears of loss or oppression can be set at rest; and that their cultural identity can be preserved. Belgian structural devices for linguistic assemblies whose membership overlaps with the Belgian parliament, informal quotas in the Cabinet and elsewhere, and equal recognition for both languages in the public services have enabled Flemish and Walloon interests to be conciliated. Again, the new nineteen-state structure in Nigeria, a strong but not overriding federal centre, and governments that are obliged to rely on widespread ethnic alliances, have established a fragile but real unity in the Nigerian state which has survived the fall of the civilian presidency. The one serious attempt to do something like this in Northern Ireland was the power-sharing Assembly and the introduction of proportional representation. Since then nothing else like it has been tried and there has been too little peace. At some stage if there are to be enduring moves towards peace, or at least towards isolating those geared to conflict, both communities in Northern Ireland will have to decide that conciliation and concessions which involve apparent immediate loss to some interests are likely to be the only way of protecting and furthering general interests in the long run. The recent Anglo-Irish Agreement, which has accepted the existence of two communities and the roles of two governments, has so far had limited success, mainly because the unionist community felt affronted by it. It may be necessary to find other agreed ways forward, but they are likely to be ways that take in the essentials of this Agreement.

(b) *Structures, interests, and the primacy of process*

By way of conclusion to this paper I want to make two general points. The first focuses on objective structures and interests. The second suggests the primacy of process.

1: *Structures and interests*

Situations in which groups and persons recognize that their interests are not incompatible with one another and may even be identical or complementary are crucial to avoiding conflict. Where there is objective conflict of interest—as in Northern Ireland, where religion has been used to allocate societal resources unevenly, or South Africa, where colour has been used to the same purpose—there is usually little hope of avoiding conflict, whatever about less immediate prospects. In this sense theories of mediation that lay exclusive stress on generosity or explaining groups to one another as relatively complete approaches to peace are—it seems to me—quite mistaken. Peace depends on a reconciliation of economic interests, historical sentiments, and ideological values, but especially on reconciling economic interests. One does not have to be a Marxist to observe that seldom do economic and political power remain at any great distance from one another. Moreover, economic interests are the meat of politics and sentiments the sauce. For a period the sauce may drown the taste of the meat but never for too long.

To put the previous paragraph into other words, and to add some nuances: groups are more likely to live in peace with one another in societies where their political and economic interests do not clash and where constitutional or other structures do not provoke competition among such interests or produce clashes of sentiment. Furthermore, peace is more likely in such societies and situations than in societies and situations where there may be greater individual integrity among leaders and people or higher levels of individual peacefulness or again greater mediation efforts by insiders or outsiders. The contrast between Belfast's low non-political murder rate (as compared with, for example, Glasgow's) and higher political murder rate illustrates this contention. Put in another way: there is more likely to be peace where social and structural temptations to violate it do not exist than in a situation where integrity ventures into or is obliged to venture into temptation. In other words again, integrity on a social level as on an individual level is maintained by avoiding temptation rather than by being strong in temptation.

2: *Process and solutions*

There is a definition of politics that can be given a cynical or pessimistic twist: politics is the art of the possible. Obviously, politics cannot achieve the impossible, but the impossible should not be too quickly defined in politics. In other words, honest, strong, and realistic efforts can stretch the possible. For that reason another less well-known definition makes more operational sense: politics consists of finding immediate solutions to problems that are ultimately unsolvable. There is never quite enough to go around within states, but politics has to seek to make it go round with as little dissatisfaction or injustice as possible. There may be conflicting ideologies in states in rapid change in our global-village world, but the function of politics is to enable their proponents to work together with as little friction as possible; in multi-ethnic states there are divergent cultural traditions and sentiments, but the function of politics is to help groups to realize that to be different is not to be better or worse but to be other—but hopefully complementary. In effect, what has been said is that in conflict situations there is need not for solutions but for process—process of a kind that accepts that no immediate solutions are available to intractable human problems but that seeks to confine, reduce, or avoid conflict and to construct structures that enable groups to reconcile interests in continuing and often adjusting ways. Much of the success of Belgian politics in the face of differing linguistic traditions and usage comes from the way that Belgians have accepted compromise solutions that never pretended to be definitive. Nigerians have learnt from the imbalance of the First Republic and the calamitous confrontation of the civil war to seek to keep a process going as newly politically conscious groups come on the political scene and as the old dominant groups are obliged to realize that they have to protect their interests in ways different from those of the past. In Northern Ireland less than in most conflict areas are ready solutions available. At least the merit of the Anglo-Irish Agreement is that it modestly confines itself to process. What is needed are brokers who come mostly, though not entirely, from the province itself; who can convince Protestants that Catholic politics is not necessarily subversive; who can convince Protestants and Catholics alike that the Irish Republic could not, and in any case would not, take on the economic and security problems of the North or want the political disequilibrium of an entirely new set of voters; and who can, finally, persuade Catholics and Protestants that their common interests lie in negotiating directly with one another and in sharing political and economic power, whatever the name given to the practice.

In short, the comparative experience and lessons of our case studies suggest that, while there may be no solutions, there is hope in a process that seeks to eliminate or ameliorate conflict-laden structures, wrests reluctant compromises out of groups, and lets them learn that all interests are ultimately better protected in not seeking to protect immediately every interest. In the last resort, however, every situation is individual. Also, if there is a science of politics, there is an art of governing and politicking. But there are comparative considerations that can throw light on the individual situations, and not least on how conciliation can be brought to bear on conflict.

APPENDIX

AGREEMENT
BETWEEN THE GOVERNMENT OF THE UNITED KINGDOM OF GREAT BRITAIN AND NORTHERN IRELAND AND THE GOVERNMENT OF THE REPUBLIC OF IRELAND

The Government of the United Kindom of Great Britain and Northern Ireland and the Government of the Republic of Ireland;

Wishing further to develop the unique relationship between their peoples and the close co-operation between their countries as friendly neighbours and as partners in the European Community;

Recognising the major interest of both their countries and, above all, of the people of Northern Ireland in diminishing the divisions there and achieving lasting peace and stability;

Recognising the need for continuing efforts to reconcile and to acknowledge the rights of the two major traditions that exist in Ireland, represented on the one hand by those who wish for no change in the present status of Northern Ireland and on the other hand by those who aspire to a sovereign united Ireland achieved by peaceful means and through agreement;

Reaffirming their total rejection of any attempt to promote political object-ives by violence or the threat of violence and their determination to work together to ensure that those who adopt or support such methods do not succeed;

Recognising that a condition of genuine reconciliation and dialogue between unionists and nationalists is mutual recognition and acceptance of each other's rights;

Recognising and respecting the identities of the two communities in Northern Ireland, and the right of each to pursue its aspirations by peaceful and constitutional means;

Reaffirming their commitment to a society in Northern Ireland in which all may live in peace, free from discrimination and intolerance, and with the opportunity for both communities to participate fully in the structures and processes of government;

Have accordingly agreed as follows:

A

STATUS OF NORTHERN IRELAND

ARTICLE 1

The two Governments

(a) affirm that any change in the status of Northern Ireland would only come about with the consent of a majority of the people of Northern Ireland;

(b) recognise that the present wish of a majority of the people of Northern Ireland is for no change in the status of Northern Ireland;

(c) declare that, if in the future a majority of the people of Northern Ireland clearly wish for and formally consent to the establishment of a united Ireland, they will introduce and support in the respective Parliaments legislation to give effect to that wish.

B

THE INTERGOVERNMENTAL CONFERENCE

ARTICLE 2

(a) There is hereby established, within the framework of the Anglo-Irish Intergovernmental Council set up after the meeting between the two heads of Government on 6 November 1981, an Intergovernmental Conference (hereinafter referred to as "the Conference"), concerned with Northern Ireland and with relations between the two parts of the island of Ireland, to deal, as set out in this Agreement, on a regular basis with:

    (i) political matters;

    (ii) security and related matters;

    (iii) legal matters, including the administration of justice;

    (iv) the promotion of cross-border co-operation.

(b) The United Kingdom Government accept that the Irish Government will put forward views and proposals on matters relating to Northern Ireland within the field of activity of the Conference in so far as those matters are not the responsibility of a devolved administration in Northern Ireland. In the interest of promoting peace and stability, determined efforts shall be made through the Conference to resolve any differences. The Conference will be mainly concerned with Northern Ireland; but some of the matters under consideration will involve co-operative action in both parts of the island of Ireland, and possibly also in Great Britain. Some of the proposals considered in respect of Northern Ireland may also be found to have application by the Irish Government. There is no derogation from the sovereignty of either the United Kingdom Government or the Irish Government, and each retains responsibility for the decisions and administration of government within its own jurisdiction.

ARTICLE 3

The Conference shall meet at Ministerial or official level, as required. The business of the Conference will thus receive attention at the highest level. Regular and frequent Ministerial meetings shall be held; and in particular special meetings shall be convened at the request of either side. Officials may meet in subordinate groups. Membership of the Conference and of sub-groups shall be small and flexible. When the Conference meets at Ministerial level the Secretary of State for Northern Ireland and an Irish Minister designated as the Permanent Irish Ministerial Representative shall be joint Chairmen. Within the framework of the Conference other British and Irish Ministers may hold or attend meetings as appropriate: when legal matters are under consideration the Attorneys General may attend. Ministers may be accompanied by their officials and their professional advisers: for example, when questions of security policy or security co-operation are being discussed, they may be accompanied by the Chief Constable of the Royal Ulster Constabulary and the Commissioner of the Garda Siochana; or when questions of economic or social policy or co-operation are being discussed, they may be accompanied by officials of the relevant Departments. A Secretariat shall be established by the two Governments to service the Conference on a continuing basis in the discharge of its functions as set out in this Agreement.

ARTICLE 4

(a) In relation to matters coming within its field of activity, the Conference shall be a framework within which the United Kingdom Government and the Irish Government work together

   (i) for the accommodation of the rights and identities of the two traditions which exist in Northern Ireland; and

   (ii) for peace, stability and prosperity throughout the island of Ireland by promoting reconciliation, respect for human rights, co-operation against terrorism and the development of economic, social and cultural co-operation.

(b) It is the declared policy of the United Kingdom Government that responsibility in respect of certain matters within the powers of the Secretary of State for Northern Ireland should be devolved within Northern Ireland on a basis which would secure widespread acceptance throughout the community. The Irish government support that policy.

(*c*) Both Governments recognise that devolution can be achieved only with the co-operation of constitutional representatives within Northern Ireland of both traditions there. The Conference shall be a framework within which the Irish Government may put forward views and proposals on the modalities of bringing about devolution in Northern Ireland, in so far as they relate to the interests of the minority community.

C
POLITICAL MATTERS

ARTICLE 5

(*a*) The Conference shall concern itself with measures to recognise and accommodate the rights and identities of the two traditions in Northern Ireland, to protect human rights and to prevent discrimination. Matters to be considered in this area include measures to foster the cultural heritage of both traditions, changes in electoral arrangements, the use of flags and emblems, the avoidance of economic and social discrimination and the advantages and disadvantages of a Bill of Rights in some form in Northern Ireland.

(*b*) The discussion of these matters shall be mainly concerned with Northern Ireland, but the possible application of any measures pursuant to this Article by the Irish Government in their jurisdiction shall not be excluded.

(*c*) If it should prove impossible to achieve and sustain devolution on a basis which secures widespread acceptance in Northern Ireland, the Conference shall be a framework within which the Irish Government may, where the interests of the minority community are significantly or especially affected, put forward views on proposals for major legislation and on major policy issues, which are within the purview of the Northern Ireland Departments and which remain the responsibility of the Secretary of State for Northern Ireland.

ARTICLE 6

The Conference shall be a framework within which the Irish Government may put forward views and proposals on the role and composition of bodies appointed by the Secretary of State for Northern Ireland or by departments subject to his direction and control including:

the Standing Advisory Commission on Human Rights;

the Fair Employment Agency;

the Equal Opportunities Commission;

the Police Authority for Northern Ireland;
the Police Complaints Board.

D

SECURITY AND RELATED MATTERS

ARTICLE 7

(*a*) The Conference shall consider:
  (i) security policy;
  (ii) relations between the security forces and the community;
  (iii) prisons policy.

(*b*) The Conference shall consider the security situation at its regular meetings and thus provide an opportunity to address policy issues, serious incidents and forthcoming events.

(*c*) The two Governments agree that there is a need for a programme of special measures in Northern Ireland to improve relations between the security forces and the community, with the object in particular of making the security forces more readily accepted by the nationalist community. Such a programme shall be developed, for the Conference's consideration, and may include the establishment of local consultative machinery, training in community relations, crime prevention schemes involving the community, improvements in arrangements for handling complaints, and action to increase the proportion of members of the minority in the Royal Ulster Constabulary. Elements of the programme may be considered by the Irish Government suitable for application within their jurisdiction.

(*d*) The Conference may consider policy issues relating to prisons. Individual cases may be raised as appropriate, so that information can be provided or enquiries instituted.

E

LEGAL MATTERS, INCLUDING THE ADMINISTRATION OF JUSTICE

ARTICLE 8

The Conference shall deal with issues of concern to both countries relating to the enforcement of the criminal law. In particular it shall consider whether there are areas of the criminal law applying in the North and South respectively which might with benefit be harmonised. The two Governments agree on the importance of public confidence in the administration of justice.

The Conference shall seek, with the help of advice from experts as appropriate, measures which would give substantial expression to this aim, considering *inter alia* the possibility of mixed courts in both jurisdictions for the trial of certain offences. The Conference shall also be concerned with policy aspects of extradition and extra-territorial jurisdiction as between North and South.

F

CROSS-BORDER CO-OPERATION ON SECURITY, ECONOMIC, SOCIAL AND CULTURAL MATTERS

ARTICLE 9

(*a*) With a view to enhancing cross-border co-operation on security matters, the Conference shall set in hand a programme of work to be undertaken by the Chief Constable of the Royal Ulster Constabulary and the Commissioner of the Garda Siochana and, where appropriate, groups of officials in such areas as threat assessments, exchange of information, liaison structures, technical co-operation, training of personnel, and operational resources.

(*b*) The Conference shall have no operational responsibilities; responsibility for police operations shall remain with the heads of the respective police forces, the Chief Constable of the Royal Ulster Constabulary maintaining his links with the Secretary of State for Northern Ireland and the Commissioner of the Garda Siochana his links with the Minister for Justice.

ARTICLE 10

(*a*) The two Governments shall co-operate to promote the economic and social development of those areas of both parts of Ireland which have suffered most severely from the consequences of the instability of recent years, and shall consider the possibility of securing international support for this work.

(*b*) If it should prove impossible to achieve and sustain devolution on a basis which secures widespread acceptance in Northern Ireland, the Conference shall be a framework for the promotion of co-operation between the two parts of Ireland concerning cross-border aspects of economic, social and cultural matters in relation to which the Secretary of State for Northern Ireland continues to exercise authority.

(*c*) If responsibility is devolved in respect of certain matters in the economic, social or cultural areas currently within the responsibility of the Secretary of state for Northern Ireland, machinery will need to be established by the responsible authorities in the North and South for practical co-operation in respect of cross-border aspects of these issues.

G

ARRANGEMENTS FOR REVIEW

ARTICLE 11

At the end of three years from signature of this Agreement, or earlier if requested by either Government, the working of the Conference shall be reviewed by the two Governments to see whether any changes in the scope and nature of its activities are desirable.

H

INTERPARLIAMENTARY RELATIONS

ARTICLE 12

It will be for Parliamentary decision in Westminster and Dublin whether to establish an Anglo-Irish Parliamentary body of the kind adumbrated in the Anglo-Irish Studies Report of November 1981. The two Governments agree that they would give support as appropriate to such a body, if it were to be established.

I

FINAL CLAUSES

ARTICLE 13

This Agreement shall enter into force on the date on which the two Governments exchange notifications of their acceptance of this Agreement.

REFERENCES

ADAMS, J. (1986). *The Financing of Terror*. London.

AKENSON, D. H. (1975). *A Mirror to Kathleen's Face: Education in Independent Ireland, 1922–1960*. Montreal.

—— (1979). *Between Two Revolutions: Islandmagee, Country Antrim, 1798–1920*. Dublin.

ALLIANCE COMMISSION ON NORTHERN IRELAND (1985). *What Future for Northern Ireland? Report of the Alliance Commission on Northern Ireland, 18 July 1985*. London.

ALLISTER, J. H. n.d. [1981?]. *Irish Unification: Anathema*. Belfast.

van AMERSFOORT, H. (1978). ' "Minority" as a Sociological Concept', *Ethnic and Racial Studies* 1. 2, 218–34.

ANDERSON, B. (1983). *Imagined Communities: Reflections on the Origins and Spread of Nationalism.* London.

ARTHUR, P. (1980). *Government and Politics of Northern Ireland*. London.

ATKINS WHITE PAPER (1980). See Discussion Paper (1980).

AUGHEY, A. and McILHENEY, C. (1981). 'The Ulster Defence Association: Paramilitaries and Politics', *Conflict Quarterly* 2.

—— —— (1984). 'Law before Violence? The Protestant Paramilitaries in Ulster Politics', *Éire-Ireland* 19. 2, 55–74.

AUNGER, E. A. (1981). *In Search of Political Stability: A Comparative Study of New Brunswick and Northern Ireland*. Montreal.

BARRINGTON, D. n.d. [1959]. *Uniting Ireland* (Tuairim, pamphlet 1). Dublin.

BARRITT, D. P. and CARTER, C. F. (1962). *The Northern Ireland Problem*. London.

BELL, G. (1976). *The Protestants of Ulster*. London.

—— (1982). *Troublesome Business: The Labour Party and the Irish Question*. London.

—— (1984). *The British in Ireland: A Suitable Case for Withdrawal*. London.

BENN, S. I. and PETERS, R. S. (1959). *Social Principles and the Democratic State*. London.

BENNETT REPORT (1979). *Report of the Committee of Inquiry into Police Interrogation Procedures in Northern Ireland*. Cmnd. 7497. London.

BEW, P. (1987). *Conflict and Conciliation in Ireland 1890–1910: Parnellites and Radical Agrarians*. Oxford.

—— GIBBON, P., and PATTERSON, H. (1979). *The State in Northern Ireland, 1921–72: Political Forces and Social Classes*. Manchester.

—— and PATTERSON, H. (1985). *The British State and the Ulster Crisis: From Wilson to Thatcher*. London.

Bico (British and Irish Communist Organization) (1970). *Connolly and Partition*. Belfast.

—— (1971). *On the Democratic Validity of the Northern Ireland State* (policy statement, no. 2). Belfast.

—— (1972a). *The Home Rule Crisis, 1912–1914*. Belfast.

—— (1972b). *The Economics of Partition*. Belfast.

—— (1973). *'Ulster as it is': A Review of the Development of the Catholic/ Protestant Political Conflict in Belfast between Catholic Emancipation and the Home Rule Bill*. Belfast.

—— (1974a). *The Road to Partition*. Belfast.

—— (1974b). *The Belfast Labour Movement, i. 1885–93*. Belfast.

—— (1984). *The Birth of Ulster Unionism*. Belfast.

Birrell, D. (1981). 'A Government of Northern Ireland and the Obstacle of Power-sharing', *Political Quarterly* 52. 2, 184–202.

Boal, F. W. (1969). 'Territoriality on the Shankill/Falls Divide in Belfast', *Irish Geography* 6. 1, 30–50.

—— (1982). 'Segregating and Mixing: Space and Residence in Belfast', in Boal and Douglas (1982), 249–80.

—— and Douglas, J. N. H. (1982). *Integration and Division: Geographical Perspectives on the Northern Ireland Problem*. London.

Boland, K. n.d. [1972]. *'We Won't Stand [Idly] By'*. Dublin.

—— n.d. [1977]. *Up Dev!* Rathcoole.

—— (1982). *The Rise and Decline of Fianna Fáil*. Cork.

—— (1984). *Fine Gael: British or Irish?* Cork.

Boserup, A. (1972). 'Contradictions and Struggles in Northern Ireland', in *The Socialist Register*, 157–92.

Boulton, D. (1973). *The UVF 1966–73: An Anatomy of Loyalist Rebellion*. Dublin.

Bowen, K. (1983). *Protestants in a Catholic State: Ireland's Privileged Minority*. Kingston and Montreal.

Bowman, J. (1982). *De Valera and the Ulster Question 1917–1973*. Oxford.

Boyce, D. G. (1982). *Nationalism in Ireland*. London.

Boyle, K. and Hadden, T. (1984). 'How to read the New Ireland Forum Report', *Political Quarterly* 55. 4, 402–17.

—— —— (1985). *Ireland: A Positive Proposal*. Harmondsworth.

—— —— and Hillyard, P. (1975). *Law and State: The Case of Northern Ireland*. London.

—— —— —— (1980). *Ten Years on in Northern Ireland: The Legal Control of Political Violence*. London.

Bruce, S. (1986). *God Save Ulster! The Religion and Politics of Paisleyism*. Oxford.

Buchanan, R. H. (1982). 'The Planter and the Gael: Cultural Dimensions of the Northern Ireland Problem, in Boal and Douglas (1982), 49–73.

BUCKLAND, P. (1973). *Irish Unionism, ii. Ulster Unionism and the Origins of Northern Ireland 1886–1922.* Dublin.

—— (1979). *The Factory of Grievances: Devolved Government in Northern Ireland, 1921–39.* Dublin.

BUCKLEY, A. D. (1982). *A Gentle People: A Study of a Peaceful Community in Ulster.* Holywood (Ulster Folk and Transport Museum).

BULL, P. (1972). 'The Reconstruction of the Irish Parliamentary Party 1895–1903' Ph.D. thesis, University of Cambridge.

BURTON, F. (1978). *The Politics of Legitimacy: Struggles in a Belfast Community.* London.

CAIRNS, E. (1982). 'Intergroup Conflict in Northern Ireland' in H. Tajfel (ed.), *Social Identity and Intergroup Relations*, 277–97. Cambridge.

CAMERON REPORT (1969). *Disturbances in Northern Ireland: Report of the Commission appointed by the Governor of Northern Ireland.* Cmd. 532. Belfast.

CAMPAIGN FOR LABOUR REPRESENTATION IN NORTHERN IRELAND n.d. [1982?]. *British Labour and Northern Ireland.* London and Belfast.

CARSON, W. A. (1956). *Ulster and the Irish Republic.* Belfast.

CIELOU, R. n.d. [1983]. *Spare My Tortured People: Ulster and the Green Border.* Lisnaskea.

COAKLEY, J. (1983). 'Patrick Pearse and the "Noble Lie" of Irish Nationalism', *Studies* 72 119–36.

COHAN, A. (1972). *The Irish Political Elite.* Dublin.

COLLINS, M. (ed.) (1985). *Ireland After Britain.* London.

COLLINS, T. (1983). *The Centre Cannot Hold.* Dublin and Belfast.

COLSON, E. (1974). *Tradition and Contract: The Problem of Order.* Chicago.

COMPTON, P. (1981). 'The Demographic Background', in Watt (1981), 74–92.

COMPTON REPORT (1971). *Report of the Inquiry into Allegations against the Security Forces of Physical Brutality in Northern Ireland arising out of Events on the 9th August, 1971.* Cmnd. 4823. London.

CORMACK, R. J. and OSBORNE, R. D. (eds.) (1983). *Religion, Education and Employment: Aspects of Equal Opportunity in Northern Ireland.* Belfast.

COVELLO, V. T. and ASHBY, J. A. (1980). 'Inequality in a Divided Society: An Analysis of Data from Northern Ireland', *Sociological Focus* 13, 2, 87–98.

COX, W. H. (1985*a*). 'Who wants a United Ireland?', *Government and Opposition* 20. 1, 29–47.

—— (1985*b*). 'The Politics of Irish Unification in the Irish Republic', *Parliamentary Affairs* 38. 4, 437–54.

CRICK, B. (1962). *In Defence of Politics.* London.

—— (1982). 'The Sovereignty of Parliament and the Irish Question', in D. Rea (ed.), *Political Cooperation in Divided Societies*, 229–54. London.

—— (1986). 'Northern Ireland and the Concept of Consent', in C. Harlow, (ed.), *Public Law and Politics*, 39–56. London.

CRITCHLEY, J. (1972). *Ireland: A New Partition.* London.

CRONIN, S. (1980). *Irish Nationalism: A History of its Roots and Ideology.* Dublin.

CSJ (CAMPAIGN FOR SOCIAL JUSTICE IN NORTHERN IRELAND) (1969). *Northern Ireland: The Plain Truth.* (2nd edn.) Dungannon.

DARBY, J. (1976). *Conflict in Northern Ireland: The Development of a Polarised Community.* Dublin.

DAVIS, E. and SINNOTT, R. (1979). *Attitudes in the Republic of Ireland Relevant to the Northern Ireland Problem.* Dublin.

—— (ed.) (1983). *Northern Ireland: The Background to the Conflict.* Belfast.

—— MURRAY, D., BATTS, D., DUNN, S. FARREN, S., and HARRIS, J. (1977). *Education and Community in Northern Ireland: Schools Apart?* Coleraine.

DE PAOR, L. (1970). *Divided Ulster.* Harmondsworth.

DENT, M. J. (1982). *The Dispute over Falklands/Malvinas: The Road to an Honourable and Lasting Peace.* Keele.

—— (1988). 'The Option of Shared Sovereignty in the Falklands/Malvinas Dispute' in Walter Little and Christopher Mitchell (eds.), *In the Aftermath: Anglo-Argentina Relations after the War.* Maryland.

DEUTSCH, M. (1973). *The Resolution of Conflict: Constructive and Destructive Processes.* New Haven.

DEVLIN, B. (1969). *The Price of My Soul.* London.

DICEY, A. V. (1886). *England's Case Against Home Rule.* London.

DISCUSSION PAPER (1972). *The Future of Northern Ireland.* Northern Ireland Office.

DISCUSSION PAPER (1974). *Government of Northern Ireland: A Society Divided.* HMSO.

DISCUSSION PAPER (1980). *The Government of Northern Ireland: Proposals for Further Discussion.* Cmnd. 7950.

DOOB, L. W. and FOLTZ, W. J. (1973). 'The Belfast Workshop: An Application of Group Techniques to a Destructive Conflict', *Journal of Conflict Resolution* 17. 3, 489–512.

DUDLEY EDWARDS, O. (1970). *The Sins of our Fathers: Roots of Conflict in Northern Ireland.* Dublin.

ENLOE, C. (1973). *Ethnic Conflict and Political Development.* Boston.

—— (1980). *Ethnic Soldiers.* Harmondsworth.

FARRELL, B. (ed.) (1973). *The Irish Parliamentary Tradition.* Dublin.

FARRELL, M. (1976). *Northern Ireland: The Orange State.* London.

—— (1983). *Arming the Protestants: The Formation of the Ulster Special Constabulary and the Royal Ulster Constabulary, 1920–7.* London.

FEA (FAIR EMPLOYMENT AGENCY FOR NORTHERN IRELAND) (1983). *Report of an Investigation by the Fair Employment Agency for Northern Ireland into the Non-industrial Northern Ireland Civil Service.* Belfast.

—— (1985). *Ninth Report and Statement of Accounts by the Fair Employment*

Agency for Northern Ireland, 1 April 1984 to 31 March 1985, together with the Report of the Controller and Auditor-General. London.

FENNELL, D. (1983). *The State of the Nation: Ireland since the Sixties.* Swords.

FISHER, R. (1964). 'Fractionating Conflict', in R. Fisher, (ed.), *International Conflict and Behavioral Science*, 99–109. New York.

FITZGERALD, G. (1972). *Towards a New Ireland.* London.

—— (1982). 'Irish Identities', *Listener*, 27 May 1982.

FORUM *Report.* See New Ireland Forum.

FRASER, M. (1973). *Children in Conflict.* London.

GALLAGHER, F., (1957). *The Indivisible Island: The History of the Partition of Ireland.* London.

GALLIHER, J. F. and DEGREGORY, J. L. (1985). *Violence in Northern Ireland: Understanding Protestant Perspectives.* Dublin.

GARVIN, T. (1981). 'The Growth of Faction in the Fianna Fáil Party, 1966–1980', *Parliamentary Affairs* 34. 1, 110–23.

GIBBON, P. (1975). *The Origins of Ulster Unionism.* Manchester.

GIBSON, N. (1972). 'Economics and Consensus', in J. H. Whyte *et al.*, *Governing Without Consensus: A Critique* (Northern Ireland Community Relations Commission; occasional publication, no. 10). Belfast.

GREAVES, C. D. (1972). *The Irish Crisis.* London.

GWYNN, D. (1950). *The History of Partition (1912–1925).* Dublin.

HAAGERUP REPORT (1984). *Report drawn up on behalf of the Political Affairs Committee on the Situation in Northern Ireland.* (European Parliament Working Documents 1983–1984: Document 1-1526/83).

HADDEN, T. and HILLYARD, P. (1973). *Justice in Northern Ireland: A Study in Social Confidence.* London.

HANDBOOK OF THE ULSTER QUESTION (1923). (North Eastern Boundary Bureau). Dublin.

HARBISON, J. (ed.) (1983). *Children of the Troubles: Children in Northern Ireland* (Stranmillis College Learning Resources Unit). Belfast.

—— and HARBISON, J. (eds.) (1980). *A Society Under Stress: Children and Young People in Northern Ireland.* Shepton Mallet.

HARRIS, R. (1972). *Prejudice and Tolerance in Ulster: A Study of Neighbours and 'Strangers' in a Border Community.* Manchester.

HARRISON, H. (1939). *Ulster and the British Empire, 1939: Help or Hindrance?* London.

HENNESSEY, P. (1986). *Cabinet.* Oxford.

HESKIN, K. (1980). *Northern Ireland: A Psychological Analysis.* Dublin.

HESLINGA, M. W. (1962). *The Irish Border as a Cultural Divide* (2nd edn. 1971). Assen.

HEWITT, C. (1981). 'Catholic Grievances, Catholic Nationalism and Violence in Northern Ireland during the Civil Rights Period: A Reconsideration', *British Journal of Sociology* 32. 3, 362–80.

HICKEY, J. (1984). *Religion and the Northern Ireland Problem*. Dublin.

HUME, J. (1979). 'The Irish Question: A British Problem', *Foreign Affairs*.

INSTITUTE FOR EUROPEAN DEFENCE AND STRATEGIC STUDIES (1984). *Britain's Undefended Frontier: A Policy for Ulster*. London.

JACKSON, H. (1971). *The Two Irelands—a Dual Study of Inter-group Tensions*. London.

JAHODA, G. and HARRISON, S. (1975). 'Belfast Children: Some Effects of a Conflict Environment', *Irish Journal of Psychology* 3. 1, 1–19.

JALLAND, P. (1979). 'United Kingdom Devolution 1910–14: Political Panacea or Tactical Diversion?', *English Historical Review* 94, 757–85.

—— (1980). *The Liberals and Ireland: The Ulster Question in British Politics to 1914*. Brighton.

JENKINS, R. (1964). *Asquith*. London.

JENKINS, R. (1982). *Hightown Rules: Growing up in a Belfast Estate*. Leicester.

—— (1983). *Lads, Citizens and Ordinary Kids: Working-class Youth Lifestyles in Belfast*. London.

JONES, T. (1971). *Whitehall Diary, iii. Ireland 1918–1925* (ed. K. Middlemas). London.

KEDOURIE, E. (1961). *Nationalism* (2nd edn.). London.

KELLEY, K. (1982). *The Longest War: Northern Ireland and the IRA*. Dingle.

KENNEDY, D. (1984). 'Joint Authority was tried and failed in the North', *Irish Times*, 6 December 1984.

KILBRANDON REPORT (1984). *Northern Ireland: Report of an Independent Inquiry*. London.

KOSS, S. (1976). *Asquith*. London.

LAFFAN, M. (1983). *The Partition of Ireland 1911–1925*. Dundalk.

LARSEN, S. S. (1982a). 'The Two Sides of the House: Identity and Social Organisation in Kilbroney, Northern Ireland', in A. P. Cohen (ed.), *Belonging: Identity and Social Organization in British Rural Cultures*, 131–64. Manchester.

—— (1982b). 'The Glorious Twelfth: A Ritual Expression of Collective Identity', ibid. 278–91.

LEYTON, E. (1974). 'Opposition and Integration in Ulster', *Man NS* 9, 185–98.

—— (1975). *The One Blood: Kinship and Class in an Irish Village* (Newfoundland Social and Economic Studies, no. 15). St John's.

LIJPHART, A. (1975). 'The Northern Ireland Problem: Theories and Solutions', *British Journal of Political Science* 5, 83–106.

—— (1977). *Democracy in Plural Societies: A Comparative Exploration*. New Haven.

LYONS, F. S. L. (1979). *Culture and Anarchy in Ireland 1890–1939*. Oxford.

McALLISTER, I. (1980). 'Territorial Differentiation and Party Development in Northern Ireland', *Studies in Public Policy*, 66. Glasgow.

—— (1982). 'The Devil, Miracles and the Afterlife: The Political Sociology of Religion in Northern Ireland', *British Journal of Sociology* 33. 3, 330–47.

—— and ROSE, R. (1983). 'Can Political Conflict be Resolved by Social Change? Northern Ireland as a Test Case', *Journal of Conflict Resolution* 27. 3, 533–57.

MacBRIDE, S. n.d. [1985]. *Ireland's Right to Sovereignty, Independence and Unity is Inalienable and Indefeasible*. Dublin.

McCANN, E. (1974). *War and an Irish Town*. Harmondsworth (new edn, London 1980).

McCARTNEY, R. L., HALL, S., SOMERS, B., SMYTH, G., McCRACKEN, H. L., and SMITH, P. (1981). *The Unionist Case*. (Document presented to the Taoiseach and the Leader of the Opposition, 8 October.)

McCASHIN, A. (1982). 'Social Policy, 1957–82', in F. Litton, (ed.), *Unequal Achievement: The Irish Experience 1957–1982*. Dublin.

McCRACKEN, J. L. (1967). 'The Political Scene in Northern Ireland, 1926–37', in F. McMANUS (ed.), *The Years of the Great Test*, 150–60. Dublin.

MacDONAGH, O. (1983). *States of Mind: A Study of Anglo-Irish Conflict 1780–1980*. London.

MacGREIL, M. (1977). *Prejudice and Tolerance in Ireland*. Dublin.

McKEOWN, M. (1985). 'Repartition: The Veto to end all Vetos', *Fortnight*, no. 212.

McKERNAN, J. (1980). 'Pupil Values as Social Indicators of Intergroup Differences in Northern Ireland', in Harbison (1980), 128–40.

McNEILL, R. (1922). *Ulster's Stand for Union*. London.

McWHIRTER, L. (1983). 'Looking Back and Looking Forward: An Inside Perspective', in Harbison (1983), 127–57.

MANSERGH, P. N. S. (1974). 'The Government of Ireland Act, 1920. Its Origins and Purposes. The Working of the "Official" Mind', in J. G. Barry (ed.), *Historical Studies: Papers read before the Irish Conference of Historians, May 1971*. Belfast.

MARTIN, J. (1982). 'The Conflict in Northern Ireland: Marxist Interpretations', *Capital and Class* 18, 56–71.

MILLER, D. W. (1978). *Queen's Rebels: Ulster Loyalism in Historical Perspective*. Dublin.

MOODY, T. W. (1966). 'Thomas Davis and the Irish Nation', *Hermathena* 102, 5–31.

MORAN, D. P. (1905). *The Philosophy of Irish Ireland*. Dublin.

MORGAN, A. and PURDIE, B. (eds.) (1980). *Ireland: Divided Nation, Divided Class*. London.

MOXON-BROWNE, E. (1979). *The Northern Ireland Attitude Survey: An Initial Report*. Belfast.

—— (1983). *Nation, Class and Creed in Northern Ireland*. Aldershot.

MURPHY, D. (1978). *A Place Apart*. London.

MURPHY, D. (1984). *Changing the Problem: Post-Forum Reflections*. Gigginstown.

MURRAY, D. (1985). *Worlds Apart: Segregated Schools in Northern Ireland*. Belfast.

NAIRN, T. (1977). *The Break-up of Britain: Crisis and Neo-nationalism*. London.

NELSON, S. (1984). *Ulster's Uncertain Defenders: Loyalists and the Northern Ireland Conflict*. Belfast.

NEW IRELAND FORUM (1983). *Report of Proceedings, Public Session, 17 November 1983*. Dublin.

—— (1984*a*). *Report*. Dublin.

—— (1984*b*). *The Macroeconomic Consequences of Integrated Economic Policy, Planning and Co-ordination in Ireland*. Dublin.

NEW ULSTER MOVEMENT (1972). *Two Irelands or One?* Belfast.

NEW ULSTER POLITICAL RESEARCH GROUP (1979). *Beyond the Religious Divide*. Belfast.

NORTHERN IRELAND ASSEMBLY COMMITTEE ON THE GOVERNMENT OF NORTHERN IRELAND (1986). *First Report* (NIA 237, adopted by the Assembly on 5 February 1986).

O'BRIEN, C. CRUISE (1972). *States of Ireland*. London.

—— (1973). 'Ireland and Minority Rights', *New Humanist*, March, 433–5.

—— (1980). *Neighbours*. London.

O'BRIEN, G. (1936). *The Four Green Fields*. Dublin.

O'DONNELL, E. E. (1977). *Northern Irish Stereotypes*. Dublin.

O'DOWD, L., ROLSTON, B., and TOMLINSON, M. (1980). *Northern Ireland: Between Civil Rights and Civil War*. London.

O'HALLORAN, C. (1987). *Partition and the Limits of Irish Nationalism*. Dublin.

O'LEARY, B. (1985). 'Explaining Northern Ireland: A Brief Study Guide', *Politics* 5. 1, 35–40.

O'MALLEY, P. (1983). *The Uncivil Wars: Ireland Today*. Belfast.

O'NEILL, T. (1972). *Autobiography*.

OSBORNE, R. D. (1982). 'The Lockwood Report and the Location of a Second University in Northern Ireland', in Boal and Douglas (1982), 167–78.

PAISLEY, I. R. K. (1972). *United Ireland—Never!* Belfast.

—— ROBINSON, P. D., and TAYLOR, J. D. (1982). *Ulster: The Facts*. Belfast.

PATTERSON, H. (1980). *Class Conflict and Sectarianism: The Protestant Working Class and the Belfast Labour Movement 1868–1920*. Belfast.

PEARSE, P. H. (1913). 'The Coming Revolution', *An Claidheamh Soluis*, 8 November 1913.

PICKVANCE, T. J. (1975). *Peace Through Equity: Proposals for a Permanent Settlement of the Northern Ireland Conflict*. Birmingham.

POCOCK, J. G. A. (1982). 'The Limits and Divisions of British History: In Search of the Unknown Subject', *American Historical Review* 87. 2, 311–36.

POOLE, M. A. (1982). 'Religious Residential Segregation in Urban Northern Ireland', in Boal and Douglas (1982), 281–308.

PRIOR WHITE PAPER (1982): see White Paper (1982).

PRAGER, J. (1986). *Building Democracy in Ireland*. Cambridge.

PROBERT, B. (1978). *Beyond Orange and Green: The Political Economy of the Northern Ireland Crisis*. London.

REED, D. (1984). *Ireland: The key to the British Revolution*. London.

REVIEW PAPER (1974). *The Northern Ireland Constitution*. Cmnd. 5675.

ROBB, William (1982). *A History of Northern Ireland Railways*. Belfast.

ROSE, R. (1971). *Governing Without Consensus: An Irish Perspective*. London.

—— (1976). *Northern Ireland: A Time of Choice*. London.

—— MCALLISTER, I., and MAIR, P. (1978). 'Is there a Concurring Majority about Northern Ireland?, *Strathclyde Studies in Public Policy* 22.

—— and GARVIN, T. (1983). 'The Public Policy Effects of Independence: Ireland as a Test Case', *European Journal of Political Research* 11. 4, 377–98.

RUDOLPH, J. R. Jun. and THOMPSON, R. J. (1985). 'Ethnoterritorial Movements and the Policy Process: Accommodating Nationalist Demands in the Developed World', *Comparative Politics* 17. 3, 291–311.

RYAN, D. (ed.) (1948). *Socialism and Nationalism: A Selection from the Writings of James Connolly*. Dublin.

SAUNDERSON MSS. Public Record Office of Northern Ireland.

SCARMAN REPORT (1972). *Violence and Civil Disturbances in Northern Ireland in 1969: Report of a Tribunal of Inquiry*. Cmd. 556. Belfast.

SHEARMAN, H. (1942). *Not an Inch: A Study of Northern Ireland and Lord Craigavon*. London.

—— (1948). *Anglo-Irish Relations*. London.

—— (1970). 'Conflict in Northern Ireland', *Year Book of World Affairs* 24, 40–53.

—— (1982). 'Conflict in Northern Ireland', *Year Book of World Affairs* 36, 182–96.

SHEEHY, M. (1957). *Divided we Stand: A Study of Partition*. London.

SMITH, P. (1984). *Opportunity Lost: A Unionist View of the Report of the Forum for a New Ireland*. Belfast.

SMYTH, W. M. (1972). *The Battle for Northern Ireland*. County Grand Orange Lodge of Belfast.

—— n.d. [1975]. 'A Protestant looks at the Republic', in *Sectarianism—Roads to Reconciliation. Papers read at the 22nd Annual Summer School of the Social Study Conference, St Augustine's College, Dungarvan, August 1974*. Dublin.

STEWART, A. T. Q. (1967). *The Ulster Crisis*. London.

—— (1977). *The Narrow Ground: Aspects of Ulster, 1609–1969*. London.

STRAUSS, E. (1951). *Irish Nationalism and British Democracy*. London.

THE SUNDAY TIMES INSIGHT TEAM (1972). *Ulster*. Harmondsworth.

THORNBERRY, P. (1980). 'Minority Rights, Human Rights and International Law', *Ethnic and Racial Studies* 3. 3, 249–63.

TOWNSHEND, C. (1983). *Political Violence in Ireland: Government and Resistance since 1848.* Oxford.

—— (1986). 'Northern Ireland', in R. J. Vincent (ed.), *Foreign Policy and Human Rights*, 119–40. Cambridge.

TREW, K. (1983). 'Group Identification in a Divided Society', in Harbison (1983), 109–19.

ULSTER POLITICAL RESEARCH GROUP. (1987). *Common Sense.* Belfast.

ULSTER UNIONIST ASSEMBLY PARTY'S REPORT COMMITTEE (1984). *Devolution and the Northern Ireland Assembly: the Way Forward.* Belfast.

VAN der STRAETEN, S. and DAUFOUY, P. (1972). 'La Contre-révolution irlandaise', *Les Temps Modernes* 311, 2069–104.

VANGUARD (1973). 'Community of the British Isles'. Belfast.

VINEY, M. n.d. [1965]. *The Five Per Cent: A Survey of Protestants in the Republic.* Dublin.

WALSH, B. M. (1970). *Religion and Demographic Behaviour in Ireland.* Dublin.

—— (1975). 'Trends in the Religious Composition of the Population in the Republic of Ireland, 1946–71', *Economic and Social Review* 6. 4, 543–55.

WALSH, D. P. J. (1983). *The Use and Abuse of Emergency Legislation in Northern Ireland.* London.

WATT, D. (ed.) (1981). *The Constitution of Northern Ireland: Problems and Prospects.* London.

WEST, T. (1986). *Horace Plunkett: Co-operation and Politics.* Gerrards Cross.

WHELAN, C. T. and WHELAN, B. J. (1984). *Social Mobility in the Republic of Ireland: A Comparative Perspective.* Dublin.

WHITE, B. (1986). 'Ulster: What a Look Back at the Opinion Polls Shows', *Belfast Telegraph*, 12 February 1986.

WHITE, J. (1975). *Minority Report: The Protestant Community in the Irish Republic.* Dublin.

WHITE PAPER (1982). *Northern Ireland: A Framework for Devolution.* Cmnd. 8541.

WHYTE, J. (1978). 'Interpretations of the Northern Ireland Problem: An Appraisal', *Economic and Social Review* 9. 4, 257–82.

—— (1981). 'Why is the Northern Ireland Problem so Intractable?', *Parliamentary Affairs* 34. 4, 422–35.

—— (1983a). 'How much Discrimination was there under the Unionist Regime, 1921–68?, in T. Gallagher and J. O'Connell (eds.), *Contemporary Irish Studies*, 1–35. Manchester.

—— (1983b). *Is Research on the Northern Ireland Problem Worth While?* (Inaugural Lecture, Queen's University). Belfast.

WRIGHT, F. (1973). 'Protestant Ideology and Politics in Ulster', *European Journal of Sociology* 14, 213–80.

—— (1981). 'Case Study III: The Ulster Spectrum', in D. Carlton and C. Schaerf (eds.), *Contemporary Terror: Studies in Sub-state Violence*, 154–214. London.

INDEX